MW00574389

Praise

The 4 Habits of all Successful Relationships

'The internet is littered with superficial, relationship self-help manuals but this "work" is quite different in three striking respects: it is authored by a husband-and-wife partnership giving different perspectives; it covers both personal and commercial, workplace relationships; and having been there and got the tee shirt, Jon and Andrea share their own lived experiences while weaving a wealth of research deep into the fabric. The conventional manuals resemble the highway code. This is the degree course for those who really want to understand the "whys" of bad relationships as well as the "how tos" of successful and fulfilling ones. And to cap it off, it is a pleasure to read and work through.'

Sir Paul Coleridge – Founder and Chairman of Marriage Foundation

'With The 4 Habits, the Taylor-Cummings have put together a template to help anyone have better relationships – whether in the boardroom or the bedroom! Dotted throughout with real-life examples, they present with clarity well-researched wisdom and strategies to enable anyone to develop their connection and communication with those who matter most. The ideas in this book aren't just something to read, but to put into practice and reap the rewards.'

Rob Parsons, OBE – Founder and Chairman, Care for the Family

'In this book Jonathan and Andrea Taylor-Cummings provide us with hands-on, practical, and timeless principles for building wholesome and enduring relationships that are urgently needed at all levels of our modern society. This book shines a ray of hope in the dark areas of conflicts in our world where the spirit of good relationships is gradually fading. Reading and applying the principles admonished throughout the pages of this book can only serve to engender and strengthen healthy relationships.'

His Excellency Seth George Ramocan CD – High Commissioner for Jamaica to the United Kingdom

'I welcome this publication from Andrea and Jonathan because I know that their "talk" in the book is based on their "walk" in life. Secondly, inclusive teams, organizations, societies or nations all require secure personal relationships; The 4 Habits provide a perfect template. Thirdly, in positioning Curiosity, Care, Asking and Connecting as habits, they display their understanding of a fundamental aspect of the human condition – we are creatures of habit, therefore in changing our habits, we change our lives.'

Linbert Spencer, OBE – Inclusive Leadership and Performance Management Consultant / Executive Coach, Author, Co-Founder of The Centre for Inclusive Leadership

'Healthy, respectful relationships focused on mutual flourishing are the bedrock of the lives of couples and families and are vitally important in the workplace as well. This is also a key social justice issue as the evidence shows that healthy couple relationships are a bulwark against poverty, so I warmly welcome this practical book on how we can all keep our relationships in good repair and iron out those bad habits.'

Andrew Selous MP – Co-Chair All Party Parliamentary Group on supporting couple relationships and reducing interparental conflict

'This book is a treasure chest of rich vignettes, reflective questions and practical exercises that deepen our understanding of factors that can damage relationships and actions we can take to develop healthy relationships. It is not just a book about personal relationships, it offers insights as to how we can build productive relationships in the ever-increasing complex work settings we now inhabit. The blend of honest reflection and evidence-based research material makes this a wonderful resource.'

Dr Sue Dopson – Professor of Organisational Behaviour, Fellow of Green Templeton College and Deputy Dean of Saïd Business School, University of Oxford

'It's one thing for someone to hand you a map. It's another thing to have an expert guide walk you to that next great place. In this case, it's two guides, Dr Andrea and Jonathan Taylor-Cummings. Their 4 Habits book can help guide and strengthen your team, workplace, and family, and improve your most important relationships. I've been blessed to get to know both Jonathan and Andrea and I highly recommend them and their hugely helpful new book.'

Dr John Trent – Author of LifeMapping®, President StrongFamilies.com and The Centre for Strong Families

'Andrea and Jonathan provide an invaluable service by distilling a deep seam of academic research and well-honed experience – professional and personal – into 4 Habits everyone can put into practice. Readers who take time to gaze through the powerful lens they hold up to relationships, whether with remote work team members, or closest friends, will be enabled to make better choices, build stronger bonds and live more resiliently.'

Dr Samantha Callan – Director and Co-Founder, Family Hubs Network

'Supporting our people's emotional health and wellbeing has always been a key priority for The De Beers Group. The pandemic experience highlighted the important link between life at home and life at work, and that strong resilience comes from strong relationships. This book provides an excellent resource for equipping everyone to get better at relationships so they can thrive as individuals, colleagues, couples and families. I couldn't recommend it more highly.'

Paul Rowley – Executive Vice President, The De Beers Group of Companies

'We all need frameworks for life and, when it comes to the complex business of making relationships work, this is as good as it gets. In a world of broken relationships and at a time such as this, these powerful insights from Andrea and Jon Taylor-Cummings are cool water in a thirsty land. For relationships at work, home life or friendships generally, these 4 Habits provide the cornerstones of a strong foundation on which you can build anything relational.'

Dawid Konotey-Ahulu – Co-Founder of Redington, Mallowstreet and 10,000 Black Interns

'Relationships matter, they are one of the most important investments we make at home and at work. Many companies talk about the importance of relationships but fail to give the support to do relationships well. This book is a clear roadmap on what to do, and how to build long-term relationships intentionally. The 4 Habits provide a clear framework for transforming good relationships into great ones.'

Robert J. Gardner – Executive Board Director of St James's Place Wealth Management, Co-Founder of Redington and Mallowstreet

'This is an essential and timely must-read that will provide a new and powerful lens through which to strengthen and nurture your relationships at work and in life. Packed with hidden gems, real-life stories and practical "how tos", The 4 Habits takes a complex subject and makes it accessible to all. Cultivating healthy relationships can have a significant impact on our wellbeing and happiness, making relational intelligence a vital skill for life!'

Kirsten Samuel – CEO and Founder of Kamwell (Employee Wellbeing Consultancy)

'The importance of relationships has never been more critical and The 4 Habits provides invaluable and tangible tools and behavior changes to build successful relationships both at home and at work. The three-part structure makes it easy to digest and implement with strong reference points so the reader can make steady and lasting changes. A fantastic toolkit for us all to build our essential relational intelligence skills.'

Chris Cummings – CEO Sonas Group (Wellbeing@Work, Future of Work Insights) and Co-Founder Inside Out Awards

'At The De Beers Group we believe in looking after "the whole person" and the things that matter most to us – especially where work impacts family life and vice versa. Building quality relationships at work and home is central to building a thriving workforce. This book provides the "how to" for developing strong Relational Intelligence and doing relationships well. A vital resource for employers and employees alike.'

Matlhogonolo Mponang – Head of Human Resources: Diamond Trading, The De Beers Group of Companies

'The pandemic has in many ways democratized the conversation about emotional and mental health while highlighting the importance of our overall wellbeing – physical, emotional, mental and spiritual health. In this book, Andrea and Jonathan provide some wonderful insights and practical tools on how we can all improve our emotional health through the quality of our relationships. A must read if we are to take a more holistic approach to maintaining our most valuable asset – our health.'

Geoff McDonald – Global Advocate, Campaigner and Consultant for Mental Health

'Having had the privilege of attending one of Andrea and Jon's live courses in the past it was a delight to read their new book. Like in the course, in their book they bare all. You'll laugh, cry and empathize with their personal stories, perhaps seeing yourself reflected on the pages you read. You'll be equipped with "how to" and more importantly understand "why to" enrich relationships across all areas of life.'

Diana Page – Global Network Marketing and Goal Mapping Practitioner

'The world is hungry for meaningful and fruitful relationships, but in the most part we lack the tools to be intentional about cultivating them. Through real-life case studies, well-researched insights and proven behavioral frameworks, Jon and Andrea's 4 Habits are a game-changer for those seeking to build healthy and successful relationships, whether at home or at work. Not just a book to enjoy, this book may prove to be one of the most life-changing books you read.'

Mark Helvadjian – Senior Pastor, Vineyard Church, Saint Albans

'*Deep within we yearn for flourishing, healthy relationships – for an antidote to the division too often normalized in modern media. We know that it takes effort to build great relationships in our work, home and community. Andrea and Jonathan offer humble examples from their own lifetime struggles and a heartfelt, deeply practical model for targeting that effort brilliantly.*'

James Entwisle – Chair of Trustees, FairLife Foundation and Agape Alive In India, Advisory Council member, TLG charity

'*We all want great relationships but do not always have the skills to develop and maintain them. This book provides an insightful guide to building strong relationships on purpose, with principles that apply both at home and at work. Full of compassion, honesty and empathy* The 4 Habits *is inspiring from page 1.*'

Jeremy Lindley, MA, FRSA – Business Leader, Non-Executive Director and Chair of Trustees, Soulmates Academy Foundation

'*This book by Andrea and Jonathan Taylor-Cummings highlights the importance of acquiring and building relational competence in our marriages as well as business situations. A well thought out manual for high achieving people.*'

Richard and Maria Kane – Founders of Marriage Week UK and International

'*This book is for anyone who's ever been in any kind of relationship – lover, husband/wife, children, parents, business, boss.* The 4 Habits *will help to improve them all.*'

Barry Phillips 'Barry the Book' – Owner of Knowledge is King and author of *Life Changing Quotes*

THE HABITS 4

of all

Successful Relationships

Improving your relationships
at home, at work and in life

Dr. Andrea & Jonathan Taylor-Cummings

Grace & Down
PUBLISHING

Cover design by Esther Kotecha
Art direction by Sarah Grace

Printed in the UK

Dedication

To our beloved Sam and Isaac, and our future generations through them. May strong, quality relationships be your rich inheritance and great reward.

Contents

PART C – TAKING RESPONSIBILITY

Why Read This Book &
What You'll Get Out Of It

Introduction

The secret to successful relationships

You've been there, we've been there. The simple truth is all relationships face challenges. A predictable set of hurdles really. Different values and assumptions, misunderstood differences, and poor conflict-resolution skills all create feelings of mistrust or disrespect. Or sometimes it's just the case of poor communication skills leading to feelings of being unvalued, unappreciated, unloved. All familiar issues.

You would expect that being familiar and predictable, we would all be good at anticipating and dealing with these issues well. Except we aren't.

Success in relationships comes from being equipped ahead of time to get over these hurdles so that we each 'turn up' better in our interactions, have better conversations and achieve better outcomes.

We learned that the hard way. And that's why we wrote this book.

Our story (perhaps in some ways, yours too)

Our story goes back to 1989, when we met at Business School. Andrea came to the UK to get her Masters . . . and, as we like to add, ended up getting her Mister as well! We both did postgraduate degrees at the University of Oxford, got married a few years later and pursued careers in Professional Services. We had the amazing experience of spending our first year of marriage living and working out in Tokyo, Japan. That was a year of bliss as DINKs – Double Income, No Kids.

On our return to the UK, we decided to set up in business together. Armed with business degrees, a bit of real-life experience in the working world and entrepreneurial courage, we followed our dream and started our own business. After all, how hard could it be?

As we shared in our TEDx Talk, it took us all of about three months to find out!

We thought we knew each other really well but quickly discovered that we had very different work styles and didn't know each other in a work context at all. The bliss we had previously enjoyed quickly spiraled down into a living hell.

Even simple things became problems as we grated against each other.

For some couples, their trigger is the toilet seat . . . up or down. For us, the predictable trigger was the state of our desks. Jon, the resident engineer, was very organized. Andrea was (and still is!) more like 'organized chaos'. The problem was, back then, we only had one desk-top computer which just 'happened' to be on Jon's desk, so we had to swap desks from time to time. Nightmare.

Andrea: 'Don't touch my papers!!'

Jon: 'How can you possibly work in such a mess?!'

Andrea: 'It's not a mess, I know where everything is. Just stop moving things around!'

That's the polite version. We both have strong 'Lion-type' personalities (we'll talk about this later). And what do Lions do under pressure? They R-O-A-R. Well, we roared . . . a lot!

And the problems followed us home. Many a night was spent in tension, hugging the edge of the bed instead of each other, making sure we didn't even touch toes.

This was a frightening and stressful time, especially against the backdrop of the peaceful, easy going relationship we had before. We were both confused by each other's behavior. Far too many times our 'discussions' spiraled downwards into heated arguments fueled by an underlying fear about what was happening to us. Life together felt desperate. We each felt the person we married had changed. We didn't enjoy being around each other anymore. Actually, we didn't really like each other anymore! We were shutting down emotionally. Drifting apart. It felt like everything was on the line – our finances, our business . . . and our marriage.

We've since come to realize that our story is by no means unique – well, certainly not the feelings we experienced. Substitute a few names and circumstances and this experience of a great relationship turning sour could describe the experience of many couples, friends, colleagues, teams, siblings or parent / child relationships. Isn't it strange how you can love someone and yet still hate having them around! That's where we were – deep down we knew we loved each other but the daily experience was tough. Fun had gone out the window . . . this was not what we signed up for!

What we learned back then became the catalyst for our work over the last 25 plus years in strengthening relationships and building Relational Intelligence. We ticked the boxes on all the common hurdles that relationships face, but we learned that our biggest problem was our different strengths – simply unrecognized, unappreciated and completely out of balance.

Learning to understand our differences changed the narrative in our heads. We started seeing each other for who we really are and appreciating each other's strengths – rather than trying to change each other to our own individual styles. We learned to agree roles based on what we were each good at and to cover for each other's weaknesses. And that's when we started to rebuild trust and respect.

We learned that we didn't need *to be each other* but we did need to *let each other be*.

So many relationships are lost simply because people are not equipped with the skills to navigate these common hurdles. Ours could have been one of them. Why wasn't this stuff more widely known and available? We determined to play our part in equipping people to do relationships well and prevent unnecessary relationship breakdown, not just for couples, but for everyone.

The tide is against us all

As it turns out, the message of this book couldn't be more timely. The world has changed significantly since we first started writing, but the issues have only intensified. The COVID-19 pandemic shut down the world and forced us all to grapple with life under lockdown. Uniquely, this experience shone a light on the quality of relationships, with many navigating for the first time the challenges of working remotely and communicating with colleagues long distance, while living 'up close and personal' with their nearest and dearest.

The thing is these relationship challenges are not new. The pandemic only made them more visible and more urgent. In fact, pre-pandemic, relationship breakdown was already reaching epic proportions:

- In much of the developed world, workplace conflict has been costing organizations billions each year in lost hours, management time and dispute resolution (£33bn per year in the UK, $359bn per year in the US![1]).

- At the same time, in those same countries, domestic partner relationships are also not doing so well. The figures for break-ups amongst married and cohabiting partnerships vary widely across countries, influenced by factors as variable as family values, religion, local laws, etc. But with between 20 percent and 40 percent of marriages ending in divorce in many countries, and multiple surveys confirming that cohabiting couples break up at much higher rates (typically two to three times higher), couple break-up rates average out at around the 50 percent mark. What that means is that, on average, one out of every two 'long-term' couple relationships don't go the distance. At the last count, family breakdown in the UK was costing taxpayers £51bn per year,[2] almost half the budget for running the country's entire National Health Service!

And then came COVID-19.

Under lockdown, participants on the numerous online webinars and workshops we ran, reported working longer and harder and experiencing different versions of pandemic fatigue. Most struggled to contain the 'bleed' of work consuming home time and missed the downtime offered by commuting between work and home (although they didn't miss the commute itself!). They also missed the social connection with colleagues in the office and were frustrated by being stuck within the four walls of home, especially those who were isolated.

As data from organizations such as The American Institute of Stress shows, for years, stress and anxiety levels have been on the increase globally,[3] as have been concerns over mental health and wellbeing. And, as you might expect, the pandemic didn't help. With opportunities for misunderstanding and conflict greatly multiplied, relationships both at home and at work have been challenged like never before. Any number of news reports, helplines, relationship therapists, and divorce lawyers all reported spikes in the cries for help and support.

For all its ills, the COVID-19 pandemic helped elevate the need for building stronger relationships to the level of strategic importance – finally!

And by all indications, this collision of work and home will continue as a feature of life beyond the pandemic.

Never before has it been more important to focus on building strong relationship skills as a strategic priority for supporting individual wellbeing and mental health, for strengthening family units, and for maintaining organizational performance.

We can and must take action

Through countless conversations over the years, we recognized a pattern of behavior. People tend to start out well with goodwill, a degree of commitment, and motivation to build a great relationship. At some point, however, they begin to encounter hurdles – frustrations because of differences, unmet expectations, conflict situations, etc. Without the skills to overcome the hurdles, these issues often remain unaddressed problems, and in time create cracks, wedges and distance in the relationship.

This pattern remains true for all types of relationships – between couples, siblings, parents and children, relatives, friends or work colleagues. Often, it starts with just one comment or conversation that makes us feel judged, criticized or 'less than' in some way. Without the courage or skills to address it, we let things slide. Or sometimes we might have the courage to address it, but they don't have the courage to hear it. Either way, without the relationship skills, the interactions begin to go sour. We start finding excuses and reasons to keep our distance. Emotionally we drift apart, and the relationship grows cold. Over time, we begin to lose hope that we can ever have a great relationship with that person, and eventually we lose the will to even try anymore. And just like that, they are no longer a part of our lives, except for the emotional scars of a broken relationship with someone we care about – a partner, a parent, a child, a sibling, a colleague, a friend.

Here is the simple truth we have learned . . .

People grow apart because they are not *intentional* about staying together.

Most of us tend to assume that because we have a *connection* in the beginning, this will automatically remain in place and will be enough to ensure our relationship survives. But we don't do life in a vacuum and relationships don't maintain momentum on their own.

Entering a relationship is much like a sprinter out on an athletics track getting ready to run a race. The big difference is that at the start of those races, the sprinter can see the hurdles laid out in front of them down the track. In 'relationship land' you can't see the hurdles at the outset. But, make no mistake, the hurdles are as real!

In relationships, as indeed for sprinters, the problems come when people aren't equipped and able to get over the hurdles. Once people start hitting hurdle after hurdle, doubt sets in and they start to question themselves – 'Can I make it to the end of this race, or should I just opt out now?'

Sometimes it's not even about major fights.

Without the skills to do things differently, people stumble their way through and keep tripping up on unmet expectations, frustrations and disappointments until they get to the point of not wanting to try anymore. This is where people drift apart, live separate lives, or opt out altogether.

> **Too many relationships are destroyed unnecessarily, simply for lack of knowledge. We can all be taught how to get over these common relationship hurdles. Except that most of us are not.**

To date, the approach to relationships has been very reactive. People tend to wait until their relationships fall over and 'emotional drifting' has set in, before trying to patch things up with counselling, mediation or other late-stage interventions. For many, this reactive approach is all too often too little, too late. Sadly, this approach is costing society in broken couple relationships, broken family relationships, broken workplace relationships and broken inter-group relationships. The financial and emotional impact is all around us in broken lives and broken people, and the model doesn't give much hope for the next generation to do better.

In light of our personal journey, we asked ourselves: 'What if everyone could become proactive and more intentional about improving their relationships?' The famous 19th-century poem 'A Fence or an Ambulance', written by the English temperance activist Joseph Malins, provides a meaningful analogy. The last line reads *'if the cliff we will fence, we might almost dispense with the ambulance down in the valley'.*[4] Where relationships are concerned, 'fences at the top of the cliff' means equipping people with the skills to build great relationships *ahead* of challenges rather than waiting to pick up the pieces with 'ambulances' at the bottom.

If we want to enjoy health and vitality in our own lives, and restore health in the lives of our families and in society, we must get better at building strong relationships, *on purpose*. When people are equipped with the skills to do relationships well – ahead of challenges – they are able to 'turn up' better, have better conversations and achieve better results.

The question then is, where do we start?

The 4 Habits® of ALL Successful Relationships

Ever since we saw the benefits of equipping in our own relationship, we have been on a mission to develop a simple, accessible way of teaching relationship fundamentals to individuals, couples, corporates and communities. Drawing from the best-in-class tools, concepts in management theory and practice, organizational behavior, relationship therapy, psychology, psychotherapy and research on team performance, we have developed and delivered workshops, seminars and one-to-one mentoring sessions that address key relationship challenges and help equip people to do relationships well.

In March 2019, we had the privilege of delivering a TEDx Talk in the heart of the City of London – the Square Mile – which forced us to distil 25 plus years of knowledge into 15 minutes! Through the process we had another real *lightbulb moment*. We reflected on all our conversations over the years with couples and individuals, and with adults and teens. We thought about the things that created 'lightbulb moments' for them, helping them become 'unstuck' in their relationships and finding a way to move forward. We thought about what worked in our own relationship and the lessons we wanted to pass on to our children and loved ones, so they could enjoy great relationships themselves. That's when we realized that there were four fundamental habits that every successful relationship exhibited. And more to the point, every failing relationship we had ever worked with was missing at least one of them.

'The 4 Habits® of ALL Successful Relationships' were born:

Habit #1: BE CURIOUS, not critical

Habit #2: BE CAREFUL, not crushing

Habit #3: ASK, don't assume

Habit #4: CONNECT, before you correct

In our experience, these habits were truly *the difference that made the difference* in successfully addressing the challenges in ALL the relationships we'd ever seen or worked with – home relationships, work relationships, and just general life relationships.

Around the world, these four habits continue to resonate strongly, confirming that they are indeed fundamental to all relationships. In addition to the very positive engagement from workshop participants across the continents, at the time of going to print, the TEDx Talk has in excess of 1.9 million views – and the views continue to climb, daily!

The great news is that we can all develop The 4 Habits®.

In fact, more than that, we *must*. And that is why we wrote this book.

Your blueprint for learning to do relationships well

Our central message is this – as individuals, we can and must take personal responsibility for developing our own level of 'Relational Intelligence'. How we 'show up' in our relationships has a direct impact on the quality of our interactions, conversations and outcomes. The 4 Habits® help us master the fundamentals of Relational Intelligence.

Our goal in this book is to help you understand – with urgency – why building Relational Intelligence is mission critical rather than just a nice-to-have, and to give you the tools to develop yours. Strong relationship skills are as vital for succeeding in the modern workplace as they are in the home – especially as the world becomes more cross-cultural and expectations of roles, responsibilities and behaviors shift.

Throughout this book, we share the key concepts, principles and techniques that underpin The 4 Habits® and allowed us, along with many others, to change our behaviors from habits that damage relationships to these four habits that strengthen relationships. Through the information covered you will learn how to reduce stress and frustrations that might exist in your relationships. You will also learn how to increase the level of warmth in relationships that matter to you, and how to stay on the journey to mastering your Relational Intelligence and influence, so all the relationships around you will be great.

It's important to note that our mindset in writing this book is *not* as 'consultants' trying to impress you with dazzling new models and ideas. Rather, we would encourage you to think of it as a conversation we are having together, sat across from each other in our living room. Our focus is on sharing principles, techniques and habits that work – proven to have made a difference in our relationship and the relationships of those with whom we have shared these insights over the decades. In some cases, we re-present wisdom that is decades old but applied in new ways relevant to the current cultural context. And where we do, we stand on the shoulders of giants in the field, and through this book we hope to honor them and the contributions they have made to relationship education.

Is this book about personal relationships or work relationships?

The question we often get asked at this point is this – is this book about personal relationships or work relationships?

Simple answer . . . it's about both.

Relationships are a vital part of everyone's life experience and yet, despite various governments' attempts at intervention, to date no formal process exists for teaching the fundamentals of relationships in a simple, consistent, accessible manner. For the most part, the quality of your relationship skills is based on the luck of the draw and what you've seen modelled to you. Chances are, in those few cases where you have been taught relationship skills, they have been for a single context – for example, how to manage conflict and build high-performance teams at work, or as pre-marriage counselling long before the challenges at home start. As a result, many people have ended up with compartmentalized behaviors – a work persona that is different from who they are in their personal lives and vice versa.

Our approach is to be proactive and intentional about who each of us becomes as a person and how we are experienced in relationships. We want to help everyone develop their overall level of Relational Intelligence and the required behavior changes to be able to show up better and more consistently as the person we would like 'to be' – in all our relationships at home, at work and in life.

Throughout the book we use examples from both home and work contexts simultaneously to help build an understanding of how the skills apply in various areas of life. In much the same way as some people are more left brain (logical) than right brain (creative) in their thinking or vice versa, some examples will be clearer for some people in one context than the other, but together they give the best chance of really getting the concepts.

Where we do sometimes default to a particular context, we tend to default to the most authentic relationships people have – their relationships at home – with a partner, with children, with parents. These are the relationships where it is often easiest for people to call you out on stuff and keep you accountable with your behaviors. In this regard, getting relationships right at home is likely to impact how you show up at work but not necessarily the other way round.

Who this book is for, and who it's not!

This book is about equipping everyone to do relationships well, whatever the kind of relationship. The ideal is that you get hold of this book and become equipped ahead of relationship challenges, although you will also find it helpful for navigating challenges you might already find yourself in. If you embrace the habits and techniques described and commit to not just trying them once, but to mastering them as fundamental life skills, you will be equipped to build quality relationships around you *on purpose*.

However, to be clear, this book is not about a quick fix or a substitute for professional counselling. If your relationship has gone badly wrong, please get the help you need without delay. (See useful links in the Appendices). Then come back and build skills that will keep you on course going forward.

How to make the most of this book

This book is structured into three parts.

- **Part A – TAKING CONTROL OF YOUR RELATIONSHIPS –** sets the context by developing an understanding of how your behavior impacts others. The more you understand this the more you are able to influence the quality of the relationships you experience and the level of WILL to invest in each on purpose. We also introduce The 4 Habits Experience Model to help you make sense of your experience in key relationships – both good and bad – based on the level of WILL to work on each relationship and the level of SKILL in knowing what to do.

- **Part B – MASTERING THE 4 HABITS®** – is the bulk of the book. Through our own stories and other examples, we unpack the concepts, principles and techniques underpinning each of The 4 Habits® to equip you to make behavior changes by replacing habits that damage relationships with habits that strengthen them. This is all about building your Relational Intelligence and developing SKILL, so you are able to build great relationships *on purpose*.

- **Part C – TAKING RESPONSIBILITY –** is about bringing it all together and making the commitment to put the learning into action by developing your own Personal Action Plan. It's easy to learn and parrot-fashion repeat what The 4 Habits® are. The challenge to all of us is to put this knowledge into action and take personal responsibility for how we 'show up' in our own circle of influence – as individuals, as organizations and as a society. When we each take personal responsibility, together we can strengthen relationships and turn the tide on the cost and impact of relationship breakdown.

We suggest you read through the book in chapter order, making notes as you go about specific things you want to focus on and improve. The worksheet in the Appendices will help you capture your thoughts and focus on things to STOP doing, things to START doing, things to CONTINUE doing, and things to CHANGE to achieve the results you desire.

At the end of each chapter are key takeaways and exercises to implement the learning. Do the exercises to help develop your thoughts and to start putting things into practice. You will find that as you inform your thinking, your feelings and behaviors will change to be more in line with who you choose to be in your relationships. Whatever behaviors and reactions you may have inherited, this book empowers you to choose how you are experienced by the people around you, especially the ones you really care about.

Time to make it personal . . .

We invite you to take this personally. Be open and be inspired. Allow the information shared to equip and empower you to become consistent in your behaviors and be experienced in all your relationships as the person you desire to be. Through the principles and techniques shared, you will gain confidence in *knowing what to do* to keep relationships healthy, to strengthen those that are weak and to thrive in life by surrounding yourself with quality relationships that support your wellbeing.

By the end of this book, you will be able to make a realistic assessment of where you are in your key relationships, develop a plan to move each one in the direction desired and become intentional about personal growth in each of the four habits, one habit at a time.

The quality of your relationships and, consequently, the quality of your life, is literally in your hands.

Ready to take control?

Time for Reflection

Key Takeaways

- All relationships face hurdles.

- Success in relationships comes from being equipped to get over the inevitable hurdles that all relationships face.

- We can and must take personal responsibility for learning to do relationships well.

- The 4 Habits® equip you with the fundamentals for changing behaviors from habits that damage relationships to habits that build strong relationships, *on purpose.*

Questions for Reflection

1. Now that you know where we're heading, what do you hope to achieve for yourself from this book?

2. What specific behavior changes would you like to make?

PART A

Taking Control of Your Relationships

Chapter One

Managing the WILL to keep relationships alive

*'We need to learn to recognise the things we do
that provoke a negative response and ideally,
stop doing them'*

The following email highlights one of the challenges of modern family life. We've changed the names and a couple of the details to maintain anonymity, but the story is real:

So, my partner is telling me that I'm spending too much time with my 12-year-old son Christian when I have him over at the weekends, and that I'm not spending any time with her. I think it's unfair as the weekends are the only time I get to spend with Christian, when I have Samantha with me the other five days. I'm expecting that very soon, once Christian becomes a teenager, he'll want to be spending more time with his friends and I won't get a look in, so I'm keen to make as much of the time as I can, while I can! I'm just wondering, am I being selfish and uncaring about Samantha? Am I missing something?

You can see why this dad (we'll call him Abe) was torn . . . Sometimes, the reason we do certain things seems so obvious to us that we struggle to understand why others around us don't just 'get it'. Our behaviors will always have an impact on the people around us (for better or worse!) so the starting point for managing the quality of relationships needs to be understanding how what we do 'lands' with others.

When Abe sent us that email, we were prompted straight away to ask what his relationship was like with his partner both in the five days they had together, and also while Christian was around at the weekend. How was his behavior 'landing' with her? Conceptually . . . what was the state of Samantha's 'Emotional Bank Account'? The fuller it was, the less likely this was to be an issue. The emptier, the more likely this and many other things would escalate and become issues between them.

But what does that all mean?

Understanding Emotional Bank Accounts

Well, to start at the very beginning, the 'Emotional Bank Account' is probably the most powerful concept we have come across for understanding and describing the state or quality of relationships.

Back in the early 1950s, one of the founders of family therapy, Ivan Borzormenyi-Nagy, introduced the concept of an Emotional Ledger to the world. He described the Emotional Ledger (or Bank Account in modern-day speech) as *'a mental record of the good or bad, experienced or perceived by an individual in their interactions with someone else'*.

Things perceived as a good deed or good treatment, or an expression of appreciation, are 'deposits' in the account. Other things perceived as negative or unkind, are like 'withdrawals'.

The net balance of our Emotional Bank Account (deposits minus withdrawals) with any particular individual, is a reflection of the quality of the relationship we experience with them.

And like with any (financial) bank account, the more deposits there are, the more tolerance there is for withdrawals.

The benefits of a positive balance will be experienced in the relationship as more flex, warmth and friendship. People are happier to make allowances for each other and go the extra mile when their Emotional Bank Accounts are full. We all know how to find ways to say 'Yes' when we have a vested interest in a relationship. We work around the system, bend the rules a bit, and go all out to support someone when the relationship is going well.

Where the balance drops to zero or even into overdraft, everything can become a problem . . . much like with our financial bank accounts! The more withdrawals there are, the easier it is for conflicts and disagreements to flare up and the experience in the relationship will be one of tension and strain. In fact, you can have the same conversation you used to have successfully with someone when their Emotional Bank Account with you was full, but get a completely different, more hostile response when the bank account is drained. The 'tolerance buffer' has disappeared.

We all know how to be difficult and unhelpful in our attitude and approach when we feel wronged in any way. In general, we tend to make decisions emotionally and justify them retrospectively with logic. And we know how to cleverly use logic or rules and regulations to justify decisions we made emotionally because of fractures in a relationship.

This is as relevant to relationships with your colleagues, your clients, your boss, your parents, your children, your friends . . . as it is to your partner or spouse. Our very language in many western cultures confirms this concept of the Emotional Bank Account. Why else do we say 'I owe you one' after someone does us a favor of some sort? It's that internal, mental record, adding up all the time, keeping account of every interaction in every relationship.

There are a couple more points to cover in order to fully understand Emotional Bank Accounts.

Everyone's got (a different) one!

As sophisticated human beings, we each hold different Emotional Bank Accounts for each of the people we're relating to. This explains why we can be totally frustrated with one person (let's say our boss) and totally at peace with someone else at the same time – like a colleague – until our boss walks in the room and the atmosphere becomes chilled!

Other people also hold an Emotional Bank Account for us.

It's all about perception – what I intended is irrelevant

It's really important to note that at the end of the day, 'what I was thinking' or 'what I intended to do' has very little impact on other people's Emotional Bank Accounts.

> **Emotional Bank Accounts are all about perceptions. How what we do 'lands' with the other person is all that matters.**

We all have our own version of living and loving . . . and sometimes we get caught short by the response our words and actions provoke. Dave and Dina's 'towel flicking' episode is a great example.

Dave and Dina's story . . .

> *In the early days of their moving in together, Dave thought it would be great fun and 'bonding time' to roll up a towel (like a rat's tail) and flick the end of it at his new wife, Dina, expecting her to burst into laughter and chase him around the room like his brother used to do. She was horrified. Never having had brothers, for her, flicking a towel and inflicting pain in any way broke every rule on how 'Prince Charming' should treat his Princess. It resulted in instant anger and upset for Dina and was definitely not the romantic frolicking*

Dave anticipated. Her Emotional Bank Account went from full (things had been pretty good up until that moment) to instantly overdrawn. At that moment, no amount of explaining his 'intent' from Dave could undo the disrespect she perceived.

The reality is nobody goes into a relationship hell-bent on having a miserable time or creating a miserable time for the other person, especially if that person is their significant other. Most of us go into relationships hoping for the best . . . but there are things that we do that land badly and cause a problem. Those are the things we need to get better at.

We need to learn to recognize the things we do that provoke a negative response and ideally, stop doing them.

Becoming better at interpreting responses *in the moment* in the context of the Emotional Bank Account will help prevent a lot of aggravation and keep things from spiraling downwards.

This is why understanding the concept of the Emotional Bank Account is so vital. It helps us manage the 'temperature' and quality of our relationship, it helps us manage our own response, and it helps us diffuse tension in the relationship when necessary.

Learning to manage the 'temperature' in your relationships

Simply being aware of the state of Emotional Bank Accounts (both yours and the people you're relating with) offers a strategy for proactively managing the quality of your relationships. It allows you to sense the overall balance of emotions based on the level of warmth and goodwill in the relationship and proactively do things to get it to the level you desire.

To illustrate this, let's go back to Samantha, Abe and Christian. A drained Emotional Bank Account was precisely *the issue behind the issue* for Samantha. Yes, she and Abe had five out of seven days together but, in that time, Abe was spending more time unintentionally draining, rather than topping up, Samantha's Emotional Bank Account. For example, Abe always wanted things done a certain way and often criticized others when they didn't match his standards. Being a relatively new relationship, Samantha was still learning his preferences but was beginning to feel told off all the time. So, by the end of the week, she was already feeling emotionally empty, only to then see Abe pour out the kind of love and affirmation on Christian that she (Samantha) would have loved to feel. Of course, she knew it was important for Abe to have a strong relationship with his son. But she longed for the kind of attention that would make her, too, feel loved and special, instead of emotionally drained and 'unspecial'.

The key to fixing this relationship was to help Abe reduce the things he was doing unintentionally to drain Samantha's Emotional Bank Account and start doing more things to actually fill it up, on purpose. The question then is how could Abe do that in practice?

For Abe and Samantha, and all of us in fact . . .

Success comes from focusing on minimizing withdrawals and at the same time, maximizing deposits.

In Abe's case, holding back on the criticism was key to minimizing withdrawals from Samantha's Emotional Bank Account, while showing her appreciation in ways that are important to her in order to make deposits on purpose. We will expand on how to show meaningful love and appreciation in chapters 12 and 13, but one of the things that is really important to Samantha is spending quality one-on-one time with Abe. That makes huge deposits for her. No wonder she was feeling frustrated! In Samantha's eyes, Abe was lavishing on Christian the very thing she desired from him and all she was getting – at least in her mind – was criticism.

You can learn to minimize withdrawals and maximize deposits with anyone and everyone – your colleagues, clients, boss, partner or spouse, parents, children, in-laws, friends. Literally anybody and everybody!

Consciously maintaining an emotionally positive balance means that conflict will not be triggered so easily, there will be more flex and more willingness to have each other's backs, and that peace is restored faster whenever conflict does arise.

Doing BOTH – minimizing withdrawals and maximizing deposits – gives you the best chance of maintaining the WILL to keep your relationships alive and healthy.

So, what makes a deposit . . . and what a withdrawal?

The question then is: 'How do we find out what makes a deposit, and what a withdrawal, for each person as we relate to them?' And when we do know, what can we actually do to increase the number of times our actions are perceived as deposits and reduce the number of times our actions are perceived as withdrawals?

This is the question that often stumps us in relationships. And, as a result, we end up stumbling along until one day we find ourselves (or the experience in the relationship) somewhere we never intended it to be. Suddenly we're opting out of project teams or corporate social events because 'that person' is going to be there or is in charge. Or at home, living with the cold shoulder, with silence, or distance.

We will look at this detail when we look at each of The 4 Habits®, but the quick answer is to *listen carefully to the other person and act on what they say.*

If you have a partner or colleague or someone else, you're relating with who is complaining, listen to what they're saying – they're probably telling you right there, what makes a withdrawal for them. If they are saying things like 'you always criticize me' or 'you never say thank you or tell me when I've done a great job' or 'you get irritated every time I forget to do something silly like clearing my mugs away at the end of the day' they are giving you huge clues on what is a withdrawal for them. Or in a home context – if they complain that you leave the kitchen in a mess, or that you never give compliments – those are clues on what withdrawals are for them and what could be deposits if you did the opposite.

There are some common examples of deposits and withdrawals which always make the list when we go through this as an exercise in our workshops and webinars. Typical examples of deposits are:

- genuinely listening

- saying please and thank you

- acknowledging contributions made by an individual

- speaking kindly (especially where people are expecting a telling off)

- using a respectful tone even in a conflict situation.

We don't need special training or qualifications to do any of the above, but they make a profound difference to the 'temperature' of the relationship when we do them consistently and often. The challenge is to change our behaviors and make a habit of the things that put deposits in the Emotional Bank Accounts of the people around us. That's the 'how to' that we cover in Part B.

Typical examples of withdrawals include the reverse of deposits, of course, but the following also generally get mentioned specifically:

- criticizing harshly and/or publicly

- belittling

- holding grudges and keeping scores

- being easily angered.

These are all things that will drain warmth from someone's Emotional Bank Account. And, depending on the personality, may put their Emotional Bank Account into instant overdraft. If we are unaware of the negative impact of our words, tone and behavior on the people around us and, worse yet, if simultaneously we are not making any deposits, it is no surprise that relationships can quickly end up in a state of permanent emotional overdraft, like Abe with Samantha and Christian.

It's important to recognize that deposits and withdrawals will land with different weights for different people. For example, lack of respect for time may be a huge deal for you, but someone else might be more relaxed about time. Maybe being criticized is the big deal for them. The important thing is to recognize what is landing badly with them so you can stop that, and then start doing the opposite, which generally results in deposits. There is no shortcut for understanding how things land with each individual or for learning to manage Emotional Bank Accounts.

The sad thing about living in permanent overdraft is that any deposits you make, any attempt to show care and friendship will generally get gobbled up by the negative balance without a moment of registering positive. In those situations, where there is no emotional cushion, life can be mechanical at best, volatile at worst.

The challenge is often we have to unlearn some habits and become intentional about replacing habits that damage relationships with habits that strengthen them. Take sarcasm for example. Many times, we excuse this as 'just humor'. Even if someone is 'OK' with sarcasm, it adds no deposits to their Emotional Bank Account and one ill-timed attempt at sarcasm can send the relationship into a downward spiral. Worse yet, in a moment of self-doubt, sarcasm can be crippling to someone's self-esteem.

Learning to manage your responses

The great thing about this concept of the Emotional Bank Account is that once you understand it, you automatically start to view your interactions through this new powerful lens which helps you make better choices about how to respond. Typically, when we feel misunderstood or when something we intended to land well lands badly, we tend to react defensively and make things worse.

> In our household, we each have our own stories to tell about some classic moments with this! Let's say Andrea does something innocently that I (Jon) get upset about. But instead of apologizing and discussing the misunderstanding, Andrea gets upset about the way I responded to something she did innocently. That becomes a whole new argument about my behavior. This scenario also happens in reverse. And then we get stuck on who did the worse crime and therefore who should apologize first. It's laughable writing it on paper but the emotions have been intense! If you're anything like us, you know exactly what we are talking about.

Thankfully, the more we understand about Emotional Bank Accounts, the easier it becomes to push past our reflex response to defend ourselves, recognize that what we did or said landed badly (for reasons which might not even have anything to do with us!) and focus on clearing up the misunderstanding. We talk more about choosing our response when we talk about minimizing and managing conflict in chapters 6 and 7.

For the moment though, just becoming more aware of the impact of our behavior on other people's Emotional Bank Account helps us choose our response and gives us the opportunity to undo unintentional withdrawals before they escalate into major arguments. It also gives us the language to describe the impact of other people's behavior on us. In this way, we can choose a better response by making it clear to the other person how their behavior landed badly and asking for a different action or approach where necessary to help things 'land better'. Much more productive than sulking, distancing or giving the silent treatment!

Caution: Emotional Bank Accounts can become toxic!

Sometimes, with the best will in the world, the quality of the relationship is out of our hands. It's worth noting that any Emotional Bank Account in long-term deficit can become 'emotionally toxic' and 'ooze out' onto other relationships. People with Emotional Bank Accounts *in deficit* can become difficult to be around, as the underlying tone in all their interactions shifts to become one of mistrust, suspicion and a presumption of ill-intent.

The more relationships they have in deficit the more toxic they become as individuals. Regardless of how you turn up to these relationships yourself, their 'poison' oozes out as a permanently bad attitude or shows up as other toxic behaviors like bullying and manipulation.

The point here is that in some cases, the right thing to do might be to 'close' your Emotional Bank Account with them. Sometimes 'managing your response' means ending interactions with toxic people for the sake of your own health and sanity. You've got that power.

Learning to diffuse tension and relationship strain

Outside of toxic relationships, understanding the concept of the Emotional Bank Account can give you clues on what to do to diffuse ongoing tension in a relationship and rebuild warmth on purpose. Whether it's with an aunt or parent who constantly criticizes, a teen that seems sulky and withdrawn, a colleague that just doesn't 'get you' or a spouse that feels emotionally disconnected, choosing to focus on things that would make deposits in their Emotional Bank Account can help to diffuse tension and open the door to open, honest conversations. At the same time, you can work to find out what you might be doing that represents withdrawals for them and develop the courage to talk about the things they do that land as withdrawals for you. We talk more about how to have these kinds of courageous conversations in chapter 11.

Meanwhile, a key point to note is that:

Sometimes tensions creep into relationships simply because Emotional Bank Accounts 'leak'.

As with standard bank charges that tend to slowly drain your financial bank account (even with no activity from you), Emotional Bank Accounts also suffer the equivalent of a 'daily living allowance' that drains the balance over time.

This has real implications for how we manage remote teams or stay connected as couples who live and work apart for extended periods. Silence and distance often breed insecurities and mistrust.

No surprises that one of the key challenges described by team members working remotely through the COVID-19 lockdown was this feeling of distance, drift or strain in relationships with their colleagues or manager, simply because they were not in touch as often as they used to be. Similar to the social media experience of FOMO – the Fear of Missing Out – silence in a relationship can breed suspicion and anxiety, with an accompanying reluctance to pick up the phone or connect in some way, causing things to get worse. For some reason, many of us tend to assume we are being left out deliberately and talked-about behind our backs!

Importantly, this is as relevant in one-on-one relationships as it is to tensions between groups of people. For example, the concept of Emotional Bank Accounts can also help us understand the tension and anger around issues like racism and injustice. Years of prejudice and inequality have created major withdrawals in the Emotional Bank Accounts of traditionally marginalized groups of people – blacks, LGBTQ+, etc. The outworking of this is that relationships with those (whites, conservatives) that make them feel on the outside, tend to start out emotionally overdrawn, riddled with suspicion, mistrust and a presumption of ill-intent on both sides.

Building relationships across such differences means becoming very intentional about doing things that land well – like genuinely listening to the distinct voices without judgement – and not doing the things that land badly (and there are many!) until trust is rebuilt. We talk some more about building strong relationships across difference in the context of diversity and inclusion in chapter 16, but we wanted to make the direct link with the concept of the Emotional Bank Account here. These issues often feel so much bigger than us, but one-on-one we can start to make a difference and begin to change the narrative – at least for the people around us.

Whether between individuals or between groups of people, tensions in relationships are minimized when we each make deliberate efforts to ensure the Emotional Bank Account with each person in our circle of influence is healthy and regularly topped up. Significantly, this means understanding each individual and what makes them tick, rather than having a standard approach to treatment across a group. There is no shortcut for knowing people as individuals. We will unpack this some more when we look at each of The 4 Habits® in Part B.

Meanwhile, if it *feels* like a while since you have been in touch with someone, it's been too long already and the only way to begin to address the situation is to make contact. Of course, communication goes both ways, and they could take the initiative to contact you too. But the tension will only build the longer the silence continues. Nip it in the bud and pick up the phone. Chances are that things are not quite as bad as you are assuming they are.

This is why being intentional about making 'deposits' in the relationships that are important to you is crucial. Along with minimizing withdrawals, doing things on purpose to make people feel appreciated and cared-for keeps the warmth in the relationship, creates a buffer to manage the inevitable leaks, and minimizes unnecessary tension.

Over the years we have found that just by explaining the concept of the Emotional Bank Account, people start to feel more hopeful and empowered to do something differently and improve their key relationships where necessary. By learning to manage Emotional Bank Accounts we can help maintain the WILL to keep building strong relationships.

Armed with this understanding, the next step is to develop the SKILL, so we know exactly what to do in order to become consistent in our behaviors and to do relationships well. That's what we will explore together in the next chapter.

Time for Reflection

Key Takeaways

- We each keep a mental record of the experience of our interactions (positive or negative) with the people around us – in an Emotional Bank Account.

- We can all proactively manage the level of warmth and the quality of each of our relationships by:

    a. becoming aware of the state of Emotional Bank Accounts (theirs and ours)

    b. minimizing unintentional withdrawals

    c. maximizing deposits.

Building Your Understanding

1. Think for a minute about a relationship that is important to you and is going well (partner, friend, colleague):

    a. How would you describe the level of your Emotional Bank Account with them?

    b. How do you think they would describe their Emotional Bank Account with you?

    c. What delights you? What are the things they do that land well and are like deposits in your Emotional Bank Account?

    d. What are likely to be deposits for them?

    e. What could you do to keep putting in deposits, minimizing withdrawals and maintaining a positive balance?

2. Think for a moment about a relationship that is *not* going well:

    a. What are the things that land badly that make withdrawals for you?

    b. What do you think is a withdrawal for them? (One big hint is to think about the things they complain (or nag!) about and the things they request.)

    c. What could you do to put in deposits, minimize withdrawals and work toward a more positive balance?

Going Deeper

How can this concept of the Emotional Bank Account help explain tensions between groups of people, like the issues society still faces with racism?

Taking Personal Action

- START / STOP / CONTINUE / CHANGE

  Based on your learnings and reflections so far, what is one thing that you could start doing that you have not done before, or stop doing because it is unhelpful, or continue doing because it is working well (and now you know why!), or change to do differently? Feel free to copy the sheet in the Appendices (or download and print) to capture your thoughts.

Chapter Two

Building the SKILL to do relationships well

*'Your level of SKILL in relationships will
either promote or expose you.'*

How can I get better at communicating?

If you've ever listened in on any talk show on the subject of relationships, or indeed if you've ever asked someone who has had a long (and apparently successful) relationship, 'What makes a relationship great?', the typical answer is . . . 'communication'. We wouldn't dispute that.

And on the flip side, if you were to ask those experiencing challenges, the biggest reason we've heard time and again is . . . 'poor communication'.

The reality is not that most of us don't know *what* to do to improve our relationships (we need to get better at communicating, duh!), it's that we have no idea *how* to do it.

The following text (from, let's call him Sanjay . . . and with details modified to maintain anonymity), sums up the challenge that many face:

I'm really struggling to communicate properly with my wife Deepti. She keeps forgetting to do simple things that I find really irritating and then she doesn't like it when I try to laugh it off with sarcasm. And on my side, I keep trying to do the things I know she likes, but I either fall short of the mark, or I don't talk to her about my plans – either because I'm still making them or because I haven't put in as much effort as I feel I should have. And then she gets upset because I haven't done some things or communicated my intentions.

I'm also not so good at communicating what I love about her in the moment – like when I sometimes peek in on her and see the really caring side of her as she teaches the kids in her class. I think she's only going to think I'm patronizing her. And then the moment passes, and it feels awkward bringing it up, and so it never gets said.

I know I need to get better at communicating. I just don't know how to do it.

Sanjay, like most of us, recognized that 'communication' is a whole lot more than simply the verbal stuff. His actions were communicating negative messages unintentionally, and he was failing to communicate positive ones when he needed to. He needed to build SKILL.

It didn't take Sanjay long to recognize that what he needed to do was develop habits that would see him *stop* making unintentional withdrawals from Deepti's Emotional Bank Account and *start* making deposits on purpose. To do that, he was going to have to learn how to:

- stop reacting negatively when Deepti did things he couldn't understand

- change the way he handled conflict when the frustrations eventually bubbled out

- start rebuilding mutual trust and respect into their relationship

- actually show appreciation in ways that would register for Deepti.

In short, to get better at 'communication', he was going to have to learn The 4 Habits®.

And by the way, there were areas Deepti could also get better at to improve their communication challenges. But for now, our advice was for him to focus on changing the only person he had power to change. Himself.

As we shared with him . . .

Living out Habits #1 and #2 will help minimize withdrawals from Emotional Bank Accounts. And practicing Habits #3 and #4 regularly, helps maximize deposits.

The 4 Habits® – The 'How To' for building Relational Intelligence

Another way to think about developing the SKILL we need for improving our relationships is to think of the habits as ways to improve our 'Relational Intelligence' – our ability to connect, and stay connected, with the people around us.

Today there are many different definitions of Relational Intelligence, and a growing number of books written on the subject. What most practitioners appear to agree on, however, is the subtle difference between Relational and Emotional Intelligence. Where Relational Intelligence most agree is about how we connect with and interact with others, consensus is that Emotional Intelligence is more about awakening (or improving) our ability to handle *our own* emotions and how they impact on the people around us.

Daniel Goleman's categorization is helpful. In fact, it was he who first popularized the notion of Emotional Intelligence, back in the mid-1990s, in his book of that name. For success in life, Goleman concluded, the data suggests that our Emotional Intelligence, or EQ, 'can be as powerful, and at times more powerful, than IQ'.[5] Over the years he has refined his thinking to discuss[6] EQ in terms of how well an individual handles themselves in their relationships against four domains:

- Self-awareness: Knowing what we're feeling and why we're feeling it.

- Self-management: Handling our distressing emotions in effective ways.

- Empathy: Knowing what someone else is feeling.

- Social Skills: Putting that all together in skilled relationship.

And when you stop to think about it, it makes intuitive sense that the better we can each get at both understanding ourselves and managing how we show up when things get tense, and also at understanding others and improving how we relate to them, the better the likely outcomes for our relationships.

And that's precisely what The 4 Habits® do, in practical terms:

- **Habit #1: BE CURIOUS, not critical** – is all about developing our self-awareness (and other-awareness!) through understanding fundamental differences, learning to give each other 'space and grace' to shine in our own strengths, and overcoming the frustration of unmet expectations.

- **Habit #2: BE CAREFUL, not crushing** – is all about self-management, building strong skills in managing conflict, learning to treat each other well no matter how heated the argument, and working toward genuine resolutions so that relationships are strengthened not damaged through conflict.

- **Habit #3: ASK, don't assume** – is all about developing the social skills to build mutual trust and respect in relationships by clarifying values, having courageous conversations about things that really matter to us when necessary and overcoming the hurdles of mistrust and distance that can creep into relationships.

- **Habit #4: CONNECT, before you correct** – is all about learning to build great rapport, warmth and connection in relationships by consistently communicating appreciation and love in meaningful ways and overcoming the hurdle of feeling unvalued because of poor communication.

The reason they work is that mastering Habits #1 and #2 help us minimize those pesky unintentional withdrawals from Emotional Bank Accounts, and guess what . . . Habits #3 and #4 help us make deposits *on purpose!*

As it turns out, The 4 Habits® are the fundamental building blocks for developing the SKILL to do relationships well. They provide a practical means of unpacking the key aspects of communication and interaction with the people around us, so that we can get better at each component part. They do that by allowing us to share intent and meaning while managing Emotional Bank Accounts and change our behaviors from habits that damage relationships to habits that strengthen our relationships, *on purpose*.

Developing the SKILL

While The 4 Habits® are simple and intuitive – they're not rocket science, anyone can learn them – developing them generally doesn't happen automatically. As with most habits, it takes a while of unlearning old, unhelpful habits before we can effectively change our behaviors. Success comes from being intentional.

As many of us have learned to our cost, oftentimes when things are too intuitive, we don't give them the attention they deserve. Like with our health and fitness. Of course, we all know that, by and large, to lose weight and keep fit we must burn more calories than we consume through watching our diet and having regular exercise. For too many of us though, this is not a natural habit – and we live with the consequences in weight gain and/or associated health issues. It's the same with our relationships. The only way to enjoy great relationships is to learn and apply the skills and principles that help us make a habit of the behaviors that strengthen rather than damage relationships.

Consistency in delivery is the key.

Performance coaches, for example in the dramatic arts or the sports world, focus on consistency in terms of breaking a skill down into its very basic components and then replicating those basic movements over and over again until they are perfected, even under pressure. Just think about drama rehearsals line by line or unending football drills. With the pressure on and all eyes watching, success comes from training your body and muscles to respond in the way you have been rehearsing the basic components.

Developing great habits produces great results in the performing arts and sports, even under pressure . . . and they will do the same for your relationships!

Your level of SKILL in relationships will either promote or expose you.

With this in mind, our approach to building strong relationships is to go back to basics, help people learn the concepts and techniques around these four fundamental habits, and then practice and apply the learning until they achieve consistency – genuine, relationship-centered behavior changes.

When these fundamental habits become our natural default responses, even under pressure, we achieve the behavior change that allows us to be experienced consistently well in all our relationships, have better conversations and achieve better results. We might not know the specific challenges that we will face, but these four habits equip us with the basic skills to overcome relationship challenges, however they appear.

Is SKILL alone enough?

Once you understand the context, mastering these four fundamental habits will help you take control of your key relationships. They will help you recognize what you are doing well so you can do it on purpose. They will help you identify what you are doing that is damaging the relationship so you can make better choices. They will also help you develop your own toolkit of things to do to improve each relationship you want to strengthen, taking the relationship from where it is now to where you would like it to be.

In time, our hope is that developing this Relational Intelligence will become a natural part of personal and professional development for everyone. Until then, however, the onus is on each of us to be intentional about being equipped to do relationships well, developing the SKILL that allows us to be consistent in how we are experienced, and change our behaviors from habits that damage relationships to habits that strengthen them.

Before we delve into the detail of mastering these four habits in practice though (the sole focus of Part B), there is one last point to cover. In the next chapter we highlight WHY in addition to developing your SKILL to build great relationships, it's also important to focus on managing the WILL . . . and the impact both your level of SKILL and WILL can have on the quality of relationships you experience. This is demonstrated through The 4 Habits Experience Model which will help you make sense of WHAT you are experiencing in each of your key relationships so that the way forward becomes clearer. Understanding where you are will help you be proactive about keeping relationships great and/or strengthening them to build the quality relationships you desire.

Time for Reflection

Key Takeaways

- The 4 Habits® are the fundamental building blocks for developing Relational Intelligence and the SKILL to be consistent in doing relationships well.

- When these fundamentals become our natural default habits, we achieve the behavior-change that builds and strengthens relationships rather than damages them – even under pressure.

Building Your Understanding

1. Which of The 4 Habits® do you think is an area of strength for you?

2. Which of The 4 Habits® do you think you need to work on?

Chapter Three

How our levels of SKILL and WILL impact our relationships

*'We cannot solve our problems
with the same thinking we used to create them.'*
Albert Einstein[7]

Alessandra and Haruto's story . . .

Alessandra and Haruto had been struggling to work together on the organizational restructure of the company's Finance Department and now things had come to a head. Much of the finance work had recently been automated or taken off-shore which meant they needed to figure out how to redeploy the Finance team and, sadly, make some people redundant. As Head of HR, Alessandra was focused on mitigating risks of employee grievance procedures and tribunals. Although she did care about the people, her concern over corporate reputation and her 'matter of fact' approach to decisions that negatively impacted people's lives came across as uncaring. Years of experience in dealing with thorny global HR issues – and men with suits and matching egos – had taught her to be both direct and directive in the way she spoke.

None of that worked for Haruto. The combination of his Japanese culture and his introverted personality meant he found her style abrasive on many fronts. As Head of Finance, this was his team. He knew all these people personally – knew their families even – and was concerned about the impact this restructure would have on them. Despite being gentle in nature, he was no pushover and dug his heels in against what he perceived as Alessandra's cold, proposed approach for communicating the changes to the team.

This was their fourth attempt at developing a communication strategy and Alessandra finally lost it, becoming so frustrated that she started shouting at Haruto – in front of other colleagues. That did it for him. The conversation was over – permanently – as far as he was concerned. She would have to find someone else to work with on this. Except ... he knew she couldn't because this was his team. Ultimately, his responsibility. They would have to figure out a way, but not now. He got up, making sure his chair screeched his grave disapproval, and left the room. Alessandra stood shocked and speechless. She couldn't understand how someone so competent at his job could be so spineless and weak.

We knew Alessandra socially and could sense her frustrations when she called and asked to meet up for a coffee. As she shared the experience, we started to recognize the tell-tale signs of lack of SKILL creating frustrations and relational impasse. In Alessandra's own words as a 'hot-blooded, passionate Italian' she needed Haruto to engage more, even if that meant having to deal with the occasional shouting, so that they could argue things through and get past this unpleasant process once and for all.

One of the most rewarding aspects of the work we do is seeing the 'lightbulbs' go on in people's eyes when we share simple concepts that help them get a better perspective on their situation. Usually, one or two key principles or techniques is all it takes to help people 'hear' each other better and become open again to having more meaningful conversations and finding a way forward. For Alessandra, the quick-wins came from sharing high-level information around how different personality types show up in conflict (Habits #1 and #2) and explaining the concept of the Emotional Bank Account to help her understand the impact her behavior was having on Haruto. In one (admittedly long!) coffee conversation, we helped her see how they could start the process of repairing their relationship, developing more mutual understanding and working together more effectively for the long term. We helped her push past her frustrations and start her own journey to improving her SKILL in having better conversations and achieving better outcomes.

Some wise words came alive to her that day, 'We cannot solve our problems with the same thinking we used to create them.'

The 4 Habits Experience Model – Developing SKILL and Managing WILL

Over the past 25 plus years of working with relationships, we have found that being proactive about building (and rebuilding) quality relationships is dependent on the two criteria of building SKILL and managing WILL.

The 4 Habits Experience Model is a two-dimensional matrix which describes the likely experience in relationships based on the level of SKILL and WILL present. To understand what that looks like in practice, let's explore each axis and the typical experience at each extreme.

Developing 'SKILL'

SKILL refers to your level of knowledge and default behaviors around relationships. If you're not particularly happy with the answer to the question 'Who am I being, especially under pressure?', building SKILL is what will help you 'turn up' better and become a 'safe person' to be around – consistent, predictable and not prone to unexpected blow outs!

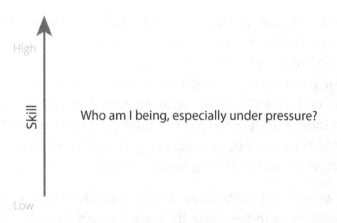

Building SKILL means building the knowledge and habits that result in a genuine change in behavior from habits that damage relationships to habits that strengthen them. As we demonstrated in the last chapter, The 4 Habits® provide the practical 'HOW TOs' for building SKILL.

Managing 'WILL'

'WILL' describes your level of energy, motivation and desire to invest in a particular relationship. It helps you answer the question 'Do I really care enough to put in the effort to maintain or improve this relationship?' As we covered in chapter 1, 'WILL' is a direct reflection of the state of the Emotional Bank Account. When the balance in the Emotional Bank Account is, on average, high over sustained periods, there is strong WILL and motivation to invest in the relationship. When the balance in the Emotional Bank Account resides around zero or below, there is very little WILL or motivation to put any effort into making the relationship work.

Managing WILL means becoming intentional about managing the state of Emotional Bank Accounts so that you can maintain the warmth, energy and motivation to build SKILLS *and* apply them to *this* relationship.

Do I really care enough to put in the effort?

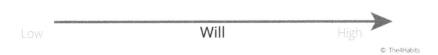

© The4Habits

In order to develop, or re-develop, the 'WILL', you need to understand what's going on in your Emotional Bank Accounts . . . and then develop the 'SKILL' so you can be deliberate about minimizing unintentional withdrawals and maximizing deposits. The more positive the balance in your Emotional Bank Account with someone, the more WILL there is to discover and do the things that make the other person feel appreciated and respected, and the more mutually satisfying the relationship is likely to be.

Understanding the state of relationships – why they 'feel' the way they do

Having the SKILL does not guarantee the WILL to invest in a particular relationship. Having the WILL does not guarantee you have the SKILL, or know what to do, to build a great relationship with this specific person either. You need both.

Together, your level of SKILL and WILL can help you articulate where you are or what you are experiencing in any of your key relationships at any point in time. They also provide pointers to what you can do to improve things, if necessary.

We like to think of WILL as the horizontal (x) axis of a graph, and SKILL as the vertical (y) axis. Where the axes cross, both SKILL and WILL are very low and increase out from there. On a graph like that, you can see how relationships will exist at different points along the continuum.

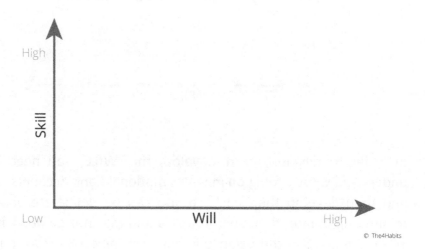

© The4Habits

Understanding what the experience in the relationship is likely to be at the extremes helps you articulate and make sense of where you are in your key relationships.

Relationships at the extremes (shown below as four quadrants) are likely to feel like:

- 'Mutual Satisfaction' (High WILL : High SKILL)

- 'Frustration' (High WILL : Low SKILL)

- 'Desperation' (Low WILL : Low SKILL), and

- 'Isolation' (Low WILL : High SKILL).

Let's look at each in turn.

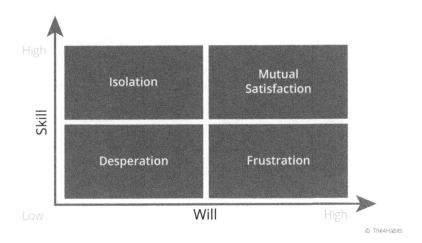

© The4Habits

Mutual Satisfaction Quadrant (High WILL : High SKILL)

For the most part, we all start out in relationships with good intentions and generally want to get on well with people so we can live or work together and enjoy a peaceful life. Our WILL is high.

Interestingly, in the early days in relationships, as long as we have some base level of SKILL, we are able to enjoy a certain amount of Mutual Satisfaction. At this stage in the relationship, SKILL plays a much-reduced role. *Goodwill* and *best behavior* tend to make up for lack of SKILL.

This is what is usually referred to as 'the honeymoon' or 'settling-in' period. The reality though is that Mutual Satisfaction is being experienced *by chance*. The relationship (and our level of SKILL) has not yet been challenged by life's hurdles. Quite often when things are working well, we don't even know what it is that we are doing *specifically* to make the relationship work.

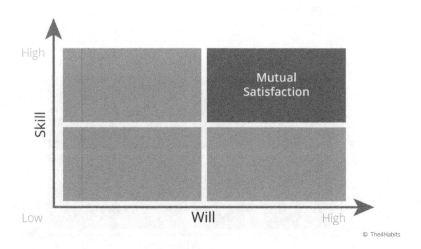

© The4Habits

Building SKILL means we get to experience Mutual Satisfaction in our key relationships, not by chance but *by choice*, because we know what to do and can be intentional in our actions to keep the relationship mutually satisfying. Specifically, we know how to look after each other's Emotional Bank Accounts, keep the levels topped up and maintain goodwill in the relationship.

Relationships in the Mutual Satisfaction Quadrant where the WILL is high, and SKILL is high, feel *great*. This is where the experience of life with your spouse, partner, children, family *feels* emotionally connected, mutually supportive and intimate. This is also where great colleague relationships and great friendships sit. People feel valued, respected, loved.

Mutual Satisfaction is what we all hope for in our key relationships. We will revisit this quadrant after we have examined the other three quadrants.

Frustration Quadrant (High WILL : Low SKILL)

Given that we're all wired differently, it's inevitable that at some stage we will experience a difference of opinion in our relationships. The longer and more often we are exposed to each other's differences the faster differences of opinions will emerge. This is especially likely during transition periods like setting up house together for the first time, a move to working from home, retirement – or national lockdown like the world experienced in the COVID-19 pandemic.

With this understanding, we can see that . . .

It is natural to flip-flop from Mutual Satisfaction into the Frustration zone as we bump up against each other's differences.

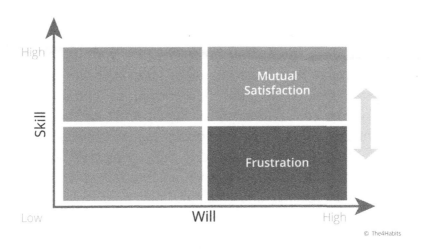

© The4Habits

Everything in the relationship could be going well and then one person says or does something that frustrates or irritates the other, and something that was innocent or even meant to be a show of appreciation or love is misunderstood. Sometimes just getting general understanding about people and their differences can help save the day.

We can all expect some level of frustration and misunderstanding in relationships but the better we get at understanding each other and having healthy conversations, the faster issues can be resolved, the more topped up the Emotional Bank Account will be and the faster we get back into the Mutual Satisfaction quadrant.

Most healthy relationships go through cycles between Mutual Satisfaction and Frustration from time to time, which is all perfectly fine as long as you keep learning and improving your understanding of each other and don't get stuck or set up camp in the Frustration zone.

However, in the absence of knowledge and the SKILL to have healthy conversations, we are left to our own devices to interpret intentions and behaviors. Usually our self-preservation mode kicks in, meaning we think the worst and our interpretation is never in the other person's favor.

In our early professional careers, we both experienced the strains and frustrations of working with different personalities, huge egos and having to battle through awkward team relationships. But at least we could leave them at work! Living and working together meant we had to learn to use the frustrations, difficult as they felt at the time, as triggers to get more understanding about each other's perspective and adjust our own approaches in order to become unstuck.

And then we set up in business together!

Sharing personally, we know what it's like first-hand to have experienced the additional life challenges that can rock a relationship and create more frustrations – severe financial stress, loss of a parent, major health challenges, surgeries and difficulties having children. We've also set up and run businesses together – putting all our finances on the line – twice! Without the SKILL to have better conversations, we too could have been stuck in a cycle of unnecessary frustrations, slowly pushing each other apart, for lack of knowledge. Although it didn't feel like a blessing at the time, the blessing for us was that we were married and so walking away was far more complicated than just resigning from a company. If we were just colleagues at work, chances are we would have started avoiding each other, found ways to make sure we didn't have to cross paths or work together, and made sure we focused on different projects to avoid getting stuck in unnecessary tensions and frustrations. We dread to think about what we could have lost if we hadn't found a way to push through.

The Frustration quadrant feels like *what it says on the tin* — moments of real hair-pulling frustration! However, in the middle of the storm is an opportunity to grow and develop more understanding, a shared perspective, and a stronger foundation for the relationship. Which is why we sometimes also refer to the Frustration quadrant as the 'learning zone'. Conflict is often a growth opportunity in disguise. But growth requires the SKILL to push past our self-preservation reflexes, have meaningful dialogue to create a shared perspective (rather than just be defensive / offensive) and treat each other well in the process so that the goodwill in the relationship remains high. We discuss this more in chapter 7 when we talk about how to do conflict well.

Desperation Quadrant (Low WILL : Low SKILL)

If we don't develop the SKILL, flip-flopping over the same issues again and again can become exhausting. When people get stuck in Frustration and don't increase their knowledge, their Emotional Bank Account drains, breeding misunderstanding and mistrust.

At that point, it's easy to *lose the WILL* to keep trying, and many relationships eventually drop down into the Desperation quadrant.

In Desperation, the oxygen in the relationship is running out and typically people are ill-equipped to breathe life back in again, on their own.

Perhaps through lack of knowledge, lack of skills, fear, or a combination of them all, things get swept under the proverbial carpet and remain unaddressed. Emotional Bank Accounts get low or overdrawn and a willingness to do anything to improve the situation drains away. Think about colleagues and friends who might have done something that disappointed you, but never got addressed and so over time, less and less effort has been put into meeting up and hanging out. Like water, we tend to follow the path of least resistance in relationships and avoid facing those niggling issues until we avoid facing the people involved all together, except where absolutely necessary.

Desperation is toxic. Differences are misunderstood, needs are mostly unmet, and the likely experience is one of tension, frequent conflicts and an unending cycle of unmet expectations followed by disappointment, followed by negative reactions either side, causing the relationship to spiral downwards.

So many relationships break down not because people don't care about each other anymore, but because they get caught in a downward spiral of action and reaction and don't know how to stop it. Good, decent people become harsh, unkind and mean in their interactions in this particular relationship that has gone cold . . . while still often turning up as thoughtful, caring people in their relationships with others.

In the workplace, relationships in a state of Desperation can lead to feelings of being bullied. Toxic cultures and low-trust work environments, evidenced by increased stress, relational tension and absenteeism, are often signs that relationships have deteriorated to a state of Desperation.

Dave's story . . . (again a real story, but with names changed to maintain anonymity)

We met with Dave, Head of Corporate Sales at a large hotel chain, to discuss using his hotel as a venue for a live workshop. As we chatted and spoke about the work we do, he opened up and described the intense frustrations he was experiencing at work. One of his colleagues seemed to be intentionally 'dragging her feet' in providing the bookings information that Dave needed to be able to respond quickly to clients and win business for the team. Turns out there was no issue around workload, need for support, delegation, etc. because others were getting the required information from this same colleague on time. This was personal. It had already led to a full-blown argument in the office, with both bosses involved in trying to address the issue.

Unfortunately, nothing was resolved, and Dave still had no idea what caused this change in his colleague's behavior. The office atmosphere was thick with tension and the cold war between Dave and his colleague impacted their work and compromised effective interactions amongst the rest of the team who felt forced to take sides. Given the daily stress with no clear way out, by the time we had our conversation, Dave was seriously contemplating leaving the company. A bad situation (broken relationships, stressful work environment and loss of business) was about to get worse (loss of talent). And all of this, not because of an unresolvable situation, but because of a lack of the relational SKILLS to work through the difficulties and misunderstandings in a constructive way.

The Desperation quadrant is also where you notice real fractures in couple relationships. 'Suddenly' couples announce they are considering divorce as they reach out for late-stage counselling or other last-minute interventions.

The scenario plays out in uncannily similar ways in all our conversations with couples in trouble. Issues and frustrations both big and small have often been swept under the carpet, creating many 'no-go' areas in the relationship and an emotional wall between them. Every conversation becomes an argument, manipulation is easier than attempting to talk things through. People who once loved each other come across as hardened and bitter. Lack of skill, fear of being hurt by being too open and vulnerable, and a huge dose of pride and ego often make it almost impossible for couples to work through this on their own. Without any attempt to get more understanding and to learn how to really listen to what is important to each other, relationships end up repeating the same negative cycle. Misunderstood actions cause one person to feel disrespected, and out of hurt they respond with disrespect in equal measure, each time taking a chip out of the foundation of commitment and belief until one or both lose the WILL to try anymore.

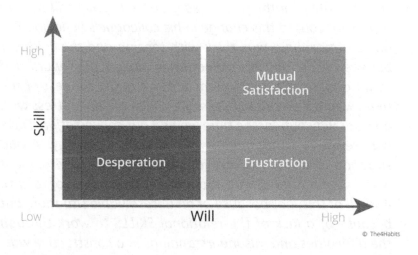

© The4Habits

Desperation is also a very vulnerable place to be. Exit options become increasingly attractive – as evidenced by Dave considering leaving a job he enjoyed.

For couples, this is where affairs become more likely, especially where attention, affirmation, appreciation and respect feel more present outside the home than in it.

Even with the best intentions, ultimately a lack of SKILL costs relationships – in both domestic and work settings.

In the recruitment business we ran in our early years of working together, we got very good at evaluating each candidate's ability based on their depth of experience developed over a period of time. For some, 10 years of experience reflected 10 years of genuine progress and development. For others, it was more like one year's worth of experience, repeated 10 times. This is the reality for many relationships.

Often, people get stuck in relationships because there is no growth in SKILL and understanding. As time passes and they stumble at hurdle after hurdle, the relationship loses life and vitality . . . and the people lose hope.

Ironically, arguments in the Frustration quadrant, are a sign of life. Silence and indifference are signs that the relationship is dying.

There are an amazing number of people who will continue living lives of quiet desperation. Yet, there is much that can be achieved quickly through gaining and applying SKILL. Simply understanding the drivers of expectations on both sides and having a willingness to respond to them as much as possible, can help people restart the journey from Desperation toward Mutual Satisfaction, and breathe hope and life into the relationship again.

Investing the effort to build SKILL can rebuild hope and the motivation and energy to try once more. But it takes commitment to the relationship and the courage to be vulnerable and open. More on that later.

Isolation Quadrant (Low WILL : High SKILL)

The Isolation quadrant is a place where no one wins. People 'check out' physically and/or mentally. They leave companies. They leave families. They leave friendships.

Typically, by this stage there have been enough arguments and 'conversations' about frustrations and expectations, often intermingled with some learning through mediation or counselling, that by default, each party has increased their level of SKILL. But the process of getting there has left them battle-scarred and exhausted.

By the time we meet some couples they have already decided that they have no desire left to struggle through with *this* relationship . . . but many openly say they are ready to learn some SKILLs for *the next one*!

Isolation also often takes a toll on mental health. On the outside people may seem strong and emotionally resilient, but sometimes the turmoil on the inside is so emotionally draining that they start considering unhealthy alternatives for finding peace. Tragically, sometimes that involves suicidal thoughts.

The frightening thing is we sometimes have people right beside us with these thoughts and we would never guess it.

We have had conversations with normal, regular-looking people who generally 'had it all together', except for that brief moment when the events of life got the better of them. The concerning thing is that each of their stories could be anyone's story. The reality is that relationships are one of the most important aspects of our lives and, when they go wrong, can eat away at our very core. The Mental Health Foundation picked up on this in their 2016 report on 'Relationships in the 21st Century'.[8] In highlighting the importance of investing in relationships, they suggested that 'failing to do so is equivalent to turning a blind eye to the impact of smoking and obesity on our health and wellbeing'. It seems the lack of SKILL for building great relationships could literally be killing us.

Could developing better Relational Intelligence allow us to be better able to navigate relationship challenges, remain resilient ourselves and offer help and hope to those around us who might be stuck?

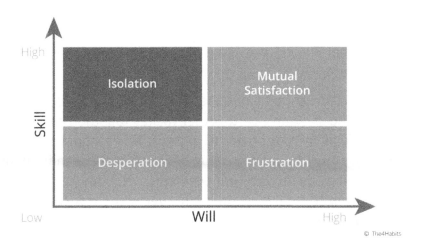

© The4Habits

Coming back from Isolation or the brink of divorce is hard, but possible. It takes time, it takes grit, it takes commitment . . . and it takes vulnerability. It requires the WILL to have courageous conversations to address the key issue(s), which often means more than one attempt at getting to mutual understanding. It requires genuine patience because changing habits and automatic responses to triggers will take time and can feel like things are getting worse before they get better. It also requires deliberate efforts to rebuild trust – like keeping your word and going out of your way to over-communicate so there is no room for questioning and doubts about intent. It requires avoiding periods of silence and distance where anxiety can creep in, and it requires demonstrating your commitment to the other person and to the relationship even in their ugliest moments – and you will probably both have them!

More than likely, it will take professional help or at least an accountability partner to help you follow through when things feel tough – because at times they will. But just knowing that, gives many people the confidence to keep working at it.

Great relationships don't just happen – they are built on purpose.

And sometimes that just requires plain hard work. But it can be absolutely worth it.

It's important to point out that this is not about trying to get people who shouldn't be together to stay together. If your life is at risk, do all in your power to get out. This is about preventing otherwise healthy relationships between well-meaning people from being destroyed unnecessarily. Nobody gets into a relationship to be in this quadrant, yet without a commitment to learn and grow together, as the statistics on both workplace conflict and family breakdown demonstrate, this is where all too many relationships end up.

However, the better way to enjoy the mental, emotional, physical and financial benefits of great relationships, is to be proactive about developing SKILL *before* things go pear-shaped and you lose the WILL. It's about learning to live in the Mutual Satisfaction quadrant permanently, *by choice.*

Mutual Satisfaction – by choice

So, back to Mutual Satisfaction. This is where a healthy understanding of differences creates healthy expectations from the relationship. A healthy understanding of *how to handle those differences* allows expectations to be met and fulfilled. Where this exists on both sides, both parties typically feel appreciated, valued and secure.

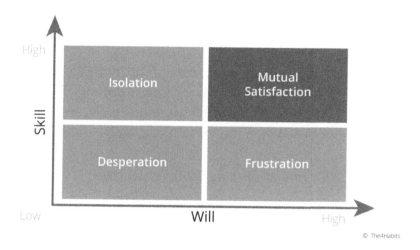

© The4Habits

Getting there and staying there is an iterative work in progress – but it is absolutely achievable. At the heart of the gateway to success are:

1. commitment to ongoing efforts in building your understanding of each other,

2. being more understanding in your responses, and

3. choosing to act and show appreciation in meaningful, specific ways.

That's not to say things never go wrong, because they do. Every now and again an issue emerges which triggers an argument and can bump you down into the Frustration quadrant.

But with the right SKILLs and the WILL to invest in the relationship, you can argue it through, get more understanding, agree a way forward and get back into Mutual Satisfaction. Typically, with increased understanding comes more patience and goodwill, the desire to understand and act better next time and an ongoing willingness to forgive, forget and move forward. This involves letting go of some things that would otherwise frustrate you, as you now have a better filter on *why* some people do what they do and realize it isn't typically to irritate you on purpose (despite the fact it might have felt like that!).

The key here is to develop and constantly improve relationship skills in order to feed Emotional Bank Accounts (both theirs and yours) and manage conflict situations well, enjoying great conversations even when the topic of discussion is a difficult one.

Building 'SKILL' and Managing 'WILL', on purpose

A proactive approach to building strong relationships is about building the SKILL and learning to manage the WILL *ahead* of challenges.

The more we learn about relationship fundamentals and the more we make a study of the people around us who are important to us, the better we get at understanding and responding to what makes them tick. This is what equips us to be intentional about working on our relationships. We learn to demonstrate the things that make them feel appreciated and recognized, and to refrain from things they view as disrespect. We learn what feeds their Emotional Bank Account and what drains it.

As we interact with others, the key is to notice when things are shifting and manage the tensions at the boundaries.

Whereas on the right-hand side of the model, the willingness to try is high, on the left-hand side, the Emotional Bank Account is drained and, without that, the willingness to do anything to improve the relationship is low to non-existent. Bringing things back to life takes genuine commitment to the relationship and a real sense of vulnerability to show your desire to make it work while trusting that the other person still thinks the relationship – and you – are worth the effort.

The great news is that there is a way forward to Mutual Satisfaction from wherever your relationships are positioned in the model.

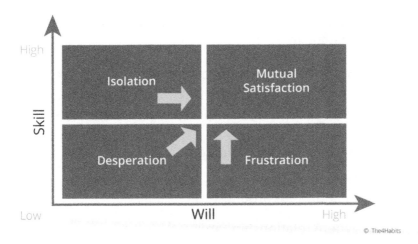

© The4Habits

However, rather than wait for chance, a better strategy is to recognize how vital relationships are to the quality of your life experience and proactively build the SKILLs to do them well. That's the focus of the rest of the book – developing the required SKILL by learning the fundamentals and mastering The 4 Habits®. This will equip you to be on purpose about doing relationships well, while learning some tools and techniques to fix the ones that feel broken.

Time for Reflection

Key Takeaways

- Building SKILL and managing WILL are the keys to being proactive and intentional about developing quality relationships.

- The 4 Habits Experience Model can help predict and describe the experience in relationships and help identify what to work on to improve them, where necessary.

Building Your Understanding

1. How does The 4 Habits Experience Model help explain relationships around you?

2. Where relationships are working well, what is making them great?

3. Where relationships are struggling, what might be missing?

Taking Personal Action

- Conduct your own relational audit – where would you position your key relationships on the SKILL / WILL dimensions of The 4 Habits Experience Model? And WHY?

- If there are tensions, what does the model suggest as an area to focus on to help improve the quality of each relationship?

PART B

Mastering The 4 Habits®

Habit #1

BE CURIOUS, not critical

Chapter Four

Overcoming our in-built tendency to criticize

'There is always strength in difference.'

The foundation for long-term successful relationships starts at the point of difference. When two people think the same and respond the same, it's easy to get along. But without the 'benefit' of working together to overcome challenges caused by differences, the 'roots' of relationships can remain weak and shallow. Sadly, this is the beginning of the end for many relationships.

Our commitment to care about each other and build a working relationship or friendship gets tested at the point we no longer see eye to eye. How we respond in that moment and what happens next determines the quality of relationship that will develop. Significantly, this is the moment when our differences can start to add real value. As a friend once wisely pointed out, 'if we were both the same, one of us would be redundant'! The challenge is to learn to treasure hunt the strengths in our differences, rather than wallow in the frustration these differences can cause. And this is where most of us could seriously benefit from developing SKILL.

Misunderstood differences are often the cause of broken relationships. For some strange reason, most of us find it a whole lot easier to be critical when faced with differences than to take the time to find out more about the differences. And as most of us tend not to like being on the receiving end of criticism, it generally doesn't bode well for the relationship.

Did you know that the number-one cause of conflict in the workplace (at least in the UK) is misunderstood personality differences?[9]

On the domestic front, citing 'irreconcilable differences' is sufficient cause for divorce in countries such as Australia, Canada and the USA and about to be the same in the UK under the 'no fault' Divorce, Dissolution and Separation Act 2020, which passed into law on June 25, 2020 (anticipated to apply from autumn 2021).

Either way, unless we can get past our differences, relationships are likely to remain strained.

The journey to successful relationships starts with understanding fundamental differences.

The more we understand, the more we are able to anticipate behaviors, and make allowances for each other . . . especially under pressure. Greater understanding of differences also allows us to benefit from each other's strengths, cover for each other's weaknesses and work more effectively as a team – whether a team of 2 or 22!

Habit #1: BE CURIOUS, not critical helps build SKILL in understanding and working with difference. Developing this habit involves learning to understand and respect all the various dimensions of difference and has two main benefits:

1. It allows us to stand strong in our own strengths and give 'space and grace' for others to shine in their strengths, and

2. It improves our understanding of *why* others do what they do – and as a result, we take offence less easily. So much stress and conflict could be avoided if we had more understanding of other people's perspectives and were more open to hearing their view of the world.

In learning to 'BE CURIOUS, not critical', we learn to suspend judgement and find strengths in differences. And it is that combination that helps us get over the hurdles of frustration that tend to come from misunderstood differences.

Understanding 'Difference' in all its dimensions

Intellectually, we all understand that we're all different. We know we are each unique individuals with different personalities, different family backgrounds, different interests, different cultures and different ways of handling stress. And that's just for starters! Our differences mean that there will be times we surprise and delight each other. But they also mean that there will be times that we frustrate and disappoint each other.

The challenge is we see our way as the norm – the right way even – and when people are different to us, we think they are wrong.

In the moment, those differences can cause real frustration. Unconsciously, we expect people to think the same as we do, process information in similar ways and arrive at similar conclusions. Many couples will confess to subconsciously thinking their partner *lives inside their heads* and that they expect their partners to be mind-readers!

One of the differences we experienced personally early in our relationship was in our expectations around physical touch in public.

Here's Andrea's recount of the experience . . .

I am very tactile and, without thinking, will touch people in conversation – a hand on the arm or on the back, greet people with a hug, etc. In my world, people who love each other will happily show affection in public and at the very least hold hands. Yet, in the early days of our relationship, when I automatically, often subconsciously, reached for Jon's hand while we were walking in public, he would grasp it for a second, gently pat it and then let go. The only way I could make sense in the moment was to feel rejected. Jon explained that the culture he was brought up in frowns on public displays of affection, so holding hands in public made him feel very awkward and self-conscious. In my mind this was something HE needed to fix because, in my world, EVERYONE shows affection to their significant other by holding hands at least! It never even occurred to me that people could have a different opinion about physical touch like that.

But then I had a few other experiences that made me realize just how differently people viewed their personal space and physical touch. On one occasion a colleague accused me of flirting with her husband because I touched his arm as we spoke. My initial thought was 'With my hunk of a husband standing right there, how could you even think that?!' On other occasions my greetings with a hug were met with a wooden, awkward pat on the back. It finally dawned on me that these were not just 'weird' people. They just had a different response to touch.

These experiences helped me learn to respect Jon's position on the hand-holding thing, and to be more discerning of other people's preferences around personal space and touch. I learned to focus more on the other ways that Jon showed me love and took the pressure off our relationship when we were out in public so that neither of us was put in a position to feel awkward or hurt. He was as entitled to feel that holding hands in public was inappropriate as I was to think it was the done thing. Being able to share and respect our different perspectives allowed us to interpret what we were each experiencing in a healthier way.

Generally, most of us struggle to embrace the fact that our world view is *not* the only world view and we end up frustrated by our *perception* of the other person's actions, regardless of their original intent – which we typically assume was against us. In truth, if only we knew how little we featured on the list of things that drive other people's behavior it would be easier for us to become more curious and take offence less easily!

The more we raise our own self-awareness of who we are – our own strengths, our own weaknesses, our own trigger points, our own reactions under pressure – the more intentional we can be about how we behave. And the more we understand about the person we are relating to specifically – their strengths, their weaknesses, their trigger points, their background, their assumptions – the better we can interpret what they mean by what they do or say and not get offended so easily. That is, the more we know about ourselves, others and how we differ, the better equipped we are to build stronger relationships.

Two fundamental differences that influence the quality of relationships

We could literally write a whole book just on the many ways in which people differ and how to understand each other better – and still have enough for subsequent volumes – because it is such a huge area. In fact, getting better at embracing difference lies at the heart of the huge global concern driving the conversations around Equity, Diversity, Inclusion and Belonging across the world today. And the problems start when we make people who have differences – in whatever shape or form – feel 'less than' and excluded because of their differences.

It's great that there are laws in most countries to protect against discrimination for certain aspects of diversity. But often that doesn't stop people feeling excluded or like they don't belong – through the subtle cues in other people's words and behaviors that don't break 'the law', but make it clear they are not part of the 'in crowd'. Sadly, this is sometimes intentional. But many times, the feeling of exclusion is unintentional, although still very real for those on the receiving end. Without realizing it, we can make people feel very excluded because of assumptions that we hold about them that are simply not true . . . or because of a misunderstanding of fundamental differences between us.

Of course, there are structures and systems that exist in society that need to be addressed to create more equity and inclusion, but we each have a part to play in how we turn up to relationships with people who are different to us.

The more we understand about our differences, the more we can challenge our own assumptions, treat each other with respect and build strong relationships across difference.

Everybody wants to feel respected and valued and like they belong, rather than criticized, 'less than' and excluded. In that context, it is no accident that the first habit for building successful relationships is BE CURIOUS, not critical. The more we understand about differences, the better we can interact with people and make them feel included, no matter how different to us they may be.

We will look at the issue of diversity and inclusion specifically in chapter 16. Meanwhile, the focus of the next few chapters will be on getting better at understanding the key differences common to ALL relationships which influence the quality of our interactions.

In Habit #2, we'll look at the different ways in which we each respond to conflict.

In Habit #3, we'll look at cultural differences and differences in assumptions, core values and beliefs.

In Habit #4, we'll focus on differences in how we each feel valued, appreciated and loved.

We could also talk about our different information processing styles, differing views on money and different approaches to parenting but we're going to have to save that for another book!

But to get us started on the journey, we have found it is helpful to begin by looking at two fundamental differences that influence the way most of us tend to 'show up' and treat each other in relationships.

The first is the 'touchy' subject of male / female differences – which we dare to venture into, because like it or not, some physiological differences exist which tend to have an impact on the quality of relationships we build at work and home. And we can't get better at issues like gender equity that continue to plague our society until we can have better conversations with both truth and grace.

The second difference, and the main focus of this chapter is on understanding fundamental differences in personality and how they play out in practice. Ultimately, relationships are about the quality of our one-on-one interactions, and personality is a huge influence on that. Think identical twins – same parents, same cultures, same sex. With all other factors of influence being equal, they each typically show up differently based on their individual personalities.

By addressing these two key friction points (male / female and personality) we get a jumpstart in understanding each other's perspectives better. This generally helps increase our level of patience and humility in dealing with people who are different to us, and helps us learn to work together successfully, while enjoying the benefits these differences have to offer.

Understanding how the sexes tend to 'show up' in relationships

As much as many of us resist the notion, there are some fundamental differences between male and female thinking styles and approaches that can cause real friction points in relationships, especially couple relationships – even if the couple are the same sex.

Before we get into it – a word on stereotypes in understanding differences!

It's true, gender stereotypes have been overused and used irresponsibly over the years to undermine and exclude people, mostly women and the LGBTQ+ community. We have no intention of adding to that pain and confusion in any way. We also acknowledge the intense debate around the use of the terms 'sex' and 'gender' and the arguments for and against binary assumptions and live in hope that healthy discussions will continue to bring *light* rather than just *heat* to those conversations.

Given all that, we recognize that venturing into male / female territory can cause an allergic reaction for some people. However, as the insights that come from addressing this are vital for the journey to developing better perspectives, better understanding and better relationships, we will tread carefully and attempt to discuss the issue with respect, with grace and with what we understand to be the truth.

Also, as in all our discussions on difference, we ask that you be especially aware of the mindset that says 'different means *less than*'. This couldn't be further from the truth and the point is as relevant whether we are talking about racism or male / female differences. Different means just that – the two are different, yet equal, and equally deserving of respect.

Biology, the brain and unique contributions

So, let's start at the very beginning . . . with a bit of a biology lesson on what happened in our bodies before each of us was even born! Multiple studies confirm that the hormone testosterone plays a huge part in our brain development. They show that, as it washes over the brains of fetuses in the womb, the brains of little girl fetuses (XX chromosomes) and little boy fetuses (XY chromosomes) develop differently.

The net result of these different growth patterns is that men tend to have around 6.5 times as much gray matter related to intelligence than women do, and women tend to have about 10 times more white matter related to intelligence than men – although the researchers[10] were then at pains to point out that this does not affect intellectual performance. Other research[11] has shown that while men seem to think with their gray matter (which apparently is full of active neurons), women tend to think with white matter (which importantly consists more of connections between the neurons).

What that means in simple terms is that women in general, tend to have not only better developed right brains than most men, but they also tend to have more connectors between the left and right hemispheres. This may well explain why *in general*, women tend to be more in touch with their feelings and have a more intuitive thinking style – which are right-brain characteristics. And why men can often be more single-minded and focused on logically solving problems in a step-by-step approach – which are left-brain characteristics. Again, remember these are in most but not all cases. Of course, some people will experience these tendencies in the reverse. The point is that differences exist and will be noticeable in a large portion of the population. End of biology lesson.

So, why is this important to understand?

A big part of improving communication is understanding the differences between typical male and female thinking styles and approaches so that we can respect how they show up in conversations and the tremendous value that they can bring to our relationships – if we let them.

A key outworking of the different 'wiring' is that in general, men tend to prefer to discuss facts, easily eliminate unnecessary data and quickly start to form solutions. Women tend to be more multitasking in their approach and simultaneously consider all aspects in problem solving, including both the emotional as well as the rational. It's only in the last few decades that society has started to embrace the idea that EQ (Emotional Intelligence) is as important as IQ (Intelligence Quotient) for success in life. If you followed our mini-biology lesson earlier, you can see why women typically have better EQ than men. Dr Helen Fisher, an anthropologist who has researched gender differences and human emotions in 130 societies globally, describes women as 'web thinkers' – highly imaginative, natural negotiators with incredible people skills.[12] And all this, like it or not, simply because their brains are different and more inter-connected across the two halves.

Understanding this fundamental difference helps explain why we have stereotypical stories of women wanting to talk through their 'feelings' on a particular situation and men preferring to keep things to the 'facts'. Indeed, in her book *You Just Don't Understand*,[13] Deborah Tanner, Professor of Linguistics at Georgetown University in Washington D.C., includes 'Information vs Feelings' as one of the six main differences between the ways males and females use language.

The problem is, rather than respect, appreciate and harness these differences, the differences have too often been used to justify discriminatory behavior and undermine each other. Unhelpfully, valiant attempts for equality have downplayed the differences and crippled the ability to have better conversations. All of society has lost out as a result.

And as roles have changed – with men no longer being the *de facto* breadwinner – multiple conversations we have had tell us that many men are no longer sure of their role in the home and are often physically and/or emotionally absent. And there is no shortage of research studies suggesting that women still struggle to get an equal seat at the top table in the workplace. In both the home and the workplace, society is missing out on huge chunks of the available skills, talents and unique contributions that could help us solve world problems faster.

Toward a better future of collaboration

The reality is we need both approaches and more collaboration between the sexes in order to create more effective solutions to today's financial, economic and social problems. Instead of trying to change one to be more like the other, we need to develop our understanding of, and respect for, the strengths in the different approaches. This will allow us all to interpret responses better, hold more realistic expectations of each other and have better conversations.

For example, one of the conversations that needs to improve is one that is typical in corporate meetings and boardrooms. One of our workshop participants shared her frustration about the countless times she would suggest an idea which seemed to fall on deaf ears . . . that is until a male colleague announced the solution he proposed they should take – which was the idea she suggested in the first place! It seems many women offer a brilliant idea with an 'I think' or a 'how about', not because they are unsure of its validity but because the female style is often more collaborative and relational than directive or dictatorial. Your stereotypical man, however, tends to hear that as hesitation and uncertainty and is more likely to listen to another man saying the same thing with more assertion . . . and suddenly it gets heard as his idea. In her book, Tannen referred to these different styles as 'Orders vs Proposals'.

Probably as a result of these and the other typical 'feminine' tendencies Tannen outlines, to survive in the corporate world, many women have felt forced to change their style to match the more 'masculine' style they perceive. But when they do, like an ill-fitting suit, their behaviors are often perceived as aggressive. They get accused of being 'too hard-nosed' at work and 'not so loving or lovable' at home. Lose-lose all round.

Of the top 10 competencies identified by The World Economic Forum in their 2016 report on 'The Future of Jobs' globally, four are purely social skills which reflect strengths of the female population – coordinating with others, Emotional Intelligence, negotiation and service orientation. In conclusion they highlighted the desperate need for women's equal participation in the workplace, in order to be prepared for the anticipated shifts in the future of work and the Fourth Industrial Revolution.[14] Yet in 2019 the percentage of women in senior management positions globally recorded an all-time high of only 29 percent.[15]

On the home front, we've heard stories of any number of men being criticized for being blind to 'obvious' things that need to be done to keep homelife ticking over, and oblivious to the emotions of the people around them. The reality is that their left-brain dominance probably means they are less able to sense the emotional dynamic in the home. But give them a task or a problem to solve and they are on it in a flash.

However, and quite sadly, this misunderstanding of strengths and differences contributes heavily to the breakdown of too many couple relationships. Meanwhile, reports on both sides of the Atlantic show prisons continue to fill up with angry young men who, more often than not, have not had the balance and security that comes from the love and presence of a father, or father-figure and a stable, healthy relationship between parents.[16]

Getting better at making room for the different skills and unique contributions made by male and female approaches will allow us to *hear* each other better, give each other space to shine in our strengths and work together to achieve more creative, inclusive solutions both at work and at home.

When all is said and done, the simple reality is that 'there is always strength in difference'. We just need to find it.

> **Instead of criticizing and judging each approach, we need to understand more about our differences so that we can listen well to *everything* being said – not just to the things that fit the way we each think and speak.**

When we pause long enough and humbly enough to really listen, we will hear things we could never have thought about and make better decisions as a result. That is the SKILL of Habit #1: BE CURIOUS, not critical. Understanding the different approaches and contributions of the sexes is just one important way to develop this first habit for success in relationships.

In the next chapter we will look at differences in fundamental personality types as another important concept for helping you develop this habit of becoming more curious than critical.

Time for Reflection

Key Takeaways

Understanding differences across multiple dimensions helps us build our self-awareness and awareness of others, so we can understand each other better, make allowances for different approaches and perspectives, and not get frustrated or offended so easily.

Building Your Understanding

1. What assumptions do you hold about males / females in terms of:

    b. Their strengths?

    c. Their weaknesses?

    d. Their role at home?

    e. Their role at work?

2. What other differences have you observed that influence the quality of relationships developed?

Taking Personal Action

1. Knowing what you now know, what could you do differently to have a better conversation with someone who has a different approach to yours?

2. If you are open to it, is there anyone you might need to offer an apology to for misunderstanding them, undermining them or shutting them down? Why not call them or go see them now . . . or at the very least make a note in your diary to do so.

Chapter Five

Mining for strengths in personality differences

*'Often, it's not our weaknesses or blind spots
that cause problems, but our strengths
pulling in different directions.'*

As we mentioned earlier, one of the key sources of conflict in the workplace is misunderstood differences in personalities and workstyles. And you've probably guessed it – the same is true at home. The challenges come when we don't understand each other, when we don't realize how our behaviors are impacting those who are different to us, and when we underestimate how our strengths can overwhelm them.

Understanding fundamental personality differences is crucial to better understanding some of the strongest drivers of behaviors and expectations. And the better we are able to interpret and filter behaviors through the lens of personality type, the better we are able to respond – we judge less, and live and work together more successfully. Putting it another way, understanding personality responses allows us to take things less personally and get offended less easily.

Understanding fundamental personality differences –
in 10 minutes

Many of you will have heard about or completed a personality psychometric questionnaire. Popular ones include Myers Briggs (MBTI), DISC, 16PF, Belbin, Colours, Hogan and McQuaig. These all give wonderful insights into our individual behaviors, strengths and areas for growth. Typically, these exercises are carried out in a work context with the focus on how to work more effectively in a team. The challenge is that the profiles are usually very complex to absorb and difficult to communicate to someone who hasn't done the same profile. This makes them not so easily portable between work and home contexts (even between work teams!) and many of us struggle to apply the learning in our everyday interactions, especially with people very different to us.

As we shared on a personal front earlier, one key difference we discovered between us was in our personalities – which showed up in our work styles and in our responses under stress. Intellectually we understood personality differences (having done our own psychometrics in the past), but in the heat of the moment the learning was not translating into how we worked through our differences as business and life partners. Worse still, the intellectual understanding had not created a change in behavior in how we treated each other.

What really helped us change was discovering a very simple, but equally robust, model that allowed us to develop a shared understanding and get on the same page. This meant we had a common language for describing (rather than attacking!) the differences in behavior we were observing and how they impacted us individually – especially our behaviors under pressure.

Very simple changes produced very powerful results. Our new understanding allowed us to interpret behaviors, comments, actions and responses in the context of our individual personality styles without taking things too personally. Instead of using up our energies to defend, explain or edit ourselves, we learned to really 'get' what the other person was saying, take offense less often, and change our behaviors to minimize those areas in which we were unintentionally damaging our relationship. Over the years this simple model has helped us reduce countless tensions and frustrations in our own relationships and in the relationships of people we have coached and supported.

If you have a personality model that you understand and can use to create a common understanding with those around you – great. You will recognize strong similarities and the following descriptions will help you communicate things even more simply. If you have not yet experienced a personality model, prepare to have some real 'aha moments'! This simple model that we share will help you understand *why people do what they do*, better. And that will be the case whether you've known them for years or for a minute. It is so powerful yet so intuitive, you can share it with anyone (even children, as we did with ours when they were less than 10 years old) and in 10 minutes instantly improve communication – and patience – in any household or any team.

Learning this model was a major game changer for us. Over the years we have taken great delight in seeing people experience 'lightbulb moments' as they *finally* understand and appreciate their own personality tendencies and start to make space for the different personalities around them. In other words, in a very practical way, this model helps us become more curious than critical.

We can't wait to help you experience the benefits, so let's jump in . . .

The Animal Personality Model – an overview

The Animal Personality Model was developed in the 1990s by John Trent and explained in his book with Gary Smalley, *The Two Sides of Love.*[17] As Certified Master Coaches for Dr Trent's model, what follows is an adaptation of his material for our 4 Habits training, used with permission. When you are ready to dig deeper, we would encourage you to get his book and find out more about the Connect Assessment® that goes into more detail and complete a profile by visiting Dr Trent's website.[18] We've listed the appropriate links in the *Taking Personal Action* section at the end of the chapter.

This model simplifies the personality traits measured in most types of psychometric testing into two key dimensions.

The first dimension looks at the extent to which people are wired to lead and take charge or are happy to let others lead.

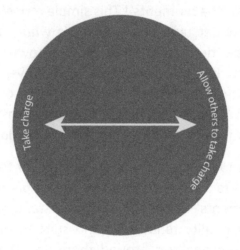

To understand that better, think of an emergency situation like a fire breaking out. The Take Charge people are wired to step up, take control and even break the rules if they deem that is what's necessary to get themselves and others to safety. Others will prefer to follow what they believe to be the right procedures and instructions.

The second dimension looks at the extent to which people are more focused on the task to be done or are more concerned about people and their emotions.

To help you process that one, think of a team getting into a boat to cross a lake. In their extreme, the task-oriented people will get you to the other side, but they might damage relationships in the process and get there with no one left in the boat. People-oriented people on the other hand, in their extreme will keep everyone in the boat but may never get to the other side.

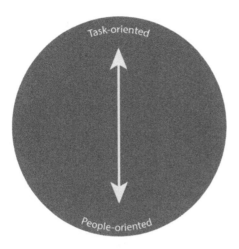

There is no right or wrong here, people are just wired to focus on different priorities.

When you put the two dimensions together, you get four distinct personality types which intuitively look like certain animal behaviors – lions, otters, Golden Retrievers and beavers (admittedly, some of them more common in the American fauna!). To be clear, this is not an exercise in labelling people or calling them animals! Rather, it provides a simple starting point to understanding fundamental personality differences, and the animal caricatures give us an easy way to remember how each personality tendency is likely to show up, especially under pressure.

- The Take-Charge / Task-Oriented people, Dr Trent called *Lions*. These are *action-oriented, goal-focused* people. As natural leaders, they have a gift for knowing the right thing to do and getting things done, and they expect everyone to keep up with their generally high-octane, energetic approach to life. But unless they are self-aware, they can drive people hard and/or make them feel lazy and incompetent. Without the right balance, they can end up with successful careers, but troubled relationships.

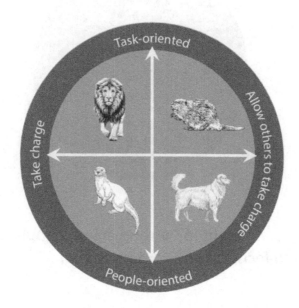

- Those who are Take Charge / People-Oriented, he called *Otters*. They are also *wired to lead but they have a gift for taking people along* with them because typically they are networkers and great communicators who are inspiring and fun to be around. But they can also get bored and run out of steam before things are finished, off to the next exciting project. Without self-awareness, they can end up disappointing people and taking unnecessary risks.

- Those who are focused on serving people and are happy to let others lead, Dr Trent called *Golden Retrievers* (not dogs! It's the particular characteristics of a Golden Retriever that are important here). These people are *wired to build warm, caring relationships*, typically becoming nurses, teachers and caregivers. They are the loyal, thoughtful people who will ask how you are . . . and really want to know the answer! However, unless they become self-aware, they can exhaust themselves looking after everybody else's needs at their own expense.

- Those who are focused on the task and are generally happy to let others lead, he called *Beavers*. These people are *wired for precision and attention to detail* and tend to be our engineers, accountants, architects. They are the reasons we have buildings and bridges that stay upright! Long after everyone else has lost *the will*, Beavers will keep going with grit until the job is done. However, without self-awareness they can be perfectionists or stifling, criticizing others for being sloppy or messy, while others may criticize them for being OCD.[19]

Of course, this is caricaturizing to make a point, and none of us is pure-bred anything. Most of us are a blend of each characteristic with dominance in one or two personality types. However, the animals and their predominant characteristics help us remember and anticipate personality tendencies in a simplified way.

Five key takeaways from understanding fundamental personality differences

Against this background of a basic understanding of personality tendencies, we can start to make some observations. There are five key takeaways to grab hold of:

1. **Having a common language helps you express and discuss feelings**

   One of the beauties of going through an exercise like this (or any of the other personality models for that matter), is that it gives you an understanding of why people behave the way they do sometimes. But perhaps even more importantly, it also gives you a common language for describing what you are each experiencing and adjusting behaviors where necessary, so you can 'land' better in each other's Emotional Bank Account.

So, for example, three of us in our house have 'Lion' tendencies, so when any of us starts getting too bossy we just say 'OK, Mr Lion (or Ms Lion), calm down' . . . and instantly we know how we are coming across and can soften our approach. Our non-Lion child has also learned to leave us to it and resurface when the coast is clear, knowing that it will only be a matter of time before we sort it out and get back to normal again. This common language for communicating helps reduce tensions instantly and helps those who don't share the same tendencies not to panic that the family is falling into a state of dysfunction! Similarly, if any of us is having a bad day, we hunt out family members with more 'Golden Retriever' tendencies who are naturals at giving reassurance. Andrea, the 'Otter', is our designated *Minister for Family Fun* and by default, all paperwork typically goes to Jon, our resident 'Beaver'.

2. **There is 'your' world view . . . and then there are at least three others!**

   Whether from this animal personality model or from one of the more complex psychometric reports, it is clear that there are at least three other views of the world aside from yours – 15 other views for some of the four-dimensional profiles! The key point though is that other people's views are as valid to them as yours is to you. You both just need to learn to recognize and respect each other's different perspectives. Of course, with each person being unique, the actual reality is that there are over 7 billion views of the world! Psychometrics and personality profiles are really just shortcuts to help us understand each other better. Just raising our awareness that other views of the world exist is a tremendous starting point for better conversations. It helps us become more open, more patient and more able to listen with respect even if we disagree.

3. **Your differences mean people will prioritize things differently to you**

The third key takeaway is the recognition that different personality types mean people different to you will value different things and make different things their priority focus. Using the understanding from the animal personality model, some people value taking charge and achieving goals, while others prefer to take time and be meticulous with structure and order. Others still focus on innovation, creativity and fun while others start with a priority of caring for people. And there are many more combinations leading to different priorities and focus points.

Each personality type offers amazing strengths. And each has blind spots as a result. But here's the thing – often it's not our weaknesses or blind spots that cause problems, but our strengths and priority focus areas pulling strongly in different directions. Too much strength can cause people to grate against each other. This is one key reason why people can end up having intense arguments and just not see eye to eye – because they are each looking at the issue through different lenses based on the thing they prioritize the most. The more we understand these inbuilt biases toward different priorities, the less critical we become of each other and the more we can play to each other's strengths. More on this shortly.

4. **Your differences will be magnified with polar-opposite personalities**

The fourth key takeaway is that differences are magnified between polar opposites. What that means is that without understanding personality differences, people will really struggle to 'get' each other and often give up on trying to build any relationship with people very different to them. It should come as no surprise that conflict and misunderstanding are likely to be most intense with the people most different to you. Just think of the people you find most difficult to get along with right now. Chances are they think, behave and respond very differently to you and you struggle to really 'get' them.

This is such an important point that we need to spend a bit more time on it. It's the classic case why people from sales or marketing might lose patience with people who focus more on the detail – like accounts or IT for example. Just building this understanding alone can save families and teams a lot of stress because it helps people anticipate behaviors, adjust their approach, communicate better and smooth out relationships.

Many of the issues being faced between couples or colleagues are often a result of misunderstanding personalities and intent or being unaware of how their behaviors 'land' with other personalities, especially those that are diametrically opposite. For example, under pressure Lions roar – and so do 'Lion-type' personalities! They don't necessarily intend to crush or dominate; they just roar because that's what Lions do. And the thing is, they expect people to roar back at them!

In giving feedback or even general communication, Lion-types tend to be very direct, which can be too blunt and hard for others to hear.

Relationships get damaged when more dominant personalities don't understand how their behavior 'lands' with others, and when gentler personalities don't have the skills to push back. Bullying and harassment are serious issues that need proper interventions to address, but sometimes the perception of being bullied is likely to exist with people who are complete opposites, until both build awareness and better respect for the differences between them and adjust their behavior and approach.

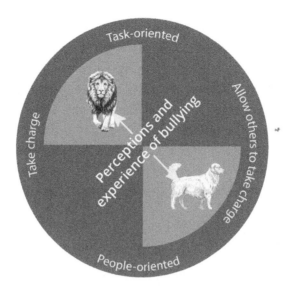

Similar tensions exist between people who are very detail-oriented and those who are more creative and free-spirited, if there is no appreciation of difference. LinkedIn CEO Jeff Weiner did a survey[20] back in 2018 which concluded essentially that people don't leave companies, they leave their bosses – and the top two reasons for leaving were being overly criticized and feeling micro-managed, two classic symptoms of personality strengths being misunderstood and mismanaged.

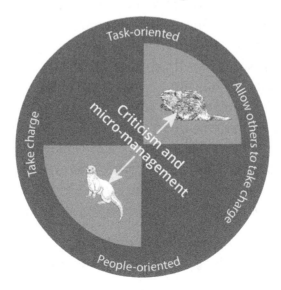

We experienced this in a real way when we ran our first business together. Jon is very much an engineer at heart and thrives on structure and process. Andrea is more of an 'ideas' person, creative and free-flowing, and finds too much structure stifling. Earlier, we shared how this was reflected in our desks. There was a lot of judgement and criticism back then! Now we have learned that for peace and sanity for both of us we need different workspaces, literally giving each other more 'space and grace'.

We also discovered we had very different information processing styles.

On one occasion we had a client proposal to develop. What we thought would have been a simple, straightforward task became a shouting match and a painful lesson in learning how to present information in the way we each need to receive it.

Here's the story as Jon tells it . . .

> Andrea had spent a long time working on the draft of the proposal. Having discussed it together coming out of the client meeting, I was looking forward to reading about the ideas and approach she had proposed, believing that it would be very innovative and a win-win solution both for the client and for us. However, what she handed to me was shocking to say the least – there was no clear structure to the presentation that I could see and, apart from anything else, the formatting was all over the place. I was annoyed that she could possibly think this document was ready for my review and worse yet, that she expected praise for half-baked ideas that, as far as I could see, were deeply buried.
>
> My reality was that I simply couldn't see Andrea's gem ideas amongst the mess. And that came out in my

words! As you can imagine that conversation didn't go down very well. (That's the polite version for describing what happened!). However, knowing that our joint success depended on us delivering something great to the client, after a bit of a timeout to calm down we got back to working on the document together. Once we had agreed the structure, I could finally see the gems hidden in the mess, and not only that . . . I realized that they had been there all along! Andrea, for her part, realized that without a clear structure her magical ideas would never be seen by me, or indeed by any clients who processed information like me! We learned that day how to work with each other's strengths (hers for ideas and mine for structure) and cover for, rather than attack, each other's weaknesses.

We both learned that there are people in the world who actually think creatively and free-flowing (like Andrea) and with more structure and precision (like Jon), and that we both needed to develop our ability to communicate with people very different to us.

There is a whole conversation we could have about different learning and information processing styles, but we don't want to confuse the issue with too many different lenses. Suffice it to say that some people have a preference for seeing things (visual), others for hearing things (auditory), sensing things (kinesthetic) or getting facts and figures (digital). So, as you probably guessed, Jon is very visual, meaning things have to look right, while Andrea is very auditory, meaning things must be explained well. Once we figured out how to respect each other's strengths and not just criticize the weaknesses, we learned that between us we get both the creativity and the structure to produce amazing results.

5. Your polar-opposites have the potential to become your best teammates

This leads us very neatly on to the fifth key takeaway – a lesson that we learned the hard way when we first set up in business together. Polar-opposites can make the best teammates – but only if you are able get past the frustrations provoked by your different approaches! The simple reason – those most different to us bring something to the table that we don't have which, importantly, helps cover our blind spots. Their different approaches provide the opportunity for genuine complementary teamwork. But without this understanding of fundamental personality differences, they can be *the most irritating and challenging* to be around. In many cases it's easier to keep them at a distance than to try to understand the way they think and pursue a meaningful relationship with them. Without this knowledge, many potentially great teams never make it off first base.

Andrea saw this in action with a client once . . .

A few years ago, I co-facilitated an executive leadership session for a team of very senior executives in the Armed Forces. On the face of it, there was no diversity in the room – eight white middle-aged men. However, the body language suggested one of them was not quite part of the 'in group'.

As we explored personality profiles, it became clear that seven of the men were similar in being dominant personalities, very extroverted leaders with 'Big Picture' thinking. The one guy – let's call him Edward – was more of a measured personality with great attention to detail. The problem is the rest of the group made it clear they saw him as a bit of a pain. He was always the killjoy putting the brakes on the exciting ideas they wanted to run with. As a result, he was often the butt of their jokes. Even the way they sat around the table showed he was excluded.

Until we did the team profile.

The combined strengths and weaknesses for the team made it glaringly obvious that Edward was their only 'safety valve'. He was carrying the rest of the team in terms of giving due consideration to safety, security and managing risk in their decision-making process – which is interesting, given that after all, this was the Armed Forces!

It was awesome to watch the shift in dynamics as the day progressed. You could feel the growth in respect from the other senior executives for Edward, and his very body language changed as he became more validated, confident and self-assured. The more they understood personality styles and tendencies, the more they appreciated the vital covering and balance that Edward's difference brought to the team.

They ended the day with the slogan, 'be more Edward' – meaning they would pay more attention to the issues and considerations he would raise, rather than mocking him for raising them.

So many friendships, couples and teams lose out on great relationships because the person who could complement them the most is often their diametric opposite in terms of skills, workstyle and approach. They can be the most frustrating to work with if you don't understand each other. Potentially awesome partnerships get cut short when differences start to grate. Ours was nearly one of them. We had to learn how to respect each other's differences and give each other 'space and grace' to shine in our respective strengths. We recommend everyone does the same.

Every team needs a mix of personality strengths, and the best teams are those that make room for each personality type, allowing them to be themselves without the need for 'editing'.

Understanding these fundamental personality types allows you to value yourself better, celebrate diversity, and becoming both inclusive and included. It allows you to stand strong and confident in your own strengths while giving others the 'space and grace' they need to shine in theirs.

If you have never done personality profiles before, we strongly encourage you to fill out your own personality inventory and get more detail on your actual profile. Use the links at the end of this chapter.

This is the model we use in our workshops, anchored by practical exercises. Time and time again we see the lightbulbs go on for people in multiple ways: in the way they know and appreciate themselves better; in the way they understand others around them better; in how they learn to anticipate their own and other people's reactions under pressure and start to relate and work with other personality types more successfully. We are confident it will do the same for you and the relationships around you.

Learning to be more CURIOUS than critical

When your first response is to judge or criticize people instead of getting curious about their different perspectives, you shut people down, kill their creativity and teach them not to speak up or be truthful. You also teach them how to find ways to blame others, rather than learn from mistakes. And you end up with 'editing' and 'exclusion' rather than 'authenticity' and 'inclusion'. This is why we must get better at understanding differences in all their dimensions and learn to have better conversations across different perspectives.

Learning to embrace difference is vital for fostering authenticity in ourselves and in others and helps everyone bring the best of what they have to give.

Understanding the influence of the different sexes and learning about personality differences are two very powerful ways to start developing Habit #1: BE CURIOUS, not critical. Together these give great insight into *why* people behave the way they do, *how* your behavior impacts others, and *how* you can minimize withdrawals from each other's Emotional Bank Accounts.

When you master Habit #1, the rewards are significant. You are able to filter your perceptions better – which means you interpret behaviors more effectively, 'hear' each other better and don't take offense so easily. It also means you appreciate yourself and others more, learn to manage expectations and anticipate behaviors (theirs and yours) better, especially under stress. In other words, you learn to 'turn up' better to your relationships, have better conversations and achieve better results.

As a starting point for developing this habit, whenever you find yourself getting irritated or frustrated because someone is behaving differently to you, instead of making withdrawals from each other's Emotional Bank Accounts you can choose to:

1. Assume the best about them

2. Suspend judgement and criticism

3. Be curious and open to their perspective

4. Treasure hunt for strengths in differences

There is always strength in difference. Our job is to be open enough to find it.

That's the essence of developing Habit #1 – BE CURIOUS, not critical.

It's about investing the time to understand differences so you can push past your natural reflexes to criticize what you perceive as 'abnormal' behavior, suspend judgement and discover the potential for amazing teamwork and partnerships.

And here's something else worth remembering – when you get close enough to someone relationally, you are inevitably exposed to their weaknesses. That's a position of privilege – long-term success in that relationship will come from learning to show empathy and cover for their weaknesses rather than criticize them. It comes from learning to be their defense.

Time for Reflection

Key Takeaways

- The person who complements our skill set the best is likely to be the most frustrating to get along with because they are so different to us – until we understand life from *their* perspective.

- Understanding differences such as male / female differences and fundamental personality types allows us to stand strong in our strengths while giving 'space and grace' for others to shine in theirs.

- Not respecting differences causes people to edit themselves and breeds mistrust and exclusion.

- Embracing difference fosters authenticity and inclusion.

- There are always strengths in difference – our job is to actively look for them and find them.

Building Your Understanding

1. How can this understanding of fundamental differences help you make sense of relationships you find difficult or frustrating?

2. What strengths have you observed in people you find frustrating to work with?

Going Deeper

1. Which people / groups do you tend to criticize more than others?

2. How could this understanding of fundamental differences help you:

    a. delegate better?

    b. give better feedback?

    c. give more meaningful support to people around you?

    d. become more tolerant of different groups of people and more inclusive?

3. How would you position people from different countries / cultures against this personality model? For example, which cultures seem bossier to you? Which gentler?

Taking Personal Action

1. Discover your Animal Personality Traits online:

    a. Take the quick free version of the Connect Assessment® by scanning the following QR code with a smartphone, or typing the following web address into your internet browser: tsl.connectassessment.com

Make a note of the code on the screen (you'll need it to complete your registration). Register with the email address where you will receive your LOGB graph when you're done.

b. Find out more and take the full version of the Connect Assessment® by visiting: www.connectassessment.com

2. Think of someone you find difficult to get along with:

a. Check the narrative in your head about things you know are different between you – what have you been telling yourself about *why* things are the way they are between you?

b. What frustrates and grates on you?

c. What judgements have you made about their differences? What criticisms come to mind (or to mouth!)?

d. How could you change the narrative in your head – for example, what do they do differently that offers strengths you might have overlooked?

e. What could you complement them for or say you appreciate about them as a starter for a better conversation on the way to improving the way you work together?

3. If you are open to it, arrange a coffee / lunch / chat with someone very different to you to start building a better relationship.

4. Using the worksheet in the Appendices write down at least one thing that you are going to START / STOP / CONTINUE / CHANGE doing to get better at developing Habit #1: BE CURIOUS, not critical.

Habit #2

BE CAREFUL, not crushing

Chapter Six

Why we end up crushing each other . . .

'Without the SKILL and confidence to do conflict well,
our natural reaction is to respond in fear.'

As unique individuals who are all wired differently, it should be
no surprise that there will be times we don't see eye-to-eye. And
that when we feel strongly enough about our different points of
view, we will end up in conflict. The simple truth is that conflict
is both normal and inevitable – in *every* relationship. The good
news is that the conflict itself is not the problem. The problem is
we often handle it badly.

Actually, us human beings deal with conflict all the time. A trivial
example would be when we need to make wise choices about
where to focus our efforts based on limited resources like our
time and our money. However, when it comes to conflict between
two people having different perspectives and emotions, and
egos get involved, the process becomes far more challenging.

Many of us feel uncomfortable in conflict situations – perhaps
because of conflict done badly in the past – and so for many the
very thought of conflict invokes a feeling of discomfort or panic
and the inclination to avoid it at all costs!

But conflict plays a vital role in creating shared
understanding and richer solutions. It is essential that
we develop our skills to be able to do conflict well.

Strong relationships are built when people have the freedom
to speak up and say 'no, that's not OK', confident that they

are safe to do that, respected for doing so and supported in finding a way forward that works for everyone involved. In its pure sense, conflict is an opportunity to create better, more inclusive solutions.

The problem most of us have is we don't have the skills to relate to each other in a healthy way when emotions are running high. Often our responses in a conflict situation come out wrong, leaving people feeling hurt and disrespected because of the way we 'turn up' and behave. Fueled by our own internal discomfort and fears around conflict, we end up resorting to poor tactics like shouting and belittling.

Without a shadow of doubt, poor conflict resolution skills damage relationships.

Knowing that we are going to 'fight' at some point, the wise thing to do is learn to do it well, so we can take care of each other in the process and strengthen rather than damage relationships. And as we don't come prepacked with the skills to handle conflict well, we have to learn them on purpose.

That is the essence of Habit #2: BE CAREFUL, not crushing. It's about getting better at self-management – learning to 'turn up' well in a conflict situation, treat people well through conflict no matter how intense the debate and come out of the process stronger together. For many of us, developing this habit involves unlearning behaviors that damage relationships and learning to replace them with behaviors that strengthen relationships.

To improve our ability to handle conflict, we need to 1) change our mindset about what it is and what it isn't, 2) understand why we default to certain behaviors, and 3) learn how to develop new, helpful behaviors that lead to more successful resolutions. Let's look at each of these in turn.

Changing our mindset: Step 1 – Addressing myths about conflict

The first step in changing our mindset around conflict is to identify some of the false thinking about it. There are a number of common myths about conflict that are unhelpful. Below are six 'true or false' questions to start debunking them. Have a go at answering them as either true or false then check your answers on the next page – no cheating!

Six common myths about conflict – true or false?

1. To avoid hurting someone's feelings when something is bothering you, it's best to say nothing.
   o   True
   o   False

2. Conflict is a sign that the relationship is damaged.
   o   True
   o   False

3. He who shouts first, wins.
   o   True
   o   False

4. Once you are in conflict, you might as well address everything from the past that is bothering you.
   o   True
   o   False

5. Sometimes it is better to lose an argument in order to win the relationship.
   o   True
   o   False

6. An argument can often strengthen a relationship.
   o   True
   o   False

ANSWERS: Six common myths about conflict – true or false?

1. To avoid hurting someone's feelings when something is bothering you, it's best to say nothing – FALSE

   Sweeping things under the carpet never works. If something is bothering you it will only fester and often will color how you perceive every other interaction. It's best to talk about things that are upsetting you but choose a time when you can both hear each other well. It never helps if either or both of you are tired, rushed or too angry. Choose your battles though. Not everything is worth a fight. More on that later.

2. Conflict is a sign that the relationship is damaged – FALSE

   The fact that we are all different, independent, thinking people means conflict is inevitable. Conflict is a sign of a healthy relationship and an opportunity to understand each other better. It's how we handle conflict that can cause damage.

3. He who shouts first, wins – FALSE

   Yup! Andrea's sister shared this gem with us when we first had children and it is one of those fundamentals that applies to all ages. It's all about being able to stay focused on the issue, treat each other well and manage your emotions while arguing things through. Shouting is a sign that you are losing control, even when you have the positional authority – like being a parent or a boss. In fact, the more weight of authority you carry, the easier it is to damage relationships through shouting and the more likely it is that you lose the respect that comes with that position. More often than not, he who shouts first, loses.

4. Once you are in conflict, you might as well address everything from the past that is bothering you – FALSE

Bringing up the past, especially unrelated issues, is unhelpful. That just tends to add more heat than light – and the last thing you need in a conflict situation is more heat! It's generally better to stay focused on the one issue at hand and work toward increasing understanding both sides and genuinely resolving it. Otherwise, multiple issues can create overwhelm and confusion. Also, distracting from the issue at hand means you are unlikely to resolve it, which means you will end up repeating this class!

5. Sometimes it is better to lose an argument in order to win the relationship – Both TRUE and FALSE!

   This is a tough one and in fact, it can be both true and false. The point here is about valuing your key relationships and 'choosing your battles' so, in this sense, the answer is true. If the relationship is important to you and the issue is really not that important in the long run, it is better to lose the argument than stress the relationship. However, if the conflict is over an important issue that will impact the level of trust and respect in the relationship, giving in is just postponing the issue – it will come back to bite. So, in this context, it's better to not give in and address it.

6. An argument can often strengthen a relationship – TRUE

   We probably already gave the answer to this one away at the beginning of the chapter. An argument is definitely an opportunity to strengthen a relationship because it offers the chance to increase understanding and perspectives both sides. Done well, an argument allows both parties to discuss their points of view and develop a shared perspective, so the issue is addressed in a more inclusive, creative, win-win approach. The challenge, of course, is to learn how to do arguments *well*.

Changing our mindset: Step 2 – The truth about conflict

Changing our mindset also involves accepting that conflict is a natural part of relationships so that we don't feel panicked or afraid of conflict and learn to 'turn up better' when it inevitably arises.

Way back in 1965, psychological researcher Bruce Tuckman demonstrated that every successful team – whether a team of 2 or 22 – goes through four stages of development, the second of which is all about conflict.[21] You might be familiar with the four stages of Forming, Storming, Norming and Performing:

- Forming – is the easy bit of just getting together.

- Storming – is what happens when conflict arises from our different perspectives, goals or values.

- Norming – is where we agree how we will consider each other's perspectives, strengths and weaknesses and find creative ways to move forward together.

- Performing – is where we develop the trust and mutual respect to be able to work to each other's strengths, anticipate reactions, cover for each other, and really pull together as a team (think Olympic rowers).

There are no shortcuts. Every successful team goes through these four stages, but the level of SKILL in working through conflict will determine how long they stay in each stage and how quickly they get to the Performing stage. This means that in any relationship, whether at work or at home, we need to learn how to 'storm' well so that we can get to performing well.

The job for each of us is to understand that the stages exist, recognize where we are and develop the SKILLS to manage how deep we sink and how long it takes to go through frustration and conflict – storming.

We also need to embrace the mindset that the role of conflict is to help us establish and agree how we're going to behave in each situation, so we can live and work together in harmony and through the relationship achieve great results.

Tuckman later added a fifth stage 'Adjourning' which is when the team breaks up because the purpose of the team is fulfilled, and tasks are successfully completed.[22] But the challenge that many relationships face, is that they tend to get to the break-up bit without really experiencing the benefits of performing well together – because they never learned to go through the Storming phase well. The added challenge is that progression to Performing is not a straight-line process, because life will throw new challenges that cause us to start Storming all over again. It's a bit like in the game Snakes and Ladders (Chutes and Ladders in the US).

How does this play out in practice?

Well, you might start sharing a house with friends and discover that they always leave the kitchen in a mess. You clean up once, twice . . . then by the third time you've had enough. You argue it out with them and eventually agree how you will each respect and manage the use of the shared space. And then soon after settling that argument, you agree with your flat mates that you're having friends over to dinner . . . but the friends end up staying later than expected which disturbs your flat mates' sleep and annoys them. You wake up to another argument about how you're not respecting each other's schedules and routines!

Or you could be a couple discovering that you have very different emotions around money – one likes to spend and enjoy life, the other is concerned about the future and has a deep need for security through saving. As you probably already know, money is one of the biggest causes of arguments between couples – and it's often because people have such different views around how money should be used. The split of household chores is another big cause of arguments between couples because of different assumptions around whose role it is to do what. We will talk about underlying assumptions and beliefs in chapter 8.

But Storming is a key part of the process of learning to understand each other more and establish norms for working together.

One classic example of redefining the rules of the game and 'norming' for us, bizarrely, was around light switches!

Here's how Jon tells the story . . .

Andrea . . . and light switches!

I find it frustrating when lights are left on long after people have left the room. I think it's a senseless waste of money and is also not helping the planet! Andrea has a habit of leaving lights blazing. In the early days I used to get really annoyed at having to go around the house constantly turning off light switches. I felt Andrea was being irresponsible or just slack (typical criticism style for my personality type!) and used to constantly complain that she had left the lights on YET AGAIN!!

Then one day I found her totally content walking into a room in pitch darkness, finding her way around, getting on with things and not even noticing that the light wasn't on. That blew my mind. It finally dawned on me that Andrea wasn't leaving lights on carelessly, she was just oblivious to light – equally happy whether they were on or off. Bat eyes apparently! So, we developed a new norm that addressed both our needs. In places like the kitchen and guest toilet where the bulbs are high energy, we now have motion sensors! The lights come on and go off all by themselves. And guess what . . . no more conflict over lightbulbs. We found our way to 'norm' on that issue.

The better you get at Storming, the faster you discover ways of behaving (norms) that will help you perform well together. Eventually you get to the point of knowing each other so well that you can anticipate how the other person (or team members) will react in certain situations and adjust your approach where necessary so you can pull in the same direction rather than pull apart. When you get to that point, it's beautiful to behold – like professional dancers out on the ice, or Olympic rowers in their flow coming up to the finish line.

But we want you to be left in no doubt . . .

There is NO path through to Performing without Storming.

So, it's crucial that we learn to storm well, if we're going to enjoy long-term success in our relationships.

The problem is that without the SKILL and confidence to do conflict well, our natural reaction is to respond in fear – fight, flight or freeze – and spiral downwards in a negative cycle of actions and reactions.

The question then becomes: 'What SKILL do we need to manage conflict well so that we get can through Storming and Norming successfully, and get to Performing sooner?'

To answer this, it's important to understand what happens in our brains when we are in a conflict situation and how this shows up in our default responses to conflict – largely driven by our personalities. The more we understand about WHY we behave the way we do in a conflict situation, the better we are able to learn and develop more helpful responses and behaviors to conflict.

Understanding why we default to certain behaviors

Here's a quick high-level lesson on how our brains respond in conflict situations.

Psychologists tell us that there are three parts of our brain that *come alive* when faced with conflict:

1. The Cortex – the logical part of our brain that does most of our information processing.

2. The Limbic – the emotional 'fight, flight or freeze' survival instinct hard-wired in our brain.

3. The Parietal – the part of our brain that stores information on values, beliefs and behaviors.

In his brilliant book *The Chimp Paradox*,[23] Steve Peters re-labels these as the '*Human*', '*Chimp*' and '*Computer*' to explain the complex workings in very simple terms – a great read if you would like to find out more.

As Peters explains, in a conflict situation, the *Human* and the *Chimp* both get fired up at the same time. However, as in real life where chimpanzees are far more powerful than human beings, the *Chimp* in our brains is far more powerful than the *Human* and easily hijacks all the *Human's* good intentions. Our ability to manage our impulsive, emotional *Chimp* is by far, one of the biggest factors determining how successful we are in conflict situations.

The only thing that can keep the *Chimp* in check, is the *Computer*.

In a life-giving nanosecond between the brain's intake and our body's response, the *Chimp* checks in with the *Computer* for instructions on how to behave in this situation. In the absence of any pre-programming, the *Chimp* assumes danger and dives in to crush the enemy, unfettered by reason.

Sound familiar?

This is *how* we can all end up saying and doing things in anger that we later regret. And it explains *why* we sometimes leave people feeling 'crushed' in conflict situations.

This really powerful analogy explains WHY it is so important to have plans or strategies in place BEFORE a conflict situation arises so that our automatic responses are more measured and effective. Our 'fight, flight or freeze' survival instinct is poised with mounting paranoia to overreact and crush whoever is causing tension – even our nearest and dearest. If we are not ready, we are likely to be triggered and respond in whatever way we have seen or developed the habit of responding. And, as our track-records show, this is usually not brilliant. Let's have a look at the four most common approaches to conflict and why they are each unhelpful.

Four common approaches to conflict . . . and why they don't work!

Most of us turn up to conflict with a combination of the skills we saw modelled to us, and a strong dose of our own personality tendency. No surprises then that the four common approaches to dealing with conflict align with the four personality types we spoke about in Habit #1. Different authors describe them with different names but for simplicity, when faced with conflict, our instincts are to either WIN, YIELD, NEGOTIATE or WITHDRAW. The bad news is that none of these approaches is helpful for creating genuine resolutions. The reason – they are all based on our 'fight, flight or freeze' survival instinct – and focused on self-preservation. Here's what they look like in practice:

- **WIN** – This tends to be the default style for strong competitive personalities (like *Lions*) who want things done their way. They tend to turn up to conflict situations determined to show you why they are right and WIN the argument. This means their approach to dealing with conflict tends to be to attack, to impose their views and to win at all costs. It is a 'me-centered' approach because instead of focusing on resolving the issue, the only focus is on winning – proving they are right, and you are wrong. But WIN / LOSE is not a long-term strategy for success in relationships. Often, if one loses, both lose.

- **YIELD** – This tends to be the style adopted by personalities focused on structure and precision (like *Beavers*), because if they don't know the *right* thing to do or say they would much rather bury their head in the sand and pretend there is no problem. As a result, they often choose to yield or give in, not necessarily because they agree but because they want to get to peace quickly and get past the discomfort of the conflict situation. The challenge is they can become a 'walking volcano' about to erupt if they are forced to yield once too often – as is often the case when they are in repeated conflict with people who like to win. On the face of it, yielding sounds like a 'you-centered' approach, giving preference to the other person but it is still very 'me-centered', focused on getting past the angst and frustration in the fastest possible way without genuinely resolving the issue.

- **NEGOTIATE** – Strong personality types that are also great communicators (like *Otters*) tend to hold on to an argument like a 'dog with a bone' and in a conflict situation opt to negotiate or compromise, trying to persuade others to come round to their way of thinking as much as possible. Agreed, this sounds like they're striving for a 'fair deal', but instead it tends to mean holding back to give away as little as possible to get as much as possible or, at worst, settling for 50/50. This is one of the biggest misconceptions that ends up crippling relationships. When we try to meet each other halfway, who decides where halfway is? There is a brilliant story of a dad, two sons and a cake which makes the point. One son said 'Dad, can I be the one to cut this cake to share with my brother?' The dad in his wisdom said, 'Yes, but your brother gets to choose the first piece.' You can just imagine the measurement and precision applied to determine exactly where the halfway mark was so that he didn't lose out when his brother chose the first piece! And that's exactly what we do in relationships through negotiation and compromise which is fundamentally still 'me-centered'.

- **WITHDRAW** – In conflict situations, those who are focused on supporting people and building relationships (like *Golden Retrievers*) typically tend to withdraw and leave the scene. Confrontation is contrary to everything they believe about having warm, relational experiences which means they generally find conflict uncomfortable – sometimes to the point of it being overwhelming and painful. As a result, their default is to try to remove themselves from the situation completely for sanity and/or safety when the conflict situation feels too intense. Usually, it's not about leaving the relationship, but about finding a place they feel safe to be able to process what is happening and come back more composed when the tension has diffused a bit. This can be hard for people who like to win or negotiate to understand. Again, this is a 'me-centered' approach, but for people who genuinely feel overwhelmed by conflict, leaving the scene for them is more about survival than selfishness.

To complicate things even further, we often end up in conflict with someone with a different approach to ours. No wonder managing conflict is such a challenge for so many of us!

Working toward genuine conflict resolution

When things get uncomfortable in a conflict situation, most of us tend to ask, 'How can I look after me?' That's great for survival . . . but not for relationships. Understanding how our brains respond to conflict and how this gets reflected through our personality types brings comfort that we are not alone but doesn't help us fix things.

The real question to be answered remains 'How can we do conflict better?'

The simple answer is that, for long-term success in relationships, what we need is a 'we-centered' approach where the focus is not on Me or You winning, but instead where 'the relationship' wins.

To get there, we will need to overcome our self-preservation drivers.

The secret lies in our ability to program our brains with the values, thoughts and behaviors we would like to become our automatic responses during conflict situations – especially in our most important relationships.

We need to program our brains with an ideal 'to be' list.

Michael Fisher, CEO of Cincinnati Children's Hospital in the USA,[24] talks about creating a daily 'to be' list so he can be intentional about who he is becoming and how he shows up every day. In an interview with McKinsey, Fisher outlined what he meant:

> *Today, for example, I want to be generous and genuine. I hope I'm that way every day. But today I want to make sure it stays top of mind. I have a couple of important meetings later with some key people from my senior team. I want to make sure it's not just a necessary, tactical interaction but also that I am generous in my appreciation for them and that they feel that, because that's really my main purpose for those conversations. On a different day this week – and, look, you can see it here in my calendar – I knew that part of my job that day was to be collaborative and catalytic. So,*

I pick out two qualities, two kinds of 'to be', every morning as part of my normal routine.

And that's why Habit #2: BE CAREFUL, not crushing is such a vital habit to develop. It allows you to be who you would like to be when the pressure is on.

We will look at how to do this in practice in the next chapter by discussing how to be better prepared for 'battle', how to develop strategies to 'fight fair' while working toward genuine resolution during 'battle' and how to restore the connection 'after the battle'.

To be clear though, we only use the term 'battle' as a metaphor – this is not about fighting physically or hurting each other. If you are being abused in any way, please get help immediately because it is likely that things will only get worse. We've included some links on where you can find help, if necessary, in the Appendices.

Time for Reflection

Key Takeaways

- Conflict is inevitable so we must learn to do it well.

- Our default habits are 'me-centered' and generally are unhelpful in genuinely resolving conflict. Success comes from finding a 'we-centered' approach.

- Understanding how our brain responds in a conflict situation helps us become more intentional about our behavior.

Building Your Understanding

1. What challenges you most in conflict situations?

2. What strategies do you have for overcoming the challenges?

Taking Personal Action

- Write a few sentences describing how you would like to be experienced in a conflict situation – your ideal 'to be' list.

Chapter Seven

Strategies for treating each other with care, during conflict . . .

'We can't change others, but we can certainly change ourselves.'

Now that we understand that conflict is inevitable and that, in the absence of any clear instructions, our brains will respond in automatic 'fight, flight or freeze' mode, we can be deliberate about developing strategies that help us be more prepared for 'battle', turn up better and 'fight fair' while working toward genuine resolutions during 'battle', and restore the connection quickly 'after the battle'. Let's look at each of these in turn.

Preparing for 'battle'

So, what are the strategies that will help us be more prepared for 'battle'?

Success comes from being able to pre-program our brain with the behaviors we would like to demonstrate no matter how intense the conflict gets.

Essentially, pre-programming is about deciding who you want to be in a conflict situation. It's about answering questions like 'What character do I want on display in the heat of the moment?', 'How do I want to be experienced, especially by the people that are important to me?', 'How do I want to leave people and/or the relationship *feeling* after the conflict?'

At the end of the day, most of us want to behave in a way that treats people well and leaves no regrets, especially where the people who matter most to us are concerned. Three key strategies are very relevant in pre-programming our responses to help us manage conflict effectively: 1) Implementing Ground Rules, 2) Developing an Anger Management Strategy, and 3) Considering how different Personality Styles impact our approach.

1. Implementing Ground Rules

For any battle or competition to go well, clear guidelines are required – rules that keep things fair, safe and on track.

In relationships, 'Ground Rules' are those lines you decide you *will not cross* no matter how heated an argument becomes. They help to keep conversations constructive and safe, even in the most intense disagreements. You may create Ground Rules for yourself, independent of relationships – for example deciding that you will never initiate a physical fight. You may also choose to have Ground Rules as a couple or as a work team, where everyone agrees to a particular code of behavior.

Here are a handful of examples of what Ground Rules look like in practice.

There are three Ground Rules that we agreed early in our marriage – 1) we would never hit each other, 2) we would never walk out of the house in anger, and 3) we would never threaten divorce just to be spiteful. Just taking those off the table have meant that arguments didn't do emotional damage that would outlast the particular disagreement and/or weaken the foundation of trust in our relationship.

Another practical example could be deciding never to respond without considered thought. One of Jon's banking bosses was awesome at that. He would never respond in the middle of a heated situation. Rather he would listen to make sure he had all the facts, then he would go away and take time to compose his thoughts before responding, in a calm and considered manner. No surprises that he went on to be one of the global heads of the bank.

We also set Ground Rules for ourselves as parents, agreeing (as much as possible!) to stay focused on a handful of life lessons we are trying to teach rather than just lashing out at our children because we are frustrated or angry. We set Ground Rules for the children too – for example they know 'it's OK to be angry but it's not OK to be rude', so no storming off and slamming doors.

Other ideas include agreeing code-words like 'time-out' or 'foul' ahead of time, to give you the chance in the heat of the battle to 'come up for air' or agree to take a break to diffuse the tension. Sometimes it's better to take a break and return with fresh energy . . . and fresh manners!

Establishing Ground Rules is a vital strategy for handling conflict situations well and a practical technique for developing Habit #2: BE CAREFUL, not crushing. Ground Rules help us pre-program our brains with the habits and behaviors that allow us to turn up better and treat the relationships that matter most to us with the care and respect they deserve.

On the flip side, if we don't establish Ground Rules, we leave ourselves entirely at the mercy of our Chimp . . . and then heaven help us all!

2. Developing an Anger Management Strategy

Developing an Anger Management Strategy involves thinking about the things that could potentially 'trigger' you or cause you to lose your cool, and then developing a strategy for maintaining self-control in the moment. This is how Jon describes his . . .

Jon's Anger Management Strategy – in the making . . .

For me, whether it's my African cultural heritage, or just the way I was brought up, showing respect to your elders is super important. When I first came to school in the UK, I remember seeing some of my classmates use four-letter words with their parents when they disagreed with them! I remember thinking to myself, 'Dear God, what planet are these kids on . . . and what planet are the parents on for letting them get away with it!' My next thought was . . . 'What if my children grow up in this country, and one day start treating me like that?!'

So, for me, I have come to realize that disrespect is a huge trigger. Disrespect from our children is like a 'red rag to a bull' for me. Having an Anger Management Strategy has helped me plan ahead for how I will behave in the moment, knowing that the long-term goal is to maintain strong respectful relationships with my kids. I also want to model how to manage anger – and to practice what we preach!

One of the things I have implemented as a strategy in the moment, is to pause and breathe and think about the 'Big Picture' of what I am trying to achieve. I use that life-giving quarter second before 'my Chimp' comes out, to say to myself something like, 'OK it's disrespect, it's not life threatening in the moment, so we can come back to that – and come back to that, we absolutely will – but for now, remember the long-term goal of connectedness and let's try and get to the bottom of what is causing them to be disrespectful.' My 'Big Picture' desire is that when I am old(er!) and gray(er!), my children will want to come and hang out with me because of the quality of the relationship we enjoy – rather than just for handouts. That helps me contain my anger and approach the situation with more care.

Now, I'm not suggesting it goes that smoothly every time, but that's the game plan. I have to confess that my responses in the face of it are not always things I'm proud of, but I'm improving.

By thinking ahead about what I can do in the moment, I am able to better manage my own triggers, treat them carefully through the process and get to the bottom of the things that are troubling them enough to provoke disrespect. Developing an Anger Management Strategy continues to help me be more conscious of the things that trigger me, choose practical steps to manage the situation better, steer the interaction away from the red zone and where necessary 'talk myself off the cliff'!

Fundamentally, it always comes back to the question 'How do I want to be experienced in the moment, especially by my wife and children?'

We all get triggered to a greater or lesser extent by things. It could be someone cutting in front of you on the road or while you're waiting in a line, poor service in a shop or restaurant, or feeling disrespected by someone's words, tone or actions. Developing an Anger Management Strategy helps us stop and think about the things that are likely to provoke anger in us, identify the actual feelings we feel when we are triggered – anger, guilt, shame – and develop effective ways to calm them so we can have a better conversation.

Changing your body language can change your mood, so think about specific actions you can take to release tension and bring more calm to your body – unclenching fists, relaxing shoulders, unfolding arms, etc. Other ideas include unclenching teeth, deep breathing, directing your thoughts to a more positive memory, forcing a smile, and whispering a prayer. The point is to give thought beforehand to how you will manage situations where you are tempted to lose control and develop strategies that work for you. Because as we all know, if we fail to plan, by default, we plan to fail.

For more detail on how to manage anger, we recommend you check out some of the work by Anger Management Specialist Dr Bernard Golden.[25]

3. Considering how different Personality Styles play out in our approach

A third strategy worth implementing as part of your proactive approach – your mental prep for the 'battle' – is to spend a bit of time thinking about the different personalities around you. Based on your understanding of their personality (from chapter 5), think about how they are likely to respond to conflict and therefore how you need to approach things in order for them to 'hear you' better and work toward resolving it. This understanding will help you 'turn up' well to the conversation.

For example, if you have a more 'dominant' personality and you have a disagreement with a 'gentler' personality, you know straight away that for things to land well you need to soften your approach and body language without necessarily softening the message.

On the other hand, if you are the 'gentler' personality in a conflict situation with a more 'dominant' personality, brace yourself for how they might turn up, so you don't feel overwhelmed or overpowered. Think about what you will say or do to get your point across and how you will handle things if you feel uncomfortable with their approach. For example, you could say something like *'STOP – I can see you are really upset about this, but I won't discuss it with you while you are shouting. I'll come back in ten minutes when you have calmed down and we can talk about it then.'* You'll find the words that work for you, but the point is to think about and decide beforehand how you will manage the likely situation.

Similarly, if you're in conflict with someone who needs structure and precision, make sure you have your facts and figures straight or you could end up arguing about minor details and not the main issue.

If you're in conflict with someone who loves words and likes to argue, expect it to go on for a while and be clear with your points of reason because they are likely to be very articulate and convincing, negotiating for as much of their way as possible.

Once you understand personalities and tendencies in conflict situations – yours and others – you can be more prepared, show up well and adjust your approach so you can have a better conversation and achieve a better result.

Practice, Practice, Practice!

Once you've created your Ground Rules and Anger Management Strategy and reflected on the different personalities and approaches to conflict (including yours), the key to changing default behaviors is practice, practice, practice. That way, under pressure your default response is more likely to be in line with the person you would like to be. The neuro-scientific update to the age-old expression 'practice makes perfect' . . . is 'practice makes Cortex!' Because it literally does that. Think of it as creating brain muscle memory – new neural pathways leading to new helpful behaviors instead of the old unhelpful or damaging ones.

One way to build confidence and develop your SKILL for conflict situations is to have a go at practicing your preferred behaviors in situations where you are pretty relaxed about the outcome. For example, let's say you have just been charged for two things when the sign in the supermarket clearly says *buy one, get one free*. Even if the money is not worth the hassle, have a go at managing the situation. Just take the receipt back and point it out politely. No need to attack the employee – everyone makes mistakes. The refund isn't out of *their* pocket so it's a great opportunity to practice your conflict resolution skills in a scenario where everyone can win. Using these instances to practice will help you get better at going into a conflict conversation to understand what happened and work toward a solution rather than to exact justice or revenge. Things can heat up a lot faster in conflict situations at work or at home because you don't have that space or thinking time, so practicing managing conflict when the outcome doesn't really matter will help you get better at working toward a healthier solution when it does.

Fighting fair during the 'battle'

In addition to preparing for battle so that we 'turn up well', most of us need to learn the SKILL of treating people well through 'the battle' and resolving issues in a 'we-centered' way that strengthens rather than damages relationships. Here are six key principles to live by and practice in order to 'fight fair' and do conflict well.

1. Choose your battles

The first point to make is to *choose your battles* and decide whether this particular issue is worth a fight at all. Not everything is worth an argument. Ask yourself the question, 'Will this matter in six months' time?' The kind of 'Big Picture' thinking we spoke about earlier helps in this regard. Sometimes we choose the need to be proved 'right' over the relationship. The more we understand differences and learn to 'cut people some slack', the easier it becomes to choose our battles and put the relationship first. There is an old proverb that says that 'Death and life are in the power of the tongue'.[26] We can choose to diffuse the situation by choosing kind, gentle words to calm anger rather than harsh words that only fuel conflict. When we make the right choices, we choose to 'give life'.

2. Listen instead of 'reload'

During the conflict, one of the most important and caring things we can do is to listen carefully and genuinely.

Unfortunately, most of us tend to use the time simply to 'reload' so that we're ready with our comeback the moment our 'opponent' takes a breath. Quite often conflicts arise because of a misunderstanding of approach or perspective when all people are looking for is the chance to be heard and validated. Sometimes the issue they complain about first is not the real issue and this is where learning to listen well is paramount. This is especially true with teenagers. Getting better at listening to the issue behind the issue has been our life-line in staying connected with our children through the stormy teen years of life as half-child, half-adult.

A huge clue that there is *an issue behind the issue stated,* is when they lash out for no apparent reason (the Chimp got triggered!). That's when we need to *really listen* the most, as Jon realized with the disrespect issue:

> *On the (admittedly rare) occasions our kids would be disrespectful (to me or their mother) I would end up shouting back at them. Disrespect was, after all, an evil that needed to be stamped out, right? Well, yes . . . but also no. Certainly not like that. The reality was that my shouting would just shut down any communication, and the relationship would quickly become distant.*

> *Actually, I learned it was much better to find out what caused the disrespect in the first place and address that. I learned that whenever our young people come out fighting with words and attitudes that, to me, sounded disrespectful it was usually as a result of them feeling hurt or afraid about something they had not yet voiced.*

I learned that at the moment of their 'Chimping', instead of getting harder, I needed to get softer, more patient and really curious about the emotions and feelings underlying their behavior. Asking questions to understand what provoked their response . . . really. What were they worried about? How was their self-worth / self-respect being compromised?

What shows up as disrespect is often frustration from not being able to articulate the fear or anxiety that something provoked in them. I try to lower my voice and soften my tone. And as we have the conversation, generally it all comes tumbling out – that they're feeling stressed about what someone said on one of their social media group chats, or about what they will miss out on if they don't get to finish some game they're playing when we told them to come off technology, or if they can't go to a particular party, etc. And then once we've had a chance to address things, they'll usually come to me with a sheepish 'I'm so sorry for how I spoke to you', and we'll hug and make up and life is good again.

For people that we truly care about, listening to get to the issue behind the issue in that moment is where real breakthroughs in relationships and conflict resolution will occur. That's not to say we can't deliver hard messages. Don't worry, I haven't gone all 'soft' and decided that disrespect from my children is fine! However, I have come to realize that there is no point delivering a hard message to a 'closed spirit'. No useful learning comes from that. Much better to stay connected, maintain the relationship and teach them the principles that way. People hear things so much better when they feel heard and validated.

The challenge is that genuine listening *in the heat of a moment* is a most unnatural response for most of us. It demands the courage to stay open and vulnerable, the strength to suspend 'our right' to attack, and the insight to listen to what is being said

– as well as what is *not* being said. It demands the presence of mind to value the other person and the relationship above your natural instincts to defend yourself. However, at that moment, any other response is likely to make the situation worse. No amount of debate or criticism or telling off will calm the gut response to a deep emotional trigger.

Taking the time to genuinely listen and find out what the real issue is – including clarifying your understanding to confirm you are on the same page – will allow you to stay on point, address the one issue and show care and concern for people and your relationship with them.

Listening skills are so vital to building great relationships that we address the topic some more in Habit #4.

3. Don't be a Shrike!

A Shrike is a bird that impales its victim on a spike or barbed wire and then gradually picks it to pieces. Yikes! Sometimes in conflict situations we become Shrikes. Out of hurt and disappointment we attack each other with everything we can find, whether related to the issue or not, to inflict hurt in equal measure. Don't be a Shrike. Learn to attack the issue and *not* each other. Be clear on what your issue is and what you want to change. Ask yourself – 'What does good look like?' – and then stay focused on resolving that issue, using as few words as possible to make the point.

As Andrea's late dad used to say, in a conflict situation, ask yourself, 'Is it nice, is it true and is it necessary?' Because if what you're saying doesn't tick all those boxes, again ask yourself genuinely 'Why are you saying it . . . really?' And 'What might saying it do to your relationship?' Thinking about it like that will help you hold your tongue.

4. Commit to a 'no-drama' zone

The story is told of a mother-in-law who was coaching her new daughter-in-law on how to get what she wanted in an argument with her husband. 'First, cry, then if that doesn't work, throw a temper tantrum and if all else fails, threaten to hang yourself!' Talk about fighting dirty!

Most of us might not go to that extreme but we each have our version of fighting dirty – things like giving 'the silent treatment', crying to manipulate things emotionally, walking out, slamming doors and delivering 'low blows' just to score points. If the desired outcome is a stronger relationship, as much as possible the process should be a no-drama zone.

This includes being careful about tone of voice and body language, recognizing that together they account for a significant part of what is being communicated, regardless of the actual words. In 1967, Albert Mehrabian and colleagues[27] calculated their often cited 7-38-55 formula – which states that the impact of a message is 7 percent verbal, 38 percent vocal, and 55 percent facial. Even if they debate the actual percentages, psychologists today generally agree that people will evaluate *most* of the emotional content of your message more by your nonverbal signs than by what you actually say. So, don't save being nice, thoughtful, considerate, polite or 'your best self' for strangers who at the end of the day don't really add to your quality of life. Determine to do conflict with no drama.

5. Avoid character assassinations

We all have a tendency to think our little quirks and annoying habits are just niggles or a result of our circumstances. Everyone else's annoying habits, on the other hand, we assume are because they have huge character flaws. For example, if you missed a deadline it's because your workload was unusually heavy. If someone else missed a deadline it's because they are fundamentally disorganized. This tendency to judge others more harshly than ourselves is so common that psychologists have a term for it – Fundamental Attribution Error.[28] Quite often, this tendency gets exaggerated in conflict situations and comes out as accusations and character assassinations.

Try to keep things in perspective and avoid using extreme language like 'you always' and 'you never' – because they are likely to provoke a whole new argument! Use more 'I' language like 'I was hurt when you said . . .' or 'I was frustrated when you did . . .' to help own your own feelings and stay focused on the issue. Equally, avoid ultimatums – nobody likes to be forced into a corner.

6. Think the best

Bearing in mind that conflict is usually caused by a misunderstanding of perspectives, it's important to think the best, assume the other person has good intentions and stay open to creative solutions.

Time for another very quick high-level biology lesson . . .

Thinking the best has a real, powerful impact on your brain function. It allows serotonin – one of the happy hormones – to flow and connect across your brain's neurotransmitters, literally setting up a *train of thought* to find creative solutions to the problem. Thinking the worst produces cortisol – the 'fight, flight or freeze' hormone – which causes nerve cells to become isolated, shutting down the neural network and with it, the creative thinking process.

The more you can approach conflict with the assumption that you are both on the same side and can sort things out, the more creative, effective and 'we-centered' the approach to conflict resolution will be.

Restoring the connection after the 'battle'

Conflict situations typically lead to withdrawals being made from Emotional Bank Accounts – and the less skilled we are, the more withdrawals we make. Once the disagreement or conflict is resolved, it's important that we focus on restoring the emotional connection and making deposits in each other's Emotional Bank Accounts *on purpose*. Doing this well requires paying attention to three key things:

1. Learn the Lessons

As we said earlier, handled well, conflict situations are really opportunities to increase our understanding about each other and strengthen the relationship. To take advantage of the opportunity though, we need to look for and learn the lesson. If we don't, chances are we will end up repeating the class! These are classes we just can't skip because they are the only route through the natural stages of Storming and Norming before we can get to Performing.

Once you have identified and worked through the key issues, it's important to discuss and agree the best next steps and a way forward. It's generally helpful to write down your own commitments around things you will STOP doing, START doing, CONTINUE doing or CHANGE as a reminder for your own personal development in the weeks and months to come. Hopefully, by implementing the strategies discussed earlier in this chapter, you can find a win-win resolution that works for both of you. Nevertheless, there will be those times where you just don't see eye to eye on a particular situation and might have to agree to disagree. Sometimes that is the best strategy to move past the conflict if the issue is not a showstopper for either party.

2. Apologize and Forgive

Apology and Forgiveness are concepts most of us don't talk about enough but are vital for building healthy relationships.

In the heat of the moment, we all get things wrong sometimes, so it's important to be able to find ways to draw a line in the sand and start afresh. Learning to take ownership for your part in any particular conflict, apologize for it and extend forgiveness to those who have offended, helps you start afresh. These are important steps in restoring the emotional connection in the relationship and rebuilding the Emotional Bank Account.

In fact, they're such important concepts, let's take a quick look at each of them in turn:

Forgiving in practice . . .

Learning to forgive and let go is as much about you as it is about the other person, especially if the relationship is important to you. Forgiveness is a healing balm for relationships.

However, while forgiveness is necessary, it is not always easy, especially when the hurt runs deep. As C.S. Lewis once said, *'Everyone thinks forgiveness is a lovely idea until he has something to forgive.'*[29]

The cost of unforgiveness runs high and it's you that pays the price – often while the other person continues in life blissfully unaware of the burden you carry.

Unforgiveness typically affects you in three main ways . . .

Firstly, anger and bitterness ooze out like acid, damaging other relationships around you in the process. They put a vice grip on your heart, constricting your ability to come from a place of love, even with people who had nothing to do with the hurt.

Secondly, holding on to resentment and bitterness damage your own wellbeing and emotional health. The emotions around bitterness and unforgiveness trigger the same 'fight, flight or freeze' hormone cortisol. Just thinking about the hurt and anger you feel about a situation can make your heart race, your teeth and fists clench, and your stomach turn to acid. The problem is that cortisol also shuts down systems like your digestion and immune systems that are not needed for an emergency escape – great as a short-term self-preservation strategy but crippling to your health if left coursing through your body long term. As the old saying goes, unforgiveness is like drinking poison and expecting the other person to die. It's OK to feel the emotions of hurt or anger but it's not OK to stay there – for your own sake as well as the sake of the people around you.

Thirdly, the reality is that it won't be long before you yourself will need to be forgiven. Remembering that everyone makes mistakes will help you stay humble and extend the grace you will soon need. As poet George Herbert so eloquently put it: *'He that cannot forgive others, breaks the bridge over which he himself must pass.'*

So, forgiveness is as much about extending grace to those who did you wrong (in the way you would like to receive it), as it is about untethering yourself from the pain of the situation and freeing yourself from the damage to your personal health caused by bitterness and resentment. We all get it wrong sometimes.

Apologizing in practice ...

Now, while forgiveness is technically independent of an apology, most of us find it easier to forgive once the other person has apologized. We get caught up in a cycle of waiting for the other person to apologize first. And we do that because we often genuinely feel the other person had a bigger part to play in the issue.

In fact, lots of research studies have shown that people generally feel that *their* pain is greater than that of others. In one experiment,[30] a group of participants were paired off with the instruction that they should take turns applying pressure to each other's thumbs for a minute. When the pair switched roles, without fail, the pressure applied by the second person was greater than the pressure they originally received.

> **We all tend to feel that the wrong done to us is greater than the wrong we did. Learning to apologize well is to humbly admit that you inflicted pain and accept responsibility for the hurt you caused.**

We can each choose to take ownership and make amends for our part in any conflict situation, regardless of what the other person is ready or willing to do. An apology is likely to help restore the connection and move things forward quicker.

The other thing that's really important to understand about apologizing is that we don't all hear apologies the same. Sometimes we genuinely believe we've apologized but the other person doesn't agree that we have. In their book *When Sorry Isn't Enough*,[31] Dr Gary Chapman and Jennifer Thomas identified five different ways in which we all want / need to hear an apology. It turns out, some people need to hear you *express regret* – that is say 'I'm sorry' (with no buts!). Others need you to *accept responsibility* for what you did and hear you say 'I was wrong'. And that's just two of the ways.

If like us you've felt at times that your apology has fallen on deaf ears, or that an apology to you didn't feel sincere enough, we recommend you check out their book to learn which style of apology might land better for the person involved, or indeed, for you.

Getting apologies right is one of the most healing things you can do for relationships.

3. Celebrate Success!

Emotions are funny things – they can cause us to sabotage 'what we really want' for 'how we feel in the moment'. Unless we are deliberate about addressing negative emotions and feelings, they can continue to fester, create distance and drain Emotional Bank Accounts long after the issue is resolved, especially if the conflict was handled badly.

Celebrating success is about drawing a line in the sand after the conflict is resolved so that the relationship can move forward, free from any left-over negative emotions. This allows us to be intentional about putting good deposits in the Emotional Bank Account by choosing an activity that rekindles friendship and creates more happy moments to enjoy. It could be as simple as a drink or meal together – anything you both feel good about that helps confirm you now understand each other better and that the relationship is restored. The key point is to find a way to re-center and bring the warmth back into the relationship after the conflict.

Learning to be more CAREFUL than crushing

How we turn up and behave in a conflict situation leaves a lasting impact on people and their Emotional Bank Accounts for better or for worse – usually for worse until we become intentional about building strong conflict management skills. In a quote often attributed to the poet and civil rights activist Maya Angelou, although it seems it was first said by Carl W. Buehner, a high-level church official: *'[people] may forget what you said – but they will never forget how you made them feel'.*[32]

Conflict done badly over and over will chip away at the foundation of trust in the relationship and ultimately cause people to lose the WILL to continue investing in the relationship. Developing Habit #2: BE CAREFUL, not crushing is vital, in order to prevent emotional distance and damage to relationships that matter to us. So often we can find ourselves repeating the same old arguments, with the same old patterns of behavior and outcomes. Learning how to anticipate and prepare for conflict, genuinely resolve issues, care for each other no matter how frustrated and angry we become and emerge stronger together, are some of the best investments you can make in your relationship and in your life. For many of us, this involves unlearning habits that damage relationships and developing new ones, by literally re-programming our brains with better responses.

That's why taking the time to develop your own 'Ground Rules' and 'Anger Management Strategy' is essential. Being clear with yourself and, where appropriate, agreeing with your partner / colleagues / children how you will choose to behave in moments of conflict will help guide your behavior when emotions run high. How are you currently being experienced by those most important to you in particular during conflict situations and, more importantly, how would you like to be experienced? Once you understand what your tendencies are and have better management strategies in place, you will be able to 'turn up better' to arguments, Storm and Norm more efficiently, and get to Performing faster in all your relationships.

Learning to apologize well and give and receive forgiveness are vital actions to stop the hemorrhaging from the Emotional Bank Account and to start restoring the connection. Also, taking the time to acknowledge the emotional cost of the process and doing something on purpose to restore the connection will help get the relationship back on track – ideally with increased understanding of each other.

The Japanese art of Kintsugi ('golden joinery'), portrays a beautiful image of how conflict done well can strengthen relationships. Instead of throwing away a broken vase, through Kintsugi (also known as Kintsukuroi ('golden repair'), they glue the pieces back together and then decorate the cracks with lacquer mixed with gold, silver or platinum. Rather than disguise the cracks, they embrace them as part of the history of the object and turn something that could be ugly into something beautiful. We have the potential to do the same in our relationships – if we learn to do conflict well. Our battles and imperfections can become part of our treasured history of growing together and becoming more understanding. The better we get at managing conflict, the stronger the relationship will be.

These are the practical ways of making the changes necessary to develop Habit #2: BE CAREFUL, not crushing and have this habit become a natural part of who you are. When we master these behaviors, we increase our chances of being 'our better self' during conflict, taking care of people around us and strengthening rather than damaging relationships. This is not always easy, but it is always worth it.

We can't change others, but we can certainly change ourselves.

Time for Reflection

Key Takeaways

- We can get better at managing how we 'turn up' in conflict situations. Specifically, we can:

    a. develop our own Ground Rules and Anger Management Strategy ahead of time

    b. learn to really listen, and pay attention to 'the issue behind the issue' when anyone starts 'lashing out'

    c. fight fair and treat others well during conflict

    d. genuinely resolve conflict and learn the lessons

    e. take the time to reconnect afterwards to ensure the conflict serves to strengthen rather than damage the relationship.

- Habit #2: BE CAREFUL, not crushing equips us with the SKILL to change our automatic response so we can treat people well through conflict and strengthen rather than damage relationships.

- Practicing Habit #2 helps us minimize withdrawals from Emotional Bank Accounts and maintain the WILL to keep investing in our relationships.

Building Your Understanding

1. What 'triggers' you and puts you at risk of losing control over your emotions?

2. Building on the description you wrote at the end of the previous chapter, who would you like 'to be', even in an intense conflict situation?

Going Deeper

1. Who do you need to be more careful with, rather than crushing?

2. Are there specific individuals or groups where your tendency is to be more defensive and crushing?

Taking Personal Action

1. Stop and think about the behavior changes you might like to work on as a result of the things we covered in this chapter. How would you like to 'be experienced' in a conflict situation with people who matter most to you? The time you invest in giving this some thought will pay you dividends for the rest of your life.

2. Make a list of your own 'Ground Rules' – your own guidelines for how you want to behave in conflict situations.

3. Start developing your own 'Anger Management Strategy' – what will you do when you feel your anger rising, to ensure you maintain control?

4. How would you describe your ideal experience of a conflict situation? Develop a dream board or collage with pictures portraying your ideal experience (e.g. pictures of people in healthy (even if heated) debate, people talking heart to heart, being tender, etc.).

5. Continue using the worksheet in the Appendices to make a note of things you want to START / STOP / CONTINUE / CHANGE including at least one thing to help develop Habit #2: BE CAREFUL, not crushing.

Habit #3

ASK, don't assume

Chapter Eight

What's driving our assumptions?

'Becoming more aware of core values and beliefs is crucial for building trust and respect in relationships.'

The tip of the iceberg

Much like with an iceberg, when we meet and start getting to know someone, whether colleague or life partner, what we see is just a small fraction of who they really are. The behavior we observe in others, or demonstrate ourselves, is just the 'tip of the iceberg' – with a whole lot more going on down below. Most of us have learned to hide our real thoughts and feelings behind the mask that we present to the world, often justifying our emotions and behaviors with logic that we think is acceptable to others. But underneath the surface, there are core values and beliefs that influence how we turn up to relationships and how we expect to be treated.

Learning to identify and talk about these deep-seated core values and beliefs is vital to building strong relationships of trust and mutual respect. But sometimes they are so ingrained in us that we tend to assume *our* way is the *only* way to think about life, and that everyone shares those values and beliefs. Often, we don't even know we hold these beliefs until someone does something that challenges or tramples on them. And because we assume that everyone thinks like us, the only narrative in our heads that can help make sense of their contrary behavior is to conclude they meant us hurt or harm . . . and that they deserve our vengeance! We feel hurt and disrespected, confused about how someone who cares about us could possibly treat us that way . . . and trust is broken, at least for that moment.

When that happens, major withdrawals are made from our Emotional Bank Accounts. Our response is often intense and visceral, and on the face of it, disproportionate to the offense. If you have ever said or done something and got blasted by someone . . . chances are you've trampled on one of their core values or beliefs. If you have ever found yourself giving someone a tongue-lashing, maybe even surprising yourself at the intensity of your reactions, you can be sure that one of your core values has been challenged.

Early in our marriage we had to set the record straight about what we each considered acceptable behavior and what was not, as Jon recounts in a couple of stories . . .

> *Andrea thought playfully pouring Coca-Cola on my head would lead to a love chase and frolicking like they do in the movies. Hmmm . . . Now, I don't do mess in general, so pouring a dark, sticky drink on me was never going to go down well, but on top of that it felt like the ultimate disrespect. Let's just say Andrea was shocked by my negative response and has found other ways to stimulate the kind of frolicking she was looking for!*

> *Equally, I used to think that rough play – like practicing judo moves on Andrea – would create moments of laughter and fun with her as it used to do with my brother growing up. But having grown up with just girls, Andrea was horrified that I could even think it was OK to inflict any sort of 'pain' on my wife. I could tell in her eyes that the Prince Charming image she had of me developed a few cracks in that moment!*

In both cases we had each made instant, sizeable – though unintentional – withdrawals from our beloved's Emotional Bank Account. We could see the hurt and feelings of disrespect, and through the responses hear the question 'If they really loved me, how could they even think of treating me this way?' The more we learned about our different values and beliefs, and our ingrained perspectives on 'the right way' to treat each other, the more we were able to do the things that built feelings of mutual trust and respect. In other words, the more we were able to make deposits in each other's Emotional Bank Accounts *on purpose*.

Becoming more aware of core values and beliefs is crucial for building trust and respect in relationships.

As self-centered as it may sound, when we come across different beliefs and assumptions in a relationship, our natural tendency is to feel that our way is the 'right' one. But that typically only leads to friction. Developing the ability to recognize when core values are being challenged, to hear and respect each other's perspectives, and have courageous conversations about tough issues when necessary, are fundamental to building long-term successful relationships. That's the essence of Habit #3: ASK, don't assume.

Fundamental to developing this habit is building SKILL in three areas. Firstly, it's about learning to identify our own core values. Secondly, it's about recognizing when our assumptions and beliefs differ from others'. And thirdly, it's about learning to have courageous conversations around deep-seated issues and things that really matter to us.

A key part of developing this habit is learning to ask questions and discuss things in a way that creates a shared perspective, rather than assuming others share our values, or that stereotypes are always true. This requires the ability and confidence to be open, vulnerable and honest with ourselves and with each other, so that we can build meaningful relationships based on mutual trust and respect.

Sadly, what most of us have learned instead is to play games of politics, manipulation and social maneuvers in order to avoid feeling too exposed by these necessary but often tough conversations, as unfolded in David and Leona's story . . .

When we first met David and Leona, it was clear that they loved each other deeply. It soon became equally clear though, that they had a couple of issues in their relationship – in the form of 'no-go' areas for discussion – that would keep causing them problems until properly addressed.

They were both professionals of pretty equal career status working in the banking industry and they both came from cultural backgrounds where the unspoken expectation was that a woman's role was to take care of the house and the children. The conflict between expectations and reality had started to play out . . .

The responsibility of cooking, cleaning and maintaining a household of two school-aged girls and a toddler son meant that Leona would come home to her second job at the end of a long day. She knew that David worked equally hard and had other responsibilities around the house like doing the garden, the never-ending stream of DIY jobs, and all the paperwork – utility bills, insurance and let's not forget the annual tax returns! But she wished he would see the weight of the daily routine and be more available and involved in day-to-day chores. Leona started growing silent and distant in communication and the warmth and intimacy between them was reduced to functional conversations around looking after the children and running the household. Behind the complaints of not helping with meals and dishes and the laundry was a growing resentment around feeling taken-for-granted and unsupported. The romance they once enjoyed was all but forgotten.

Leona's parents and siblings lived locally and tried to support where they could. They would often pop in to help with the chores and to spend time with their grandchildren / 'favorite nieces and nephew', on whom they doted. David resented the fact that Leona's family was always around, but that having 'his family' come round was always seen as a problem. Leona never told him how judged and intimidated she felt by his family. In David's family culture, a good hostess should prepare an elaborate meal of multiple dishes to show honor and welcome for guests. In Leona's eyes, other people's homes were always immaculate while she was barely able to keep piles of laundry out of sight! She felt overwhelmed by the expectations of his family's traditions and so resisted having his family over. But because they never talked about these issues, David read that as her not liking or caring for his family. Whenever he tried to discuss it, Leona would get so angry and disrespectful in the way she spoke that he found ways to work around her rather than having to talk things through. Her unspoken fears and insecurities made this a real 'no-go' area in the relationship.

Everything came to a head when David's brother Joshua, a newly qualified junior doctor, needed a place to stay for three months. Of all his family, David was the one with the space at home to accommodate him, and the family expected him to offer to help his brother. David also really wanted to help Joshua out, thinking it would be fun for them to spend time together as brothers, to have his girls get to know their uncle more, and to give his best man a chance to bond with his nephew. Knowing that Leona would be very anti the idea of Joshua staying, and find all kinds of excuses, David just said that he was coming to visit for the weekend because they had an event to attend together. He convinced himself that once Joshua was there with his suitcases, they would figure out the rest. Little did Leona know that the event the brothers had planned was the traditional circumcision ceremony for her only son!

Leona was adamantly against circumcision. In her opinion it was barbaric, outdated and no longer necessary on medical grounds. Another 'no-go' area.

Joshua arrived with a truckload of luggage and boundless excitement, chattering away about all the things they would get up to over the next three months and how honored he felt to be around as his first nephew went through this most important of traditions handed down through the generations!

David tried to signal to Joshua to stop talking but the proverbial horse had already bolted.

Deeply held values and beliefs – and undiscussed and unresolved issues – were suddenly propelled into the open, provoking anger and pitching them against each other in violent argument across the kitchen table. Frustration and resentment over the years came tumbling out in harsh accusations. Leona felt ambushed, hurt and betrayed. David tried to defend his feelings of constantly being made to feel overruled in his own home. Joshua was shocked by the issues that his brother and wife had been facing, devastated that he unknowingly caused this volcano to erupt, but hopeful that together they could find a way to sort things out. But as Joshua was unpacking and settling in, Leona was mentally packing to move out with the children. For her that was the last straw – barring a miracle, their marriage was over.

In chapter 7 we spoke about listening for 'the issue behind the issue' in a conflict situation. We mentioned that unexpected anger and 'lashing out' are often clues that a core value has been trampled on. In these situations, a courageous conversation is essential.

Not having the SKILL to have courageous conversations doesn't mean we get exempted from dealing with the issues.

They cannot be wished away . . . and while sweeping issues under the proverbial carpet may put them 'out of sight' for a while, they are definitely not 'out of mind'. They continue to fester and create distance in relationships, as the stories we tell ourselves about the other person being intentionally mean, unkind, selfish, inconsiderate (feel free to insert your own words here . . . basically evil!) remain unchallenged. Left unaddressed, over time, Emotional Bank Accounts get drained, the emotional distance in the relationship feels like a gorge too wide to cross and people lose the WILL to try any more.

Sadly, this was the case with David and Leona. As they discovered, when we are ill-equipped to have brave conversations around deep-seated, emotionally charged issues, manipulation and other forms of dysfunctional behavior sabotage the potential for strong, quality relationships of mutual trust and respect.

Building the SKILL to identify our own core values and beliefs, to recognize where they differ from others and to have courageous conversations around these issues is essential for building openness, honesty, trust and respect in relationships and preventing the creation of 'no-go' areas. It's true, not everything will get resolved immediately, but being able to discuss issues in the open prevents festering and decay, even if it takes several goes at the conversation. That is the essence of Habit #3: ASK, don't assume, and that is what we will be expanding on in the next few chapters.

Obviously, this is a huge subject to tackle so we will focus on a few key areas that offer real breakthroughs in developing this habit. As a heads up, in this chapter we will focus on understanding some of the cultural influences on our assumptions and expectations to increase awareness of our own values and the fact that in a relationship we can each be starting from very different beliefs and values around certain key issues. In the next chapter, we'll look at three prevailing assumptions that are at odds with the way we live our lives now and challenge the quality of our relationships at work and home. And then given that our own values and beliefs have such a strong influence on the way we turn up to relationships, there is a whole chapter dedicated to helping you identify the things you hold dear so that you can become more intentional about living to your values. This includes clarifying what is important to you, creating healthy boundaries, learning to ask for what you need and having tough conversations when necessary.

How our backgrounds influence our assumptions and expectations

Cultural and family values play an undeniably large part in shaping our perception of the world, the underlying expectations we bring to relationships, and the assumptions we make about how others 'should' behave. The more global and interconnected the world becomes, the more crucial it is that we each develop our cultural fluency – that is, our understanding of *what is acceptable* and *what is untouchable* in different cultures, and the values and assumptions that underpin them. And as relationships become increasingly cross-cultural, it is even more important to understand these big influencers on our expectations. Increasing our understanding allows us to show more empathy for other people's views and enjoy more peace and harmony in our relationships.

We learned some of these foundational principles first-hand while living and working in Japan in our second year of marriage. One lesson that stood out for us was how impolite it was considered to say 'no' directly to someone's face. In our early days of eating out in downtown Tokyo, in her typical creative approach, Andrea, seeing all the ingredients she wanted in different parts of the menu, would ask for customizations – 'Could we have item 5, with a bit of item 8 and part of item 10 on the side, please?' The waiter would just smile politely, if a little uncomfortably, and then with a sharp intake of breath say '*Muzukashii desu*' – which literally translated means 'that's hard or difficult'. We soon learned that what they were actually saying was 'No, not a chance – never gonna happen'. Just with a lot more grace. Andrea eventually learned to just stick to the menu options presented.

We had to learn to be more gracious in our responses too, so that we didn't offend others by being too direct, especially when we had to disagree with something or say 'no' to someone. Not a bad lesson for us. The key takeaway, though, was that – on some things, different people and cultures will have different views on the 'right thing' to do, and on what is considered respectful or disrespectful. Those cultural differences can spark quite strong gut responses to the point of making some things 'show-stoppers' – like the issue of circumcision was for Leona. As we learned back then, and now teach as a fundamental part of Habit #3, the more we can all understand how different cultures influence values and assumptions, the better we can get at recognizing when different perspectives exist, and the easier it becomes to create the room to talk about them in a way that builds mutual trust and respect.

Social psychologist Geert Hofstede is best known for developing one of the earliest and most popular frameworks for measuring cultural differences in a global perspective. Leveraging his experience at what some would argue was the first truly global organization, IBM,[33] over the last several decades Hofstede and his colleagues have identified six different dimensions[34] which distinguish between national cultures across the world: Power Distance, Individualism vs Collectivism, Uncertainty Avoidance, Assertiveness (Masculinity), Long-Term vs Short-Term Orientation, and Indulgence vs Restraint.

These dimensions highlight different (though not necessarily opposing) values which influence our perception of what is right or wrong, as well as the decisions and choices we make in life. Learning how these fundamental assumptions, values and beliefs can differ between cultures / countries will help us anticipate where people might be coming from in their perspective on an issue. It's important to emphasize the point that this is not a shortcut to knowing people as individuals because culture is just one, albeit powerful, source of influence on a person's values and beliefs. Life experiences might position them somewhere completely different to what might be expected culturally. So, rather than just stereotyping people and assuming we know where they are coming from, understanding these cultural dimensions allows us to have a better conversation on where they might be positioned relative to us. The more we learn about these cultural cues, the easier it becomes to create the environment for open, honest conversations, build mutual trust and show people respect in the ways that matter most.

We tested the assumptions and values around power distance in a live setting and the experience was electric. We ran a community workshop on building strong relationships for a local community with about 40 people in attendance and posed this question:

When interacting with people outside your peer group (business acquaintances or perhaps your children's friends) do you prefer to be addressed by your title of Mr, Miss, Mrs, Dr, etc., or are you happy to be called by your first name?

Participants in the room that day aged between late teens and early eighties. The debate was intense. The older generation, mostly from West African cultures, were adamant that the 'right' way to behave and show 'proper respect' was to defer to elders and use titles when addressing them. The teens and twenty-somethings, mostly brought up in the UK but also of West African descent, were equally adamant in their opposition to the idea of 'deference based on age'. In fact, they went on to assert that this insistence on seniority-based authority was possibly the reason why child sexual abuse often went undetected. In their view, sexual predators were able to take advantage of the associated assumption that adults were right, and children should be 'seen and not heard' – or believed.

Strong emotions, visceral responses and firmly held beliefs on both sides. Both equally valid. Both desperate to be heard and understood. And that was exactly the objective. We were not trying to prove who was 'right' or 'wrong' but to allow both sides to hear each other and make room for a different perspective on behaviors around the issue of respect, deference and negotiating power distance in relationships.

It goes without saying that no one likes to feel insulted or disrespected, but that is what we invariably inflict on others, or experience ourselves, when we don't understand how differently we think about life on key issues.

Understanding expectations around power and deference between cultures and generations also helps explain some of the generational tension being experienced in the workplace today. With three or four generations present in the workforce today, there are very different expectations around speed of career progression and power distance in the hierarchy. Older, more traditional workers (typically Baby Boomers and Generation X) generally expect to be deferred to, and expect that others coming behind will 'pay their dues' in time and commitment before being promoted. Younger members of the workforce – Generation Y (also known as Millennials) and Generation Z – tend to expect promotion every two to three years, a closer mentoring relationship with their manager rather than the traditional 'command and control' style, and flexibility in work hours and location.[35]

The point is this – our cultural and family values shape our perceptions of the world and our underlying assumptions and expectations of how others *should* behave. Without this awareness, assumptions and strongly held views can cause real tension points in relationships.

Learning to live and let live

Just realizing that there is a spectrum of opinions around each of Hofstede's six dimensions will help you become more conscious of where you are likely to be positioned on a particular issue and will also help you recognize that people you relate with might be coming to the conversation from a different direction. For example, where do you stand on the issue of deference and relating to authority? You can have better conversations at work and at home simply by understanding that you might be coming at the issue from different perspectives.

Our Japan experiences also taught us to do the hard work of meeting people one-on-one if we were ever to understand how they really felt about a particular topic. Back then at least, once people got together in a room, somehow individual ideas appeared to magically dry up. Going with the group – and indeed with the seniors in the group – was generally the preferred option. This helped us really understand how cultural values and perspectives influenced the way people behaved and what we needed to do differently to respect their values and approach, while still getting the job done.

Of course, becoming aware of different cultural assumptions means you also get challenged to confront your own. In your meetings for example, do people feel obliged to go along with the rest of the team or are they comfortable being the lone voice in the group? Do you encourage or frown upon those who choose to voice their dissent? What about relationships with your extended family? Are you free to say what you really think, or does it have to be in line with what the rest of the family think? How do you resolve issues around living with *the in-laws* or having them live with you – or including them in your decision-making?

The key point to remember here is that, outside of breaking the law, some things are not 'right' or 'wrong', they just *are*.

The more you understand about how cultures influence the way you and others think, the better you are able to anticipate their perspective and 'meet them where they are' in your conversations. And when you do that, even more importantly, you learn to treat people well and build relationships of mutual trust and respect.

How we often get it wrong at home, at work and in life

Against this background of cultural differences, it's easy to understand how we can each turn up to our relationships with a 'box of expectations' around what makes a good friend, or partner, or husband, or wife, or parent, or colleague, or boss. If the expectations and assumptions are shared, happy days! If they are not, we can end up in heated debate about surface issues ('you didn't use the proper title', etc.) without recognizing the intense emotions and huge withdrawals from Emotional Bank Accounts being made because of broken cultural cues for respect and treating people well. These challenges to our core values and assumptions can go deep, shaking our sense of security, identity and self-worth at home, at work and in life.

At home

Gina and Arjun's story . . .

For Gina and Arjun, their different assumptions around roles in the home and the role of money in creating a sense of security showed up dramatically 10 years into their relationship. In the aftermath of the 2008 market crash, Arjun was made redundant from his job as the IT manager at an insurance company. Gina did everything she could to help Arjun find another job – because for her, security came from full-time employment and a predictable income. Arjun spent more time focusing on setting himself up as an independent contractor. For him, security came from being his own boss, taking charge of his own destiny and eliminating the risk of being made redundant again.

It was a tough market, and it took Arjun the better part of nine months to get his first contract. By then, all of their savings were a distant memory and they had started to run up credit card bills. The day rate from contracting was good but finances remained a challenge because of the unpaid gaps between contracts. Gina's aversion to financial risk – and her patience – were constantly being tested. Arjun couldn't understand why she was not excited about him starting a business and the potential freedom it offered – financially and otherwise. Gina kept on Arjun's case about going back to a permanent job. And she also had her mum and dad get on Arjun's case too – after all, that was what all 'responsible providers' did in their book too! That grated against Arjun. He felt her parents should not interfere and should keep their distance like his parents did.

As the situation continued with them living from month to month without any financial cushion, Gina decided to go back to work and try and manage things around the children. The regular income eased her anxiety around their financial situation, but she struggled with resentment for Arjun putting her in the position to have to take on 'his role' while still doing hers. This along with everything else created huge ongoing tension and emotional distance between them. So much so that even after Arjun finally landed a one-year IT contract in the City – which meant they would recover financially and potentially come out of the situation better off – it was clear their issues went much deeper than just the presence or absence of funds. They needed to have some tough, honest conversations about values and disappointed expectations both sides. The problem is, they weren't aware of their very different core values around security, roles in the home and involvement of the wider family so every attempt at a 'conversation' ended up in very emotionally charged arguments . . . and blame.

In chapter 6 we mentioned that one of the top reasons for arguments in couple relationships is different core values and assumptions over money. And the problems usually come from one party having a deep need for security through finances. But many of the intense arguments around money never get to the bottom of the core need being challenged. Without an understanding of how values and assumptions differ, many couples fall into the trap of blame, judgement and needing to prove who is right, and never get to address the real concern.

But you can't talk about what you don't know about.

The more you understand how differently people can think about key issues, the more you can be open to discuss them, show people respect for what they genuinely feel is 'right' and articulate what is important for you to feel respected.

Investing the time to understand different perspectives, allows you the opportunity to gain new insight, do honest reflection, accept loving challenge and develop new approaches.

It's a bit like in the old movie *Yours, Mine and Ours*[36] . . . we need to understand what's *yours* and what's *mine* so we can have a meaningful conversation to agree what's *ours* and how we will move forward in the relationship.

Sometimes assumptions about what is 'right' can be so ingrained that we feel powerless to even broach the conversation, as was the case with Arjun and Gina. However, just by understanding that core values and assumptions drive our behavior, and that we may be coming to the relationship with different mindsets and emotions around them, we can approach conversations with more empathy, curiosity and mutual respect to find a way forward that works for the relationship. By developing the habit of ASKing, rather than assuming, we change the narrative in our heads about people's intent and behavior and give each other the space they need to think differently about things.

At work

Just knowing these differences exist helps give permission to bring the conversation out into the open so you can ask and discuss rather than assume values and perspectives are shared.

It also means you can choose not to be offended so easily.

It always stood out for us how many of our American colleagues will happily say what they are good at without an ounce of boasting intended. To our British ear it sounded like inappropriate self-praise and felt a bit 'off-color' until we realized we just held different assumptions about how assertive and confident people should be in discussing accomplishments.

This assumption around assertiveness shows up in a real way in workplace relationships and has significant implications for performance reviews and promotions – especially for women. As Sheryl Sandberg highlights in her international bestselling book Lean In: Women, Work, and the Will to Lead,[37] a lack of understanding of the underlying assumptions around whether or not it is OK to be assertive has been a major factor influencing gender inequalities in the corporate world. Men tend to be more assertive and often overly optimistic in predicting their performance. In general, women tend to be understated and less vocal / forthright about their competencies, so others assume they are lacking in skill when they are not. (Of course, there are those who experience this in reverse.)

Women also tend to get judged harshly in perceptions around their character when they are more naturally competitive and ambitious. When they do, they are criticized for being too bossy, not a team player and 'not nice'. In her TED Talk 'How to Design Gender Bias Out of the Workplace', Sara Sanford shared the observation that when performance reviews are done once a year, the focus tends to be on overall impressions rather than specific accomplishments. This is where women tend to lose out. Their research showed that two-thirds of the reports on women were about personality – 'watch your tone', 'don't be so aggressive' and only 3 percent of men's reviews mentioned their personality.[38] Changing performance reviews to be more frequent – like weekly – and focused on tasks, led to a disappearance in differences in performance between men and women.

So . . .

Next time you find yourself 'grizzling' at someone else's behavior, check your assumptions around acceptable levels of assertiveness – theirs and yours.

Similarly, different cultural assumptions around the need to control things and avoid uncertainty influence management styles. Under COVID-19 lockdown, many leaders were challenged on their assumptions of what good management looked like because they were no longer in full control of people's working hours and physical presence. Those who managed by visibility and presence struggled with the perceived loss of control and uncertainty that comes with people working-from-home. In response, by all accounts the sales of software to monitor online presence and screen flow of users soared. The underlying assumption was clearly that people could only be trusted to work well if they are being constantly supervised. Workshop participants have voiced frustrations at both ends of the spectrum. Some have felt micro-managed, while others have felt exposed due to a lack of sufficient direction and guidance. There is still much work to be done to help leaders and organizations make the massive culture change to develop the trust and leadership style that fosters stress-free remote working for both managers and employees in the new world of work. We talk about this some more in chapter 15.

In society

The key point is that these and other cultural assumptions influence our perception of what's 'right' and what's 'wrong', what's 'acceptable' and what's not and by so doing dictate the quality of our interactions.

This is as relevant in one-on-one relationships as it is to relationships between groups of people and cultures different to ours. What's needed is a shift in mindset to challenge faulty assumptions and stereotypes so that people can be more intentional about showing respect to others. This includes acknowledging just how disrespectful and hurtful some of the jokes and stereotypes that are often made about other people and cultures are.

Regardless of background or culture, it's fair to say that we all know what it feels like to be disrespected or for trust to be broken in relationships. Deep down, our desire to be valued and respected is the same as everyone else's. We can each invest the time to understand more about the assumptions and beliefs that drive people so that we can build trust and respect on purpose, no matter how different people might be to us.

Over the years, society has taught us to shy away from these kinds of conversations, when what's needed is for people to develop the SKILL to recognize and talk about these deep-seated issues in a way that is honoring and maintains mutual respect. That is how we can all go on to build meaningful relationships, uncluttered with misunderstanding, resentment, anger or hurt, no matter how different we are.

In our experience, three prevailing assumptions that are at odds with modern life provide great places to start having better conversations. Addressing them will help us develop approaches to work and home that are more aligned with life in this digital age and will help to improve the level of trust and respect in relationships at work and at home. We will look at these assumptions and how to address them effectively in the next section.

Time for Reflection

Key Takeaways

- We all have core values and assumptions that drive our behavior – some we are conscious of; others are more ingrained.

- The better we get at identifying core values, assumptions and expectations, the better conversations we can have around what is important to each of us and the more empowered we become to build relationships of mutual trust and respect.

Building Your Understanding

1. What experience have you had of different views on respectful / disrespectful behavior?

2. Which assumptions leave you feeling disempowered or present you with the most challenge in a relationship? Why do you think that is?

Going Deeper

- What jokes and stereotypes have you heard or said about people / cultures different to yours that work against building trust and respect in relationships?

Taking Personal Action

- Find someone who thinks completely different to you on an issue – for example around money or acceptable levels of in-laws' involvement – and invite them for coffee or a drink. Spend some time just talking about why they think the way they do, asking questions to understand without any attempt to change their perspective.

Chapter Nine

What would be most helpful to ASK for?

'If we can't talk about them, they're already problems.'

There are a number of underlying assumptions about work and life that are no longer relevant in today's modern, global, digital age, but three of them left unchallenged tend to have the greatest negative impact on relationships – both at work and at home. Recognizing these assumptions and then making what we call 'a big ASK' in each of them helps us be more authentic, 'turn up' better, and achieve a more sustainable work-life balance. We call them 'big ASKs', not because we shouldn't be asking for them, but because sometimes it takes a lot of courage to even broach the subject.

But if we can't talk about them, they're already problems.

The fear that conversations challenging these assumptions will be emotionally charged and not well received often makes us reluctant to 'go there' and bring the issues they provoke out into the open. However, the reality is that unless we do, we will end up 'breaking' people or 'breaking' ourselves.

We will address the important issue of *how* to approach and have these kinds of courageous conversations successfully in chapter 11, but first let's take a look at the assumptions themselves and the kinds of questions we should be asking to help us prevent them from derailing our relationships.

Three damaging assumptions . . . and the 'big ASKs' we need to make

The three assumptions that cause the most damage to relationships do so because they lead to unhelpful narratives in our heads.

They prevent us from having necessary courageous conversations around things that matter because of the faulty thinking that results. While the actual words for each individual are likely to be slightly different, the following captures the theme for most:

- *'Professional' means no 'personal' allowed* which tells me: *'Work and home life must be kept completely separate'*

- *Gender stereotypes in the home are both real and valid* which tells me: *'Roles and responsibilities at home are fixed and non-negotiable'*

- *Busy means important* which tells me: *'I have no time for anything else'*

The barriers created in our minds around these assumptions tend to be so strong that they shut down conversations in relationships both at work and at home before they even start.

When we stop to think about them though, we know these assumptions aren't really true, but most of us live our lives as though they absolutely are! A big part of the reason many work and domestic relationships continue to struggle is that many of us haven't yet managed to successfully challenge and negotiate some (or all) of these assumptions. As a result, we're not able to discuss and discover creative ways forward that are more aligned with our respective realities.

This approach to life based on invalid assumptions has troubled relationships for decades, and the clash with the realities of life under COVID-19 lockdown only brought the issues into sharper focus.

Success comes from making an appropriate 'big ASK' to address each of these assumptions – a big ASK of our boss(es) and colleagues, a big ASK of our partner and/or family, and a big ASK of ourselves.

'Professional' means no 'personal' allowed . . . really?

Without a doubt, confusion over where the divide between what should be considered 'personal' and what's 'professional' continues to cripple meaningful conversations in the workplace, challenging relationships between individuals and their employers in any way, shape or form.

Now don't get us wrong. Of course, it would be inappropriate to start going into the details about your sex life in the office – and that's not likely to change any time soon – but that's not what we're talking about here. What we're talking about is that unspoken underlying understanding buried into the 'psychological contract' of many employees, that personal issues must be left at the office door and not be allowed to interfere with the relationship between the organization and the individual. Except the problem is, the personal / professional divide we perceive has a one-way filter in it – we try to block home from impacting work, but we're less convinced the other way around.

The reality is the boundaries between work and home have been seriously blurred over the last couple of decades with the introduction of laptops, mobile phones, Broadband and increasingly decent levels of Wi-Fi. For many, working from home means there is no corporate office door to leave 'personal stuff' behind. The net result is that in today's global 24/7 working world, many feel the constant, though silent, pressure to keep working outside official office hours as necessary, especially in dealing with multinational offices in different time zones. For sure, this expectation of constant availability is hot on the agenda for conversations around the dining table at home, but one of the big unresolved challenges is that many of us have not yet given ourselves permission to bring the home-life conversation into the corporate room.

Consequently, many people feel pressured into presenting their 'official' selves and shoving out the things they care about

– sometimes literally – for fear that they might look less than one hundred percent professional. The Robert Kelly interview with *BBC News* that went viral comes to mind.[39] There he was in his home office on live TV when one, then both, of his children merrily wandered in. He tried to ignore them – unsuccessfully. His wife rushed in to get them, clambering on her knees and trying hard not to be seen. Except the whole world saw! The funny thing is the TV host attempted to bring the conversation into the room by mentioning that one of the children had walked in, but this personal / professional divide is often so hard-wired, that Kelly, in trying to wish away this collision of his personal and professional worlds, gave a moment of light relief welcomed by those of us watching. And we say this without judgement because chances are, we would have responded the same, but for the experience of seeing it modelled differently.

Contrast that with another experience we had at a conference a few years ago. In a packed room of about 200 people, as the speaker presented, his seven-year-old daughter walked from the back of the room right down the center aisle and right up to him. As more and more of us in the room realized what was happening, our eyes shifted to the little girl and wondered what would happen next. Without losing stride, the presenter bent down, lovingly scooped her up in his arms and continued presenting. The room let out a collective 'Ahhhh . . .' In that moment he was fully authentic as a professional speaker and as a dad. Personal / professional divide successfully crossed.

By paying constant homage to the assumption that 'professional' means 'no personal allowed', many of us attempt to remove all things personal from the language of work. Most problematically, we remove the ability to talk openly about the things that really matter most to us, help give us purpose in our work, and facilitate our engagement as a 'whole' person. As a result, most of us have not been good at having essential conversations at work about the things in our personal life that influence if and how we show up to work, for fear of how we will be perceived and/or how it could impact our career progression.

Further, the prevailing personal / professional divide assumption means that most attempts to develop any sort of 'relationship capability' proactively have been piecemeal and work-centric. Most training around building Emotional Intelligence or becoming a high-performance team is processed with the 'office hat' on, rather than as developing core skills to apply to relationships in all of life and influence who you become as a person. As one Global Head of People Development we spoke with commented, 'we know some of this relationship stuff and can hold it together for work, but at home it's a disaster zone'.

Closing the divide

It's true, work pressures have always impacted home life . . . and relationship troubles at home have always impacted people's ability to deliver on the job. For us, Steve's story always serves as a powerful reminder of just how much wellbeing, performance and mental health are inextricably linked . . .

> *Steve was Global Head of Transformation in a professional services firm in London. His role involved coordinating teams across Europe, America and Asia-Pacific which meant working under intense pressures and deadlines across three different time zones, travelling overseas frequently and quite often working after-hours from home.*

> *The constant stresses of work, and the added pressure in the last year of having to look after his ageing parents – not sufficiently badly off to warrant being in a care home but needing lots of extra visits and ferrying to unending doctor's appointments – meant Steve was not able to be the emotionally present husband his wife Lola expected. Communication between them started to spiral downwards and cracks in the relationship were beginning to widen.*

Steve felt Lola was constantly undermining him, criticizing his every move – especially his decisions around how he handled his parents' care, calling him incompetent and an absent father, questioning him about money and controlling how much could be spent from the family budget, although he was the main breadwinner. He felt he had lost his influence at home and that Lola no longer loved nor respected him.

To manage some of the home / work / life tensions he started taking work calls in the car, adding to the image of him being physically and emotionally absent from the pressures of home life.

Steve felt he was falling apart on the inside, but couldn't turn to his friends because, in his words 'well, that's not what guys talk about'. He had also stopped meeting with colleagues and clients for lunch or a coffee, not wanting to show how vulnerable he was on the inside. Life had become a routine of heading off to work – to stress, and home – to arguments.

Despite the challenges at home, all his colleagues could see was Steve's very well-groomed appearance and façade that he had it all together. However, his home tensions started to leak into his management style and his 360-degree feedback from colleagues and team members indicated he was becoming intense and critical, micro-managing in a way that made people feel incompetent. But it also showed he was starting to drop some balls.

Steve didn't feel his boss had his back, so he bottled up what he was going through.

Without information to the contrary, Steve's boss questioned his commitment and line management capability, made worse by a pattern of behavior. Some days Steve just never made it into work. Other days he put in a last-minute request for sick leave.

Unknown to his boss, for his own sanity's sake, Steve was choosing to stay home on the days that his wife was at work (she worked part-time as the nurse in their local doctor's office) just to have some mental space to process how he could move his life forward. He found himself having thoughts about the relief offered from the bottle of aspirin in the medicine cabinet . . . not for a headache . . . but for life . . .

As you might imagine, Steve's story is by no means unique. And for so many, what happens next depends on the Relational Intelligence of the leader and their ability to have compassionate conversations that cross the personal / professional divide.

Steve had a number of very challenging performance review meetings with his boss – one of which included an official warning – but he still refused to open up about what was going on. Thankfully, as a result of an internal re-organization, Steve's new boss quickly worked out that there was more to this than met the eye. He recommended Steve get some leadership skills coaching and through researching the company resources together, they stumbled upon the relationship coaching support the company offered through their Employee Assistance Program. Steve was finally able to get the help and relationship support he needed – and not a moment too soon.

Most often, the realities of work pressures impacting home, and home pressures impacting work, are buried in the statistics on the uptake of programs like the one Steve ended up on, and the private conversations between individuals and their after-the-fact coaching / counselling support.

Over the last few years, concerns over employee mental health and wellbeing have become regular boardroom agenda items. In response, many organizations have attempted to be proactive about emotional health and wellbeing, offering programs that range from enhanced workspaces and flexible working arrangements to yoga, mindfulness and exercise classes. Yet still, very few proactively focus on strengthening and supporting home relationships, despite the growing pressures of work on home life and the research evidence showing the vital role that quality relationships play in maintaining individual mental health and wellbeing.[40]

It seems the dots are not being joined up. As a recently retired partner from one of the Big Four global management consultancies reflected in our conversation: *'Now that I think about it . . . isn't it interesting that nothing on Relationships was included in our "New Partner Induction Program", despite HR having endless amounts of anecdotal evidence confirming that the divorce rate among the partnership is around 60-70 percent.'* It would appear these are the hushed conversations in the boardroom that never seem to be tabled as part of their strategic conversations. But given the huge demands that the nature of the work (long hours, tight deadlines, extensive travel, etc.) places on relationships at home, there has to be a whole lot more that these and other organizations could be doing to equip their people to do relationships well.

In January 2020, we reported on the findings of 'Relationship Breakdown and the Workplace', a joint YouGov research project[41] conducted in partnership with London law firm Howard Kennedy LLP and think tanks Marriage Foundation and Relationships Foundation. The surveys revealed the staggering results that high earners (those with *household incomes in excess of £100,000 per year*) were 3.5 times more likely to have experienced significant domestic relationship challenges, and when they did, productivity suffered. Often work pressures were the cause.

The survey also revealed that in most cases employees did not discuss their challenges with their employers, and even when employers were aware, the most popular response was to offer time off and/or signpost people to counselling. The nature of the work they did, fueled by the blurring of home / work boundaries, increasing trends to remote / flexible working practices and 'always on' cultures all featured as sources of increased stress on people and relationships. Where there were already cracks in relationships at home, stress at work made them worse. Problems at home led to problems at work, health challenges and in some cases, the loss of great employees.

Significantly, while the survey respondents included a number of the nation's high-flyers and senior decision makers (with 65 percent of them operating at board level), they also included a good representation of the next generation of leaders. Young ambitious millennials who were part of dual-income couples also matched the criterion of household incomes equal to or in excess of £100,000 per annum. However, as the research reveals, this younger workforce are not generally as willing to sacrifice work-life balance for a pay-cheque.[42] They expect to be able to talk about work-life challenges and be supported by their bosses and peers in finding a balance that works. Yet still, far too few organizations have these kinds of conversation on their strategic radar.

And then the COVID-19 pandemic exacerbated the problem.

Under lockdown, many came to realize that working-from-home involved a whole lot more than simply replicating office hours and activity in the location of home. Helping employees sort the physical space and practicalities needed to get work done from home proved far more straightforward than managing the mental and emotional impact of what for many felt like work invading the safe haven of their homes. Many echoed the sentiment that life felt less like 'working from home' and more like 'sleeping at the office'. A McKinsey article in March 2020[43] spoke about an employee at an internet company in China commenting that the move to work from home made his official work hours of 9-9-6 feel more like 0-0-7. Sounds cool! Except it meant his reality changing from working 9am to 9pm six days a week, to working all day, every day.

Various research studies over the last 12 months confirm that, as a result of the pandemic, there have been global increases in the prevalence and severity of depression and anxiety as well as increases in post-traumatic stress disorder and substance abuse.[44] As reported in *The Guardian*, in June 2020 the UK Office for National Statistics confirmed that anxiety amongst the parent demographic had doubled since lockdown.[45] Pre COVID-19 research (March 2020) had shown this demographic to be the least stressed and anxious in the nation. Three months later this same demographic had become the most stressed in the country, above the elderly and those living isolated. The most likely conclusion was the result of the significant challenges of this demographic having to juggle work with real life – home-schooling, childcare responsibilities, supporting vulnerable relatives, increased household chores and/or playing tag team with partners who also needed to get work done.

So many of the conversations with employees on our various online webinars and workshops in the season revealed the stress and guilt employees felt around having to juggle work and home life, not being fully present in either role, and constantly feeling pressured to be seen as 'logged on' and available during conventional working hours. Where there was a conflict with work and home demands for availability, work generally won, putting significant strain on couple / family relationships. Yet many still felt unable to discuss their home situation and the flexibility or support they would need to remain productive and work effectively around household commitments while looking after their own wellbeing. This also created internal conflict for a number of leaders who needed to keep a handle on team performance while also trying to hold things together in their own home circumstances.

By the start of 2021, people were describing different versions of 'pandemic fatigue' and how ongoing restrictions were affecting their mental state. Many spoke about the physical and mental strain of working even longer hours, with work constantly bleeding into home time and invading their safe haven, especially where work had to be done from their bedroom – for some, literally the end of their bed. Others highlighted the absence of the mental downtime they enjoyed on the commute between home and work and the opportunity that offered for them to mentally switch roles. (To be clear, they did not miss the commute itself!). Pretty much everyone spoke about missing the social contact with work colleagues and the casual office banter, especially those who were isolated and lived alone.

No surprises that those who felt supported and cared for as individuals spoke about a sense of trust and respect in their relationships with their managers / team leads and strong engagement with the organization. Those who felt their boss's focus was on bottom-line results with little or no regard for their personal wellbeing seemed to be quietly emotionally disconnecting from their organization. As we go to print, the world waits with bated breath hoping and praying that the successful global roll out of multiple vaccines will mean a return to some kind of normality soon. However, the fallout from the quality of conversations around this personal / professional divide will only become clear once the job market becomes buoyant again, confidence is re-built, and people feel able to vote with their feet. Our bet is that leaders who have taken the time to nurture relationships and support their colleagues through both professional and personal concerns when it mattered, will win.

Sadly, a number of research studies over recent months also suggest that as a direct result of these underlying assumptions, the collision of home and work life under one pretty much global lockdown, has set the world back on efforts made to reduce the gender pay gap in the last decade.[46]

Here's the point . . .

> **What may well seem like very personal issues will continue to have a direct impact on corporate performance – and show up in challenges around issues like wellbeing, employee engagement and gender equity – until we can all get better at having these conversations.**

Given that increased levels of working-from-home are likely to be a permanent feature of the work experience post-COVID, it is vital that this assumption of a personal / professional divide is addressed head-on. Getting better at having conversations that cross this divide is an essential part of creating a healthier future and workforce, where work and life happily co-exist, and relationships are based on mutual trust. This is as important a conversation for those who lead organizations as it is for the individuals who work there.

The 'big ASK' of bosses and colleagues

Now it goes without saying that challenging these kinds of ingrained societal assumptions takes courage, but the reality is that your performance, health and wellbeing depend on it. Developing the courage to think outside the box and to dare to believe that the work experience could be altogether different is crucial for creating a more sustainable approach to your rhythm of work, home and life. The starting point is to challenge the assumptions and cultures in your *own* head that stop you from exploring the possible options for being productive while still being present for the people and things that are most important to you.

Without these conversations, relationships with bosses and colleagues tend to suffer from tension, frustration and resentment.

So, the 'big ASK' of bosses and colleagues is . . . Can we renegotiate HOW we deliver?

For some that might mean asking: Can we renegotiate core work hours, availability, key tasks, deadlines? Can we become more creative and supportive in how we work together and cover for each other as a team? Can we have more, open, honest conversations about what it will take both sides to stay healthy and get work done?

To be clear, having these open and honest conversations with your boss(es) and colleagues means getting comfortable talking about personal circumstances and owning up to the fact that you have a life outside of work that also needs your time and attention. Absent that, the ongoing assumption of a rigid personal / professional divide will continue to cripple the discovery of creative solutions to a healthy work-life balance that is more relevant for this digital age. Worse yet, it could compromise your performance, undermine work relationships, and negatively impact the mental and emotional health of both you and those around you.

Gender stereotypes in the home are both real and valid . . . really?

In our experience, the second assumption of fixed roles and responsibilities in the household is often one of the biggest challenges to the quality of relationships in the home. As we mentioned previously, we each turn up to relationships with our own expectations of who does what in the home, influenced by our culture and family-of-origin experiences. Where the assumptions around gender roles are shared and agreed, life is generally more straightforward around this issue. Some couples are very happy with, and accept, the stereotypes around gender roles. The challenges come when expectations are very different and *not discussed*. The more global and intercultural we become in our personal relationships, the more vital it is to be able to have these conversations about expectations of roles and responsibilities in the home.

Moods and expectations around roles and responsibilities in the home have certainly shifted in the three decades that we personally have been working with relationships. Financial security used to be a more significant consideration in marriage for the baby boomer generation, with the stereotypical model having the man as the main breadwinner and the woman being the main caregiver, typically with a lower-paying job or no job outside the home at all. Though most of us Gen X'ers were born into that environment, and many of us lived out that model to some extent, it has been increasingly clear that change was afoot.

In a study of 130 societies through the demographic yearbooks of the United Nations, anthropologist Dr Helen Fisher reported that in all but one society, women have been moving back into the workforce and have been slowly closing the gap between men and women in terms of economic power, health and education.[47] And the trend over the years has led to women becoming their own economic power globally – with them quite often becoming the main breadwinner themselves.

For many in heterosexual relationships, this has shifted the perceived power balance and expectations in their relationships at home. Millennials, for example – by all accounts the generation with the greatest percentage of intercultural relationships and dual-income couples – expect more 'matched efforts' in the home.

But, while women have been moving steadily into the workplace, there is far less reciprocity among men taking on roles such as housework and childcare, traditionally perceived to be the 'woman's domain'. Figures from the UK's Office for National Statistics (2016) reveal that while fathers today generally spend more time with their children (and also do more of the 'ferrying around' to various after / outside-of school activities), mothers still do almost 60 percent more unpaid work than men – largely cooking, childcare and housework.[48]

Like it or not, there is still a gender imbalance in the home.

In 2018, the International Labour Organization shared their research finding that around the world, without exception, women perform three-quarters of unpaid care work.[49] Against that background you can begin to see how this placed an enormous amount of pressure on women and their careers under COVID-19 lockdown, as routines went 'out the window' and the volume of household chores went 'through the roof'. An online survey of 3,500 heterosexual couple families revealed that during lockdown, mothers were only able to do on average one hour of uninterrupted work for every three done by dads.[50] Many women found themselves juggling roles in 'the simultaneous second shift' of working while home-schooling / doing childcare, with the associated overwhelm of stress and guilt around not doing either very well. What's clear is that multitasking of this nature is overrated at best, and at worst unsustainable as a long-term strategy.

One US study showed that from February to April 2020 alone, mothers of young children reduced their work hours four to five times as much as fathers, growing the gender gap in work hours by 20-50 percent.[51] Reduced hours also meant women were likely to be penalized in the next round of promotions . . . or redundancies. The 2020 'Women in the Workplace' report raised the alarm that one in four women were considering downshifting their careers or leaving the workforce altogether, due to the impact of COVID-19.[52]

No surprises then, that research confirms the anecdotal evidence we have seen time and again – household tasks are one of the most common reasons for disagreements between couples.

Research has shown that in heterosexual couples, perceived inequity around the split of household chores, especially where the woman is disadvantaged, leads to higher levels of dissatisfaction with the relationship, relationship instability and risk of divorce.[53]

On the other hand, where roles are *perceived* to be more fairly split, couples enjoy higher levels of satisfaction with the quality of the relationship . . . and more sex.[54] Note the emphasis there on the word *perceived*!

What's clear is that without a conversation around roles and responsibilities at home, relationships can be weighed down with tension and resentment over how responsibilities are split. Unless and until assumptions and expectations are brought out into the open and discussed, the warmth and intimacy in relationships at home can be replaced by bitterness and resentment . . . and ultimately, separation and divorce.

The UK charity Relate recently confirmed that as a result of lockdown, while many realized relationships were the most important thing in their lives, 8 percent of respondents found that lockdown had highlighted the cracks in their relationship and triggered the decision to divorce or separate.[55] High on the list of pressures causing relationship strain was the stress of juggling work and home-schooling.[56]

But it wasn't all gloom and doom. Couples that were able to stand together to address the challenges from the same side – rather than turning inwards on each other – found strength and resilience in their relationship. This often meant finding new ways to live and work together and cover for each other, including new approaches to the division of roles and tasks in the home. In some instances, the main breadwinner role was reversed because of redundancies or loss of businesses, and couples and families were forced to reinvent how they did life together and mutually support each other in finding a way forward.

Either way, the key point for all was a realization that in the shifting seasons of life, assumptions about what works and what doesn't can quickly become outdated and need to be renegotiated in a way that makes everyone involved feel mutually supported.

The 'big ASK' of Partners / Family

In each new season of life, it's important to think about all the demands on your time for work, chores and the people who matter most.

If you live alone or apart from loved ones, think about the kind of remote support you may need or how you may need to renegotiate the support expected of you.

If you live with a partner and/or other family members, think about the help and support you might need to make life under one roof work well. And then ask for it. Regardless of whose role it was to do what in the past, it's important to talk about all the things that need to be done to keep the household fed, healthy and ticking over and to renegotiate roles and responsibilities based on capacity and ability to share the load. It also involves discussing schedules and availability, especially if you need to 'tag team' around caring responsibilities. To reduce stress and frustration in situations where you both work, each person will need their own focus time to work and have others respect their space to do that. This helps counter the false, but often made, assumption that because you are physically present in the home you are available at people's beck and call.

We were reminded of how challenging that can be just as the world prepared for COVID-19 lockdown 1.0. As the wave of countries locking down continued sweeping across Europe in the first few months of 2020, we decided to take what we figured would be one of our last opportunities to work outside the home for a while and headed off to spend the day working from one of our local cafés. About 11am, a friend popped in. It turned out he had been cruising the shops since dropping his children at school that morning and that he was reluctant to go home because his wife had started working from home the week before. Already it was a nightmare for him! He was accustomed to working from home on his own and as an accountant needed quiet and focus to concentrate. His wife, on the other hand, was accustomed to the buzz of an open-plan office and working from home was a novelty. Her expectations were that they would have lots of casual conversations, lunches together and basically more of a social experience than he had the time or patience for. However, he was reluctant to tell her that her approach wasn't working for him because he didn't want to hurt her feelings. Anyway, he wasn't sure how to broach the subject.

One of the ideas we shared was a lightbulb moment for him. We suggested that they discuss and agree the times when they could hang out together versus when he needed uninterrupted focus time. A couple of weeks later he confirmed that having 'a schedule' had really helped them manage expectations on both sides and gave them both the chance to look forward to and welcome breaks for lunch, teas, and also just for casual conversation around the latest unfolding news announcements. It had instantly helped to ease the tension and allowed them to mutually support each other in getting work done under new lockdown arrangements. Phew!

Four years ago, when we started working together full-time again in this Relationship Education business, we too used to frustrate each other by walking up to each other's desk and diving into a conversation, ignoring the fact that the other person might be deep in concentration creating content. Developing the simple habit of saying 'knock, knock' even if the door was open – to give each other the respect and opportunity to say something like 'give me 10 minutes or so' made a huge difference. We also learned to agree start times, stop times, when we were each unavailable because of work focus time, and when we would make ourselves available for family pressure points or family time together.

It's also important to recognize the need to tread gently with each other, because often it takes both a mindset shift and a willingness to learn new skills. Don't be surprised if it needs more than one courageous conversation to get the right result. For many of us just introducing the conversation is a real challenge to our underlying assumptions and beliefs around what is right. Here's our story as Andrea tells it . . .

For 15 years Jon had been the main breadwinner in our family while I ran a home-based business part-time around looking after our two kids and running the home. As we slipped into this new season of life though, we both carried on at home as normal, except I now found myself working double time, shoulder to shoulder in building the business, but still carrying the lion's share of household responsibilities in the evenings.

I found myself starting to get really resentful about what I perceived as an 'unfair balance', but it also challenged my mindset about what it meant to be a good wife and mother. I felt guilty that I wasn't the 'Super Mum' I thought I was and struggled to bring up the conversation. Of course, it challenged Jon as well – both in his mindset about what his role and responsibility as a good man / husband / father should be, as well as his ability (willingness?!) to physically take on tasks he never had to do before. And thank goodness for that start, because it meant that under lockdown, he wasn't averse to going further and helping to clean toilets too!

Given our different underlying assumptions of what our roles and responsibilities 'should be' it took a few goes at having the conversation for us to really 'hear' each other and to find a new balance of chores that worked for us. But we got there . . . and so will you.

If ever you find yourself getting resentful or frustrated about help or support or the split of chores at home, here is your three-step guide to less stress:

1. pause and ask yourself what is causing the frustration,

2. push past that to think about what a better approach might be, then

3. lovingly make the ask of your partner and/or family.

> **So, the 'big ASK' of partners and family members is: 'How can we share the load and be mutually supportive of each other?'**

Without these conversations out in the open, feelings of resentment, distance and disrespect will ultimately drain Emotional Bank Accounts. Strategies for managing the work-from-home environment are covered in more detail in the next two chapters, but the key point is that relationships at home can be strengthened and feel more mutually supportive when you actually talk about these issues.

Unless assumptions and expectations are voiced, the warmth and intimacy in relationships can quickly be replaced by bitterness and resentment.

At this point it's worth noting that the strategy of waiting for others to 'just see what needs to be done and do it' doesn't work ... we've tried it!

We assume others see what we see – but they don't. Sometimes chores are not even on their radar. Not only do we assume they see it, but we also become convinced they have chosen deliberately not to do anything about it because they are being selfish and inconsiderate on purpose. And then out of frustration, instead of asking for what we want or need, we grumble, complain, accuse . . . and provoke a natural, though unhelpful, defensive response in return. And suddenly you are in the middle of a heated battle about chores.

Unbelievable as it might seem, being deliberately inconsiderate is usually the furthest thing from the minds of the people at home who love you. Be careful with the language you choose around chores though. Saying something like 'help me out' versus 'let's share the load' can set you up for being solely responsible for things and removing it from other people's radar without intending for that to be the case. As our eldest said to Andrea once, 'Mum, stop playing victim and ask for help . . . otherwise everyone will happily assume you will do it!'

Challenging assumptions and having these courageous conversations around how you will work together to make life at home peaceful and happy can be tricky. Nevertheless, these conversations are crucial for building trust and respect in home relationships and for getting the support needed to create a sustainable work-life balance.

More than the actual tasks though, is the sense of feeling supported and cared for especially through pressure points or feelings of overwhelm.

Busy means important . . . really?

The third assumption that 'busy means important' and that we have no time for anything else, challenges our ability to create and maintain quality relationships – even quality relationships with ourselves! We were already a stressed out, exhausted workforce before lockdown. Many of us had been hurtling through life at full speed in an 'always on' digital culture, barely catching our breath at the weekends before racing full speed ahead again on Monday morning, week after week. The signs of stress, fatigue and burnout were already there, elevating concerns over mental health and wellbeing to the corporate strategic agenda.

In their 2019 UK Working Lives Survey,[57] an annual assessment of job quality, the Chartered Institute of Personnel and Development (CIPD), reported that one-in-four workers experienced intense and stressful working conditions – including feeling exhausted, miserable or under excessive pressure – and that 'work acts as a considerable stressor for a worrying proportion of us'. The way we work has been creating its own cycle of stress and ill-health.

It's clear that life in the fast lane in the 21st century is very different to life in previous generations. Not that long ago, our rhythm of work and rest was mostly governed by daylight and sunset. We worked when the sun was shining and rested when the sun went to bed. Pre-internet and mobile devices, people were at least able to switch off when they finally left the office and went home. However, like a well-crafted stealth move, our lives have been taken over by technology. Without resistance or question, we have suddenly become available to anyone, anywhere in the world, at any time of day – 'always on'. Now, of course, being able to work flexibly day or night and connect with any part of the world has its advantages, but unless we learn to create *healthy boundaries* around the people and things that we value, the non-stop demands on our time, energy and attention will continue to erode our health, wellbeing, productivity and relationships.

One silver lining to the COVID-19 cloud is that it has brought the urgency of this concern for investing in relationships into sharp focus. It is clear that people are working longer, more intense hours from home, taking fewer breaks and struggling to contain the bleed of work into home life. Finally, there is the recognition that to help people manage their stress levels and mental health, we need to encourage them to push back on the never-ending demands on attention and availability and create healthy boundaries around the people and things that matter most.

And this 'New Normal' is likely to become 'Future Normal' too.

According to McKinsey research,[58] 80 percent of people questioned reported that they enjoyed working from home. Over two-thirds of the people polled were as productive, if not more productive, than before. Many are looking to create a future normal with more work-from-home flexibility, and many companies are capitalizing on this as a way to reduce costs on office space in prime real estate.

To make a success of all that the work-from-home strategy promises, it's essential that we each develop a more effective coping strategy than juggling and multitasking or we will continue to bear the huge cost in stress, burnout and damaged relationships.

What ultimately makes the difference . . .

The challenge many of us have is that we've bought into the 'busy means important' mentality and wear 'busyness' and 'exhaustion' as badges of honor. We are so busy being 'busy' that we rarely take the time to identify and articulate what matters most to ourselves, let alone to anyone else. This means that we live for the most part at the mercy of our 'to do' lists which often don't reflect our real values and priorities. That's perhaps a big part of why so many people end up with mid-life crises . . . 'waking up' in their mid-forties or fifties and realizing they've spent life climbing the wrong wall. The default assumption seems to be that if we plan and schedule well around the white space in our diary, we will live out our values automatically. However, for most of us, living out our values is anything but automatic. Unless we each become intentional about identifying and valuing our own values, we will inevitably end up living to the beat of someone else's drum. With urgency, we must get back into the driving seat of our lives.

The 'gift' of COVID-19 for many of us was the chance to reconnect with our core values, and the people and things that matter most to us. Perhaps for the first time, many were forced to think about the mental and emotional boundaries they needed to draw to protect the relationships and things of most value. And having had a chance to experience a different pace of life and balance under lockdown, many became bolder in their requests about the aspects of lockdown flexibility that they wanted to keep post-pandemic.

In reality, we can all choose to think more creatively and re-imagine a more sustainable work-life balance that gives time and space to the *important* – like health, relationships and recreation – and not just the *urgent*. For the sake of our own wellbeing, we need to challenge the prevailing assumption of obeying a never ending 'to do' list and learn to value our values enough to live by them. This is no longer just a good idea; it's a matter of survival.

Before we can make meaningful ASKs of our bosses and colleagues or partners and/or families, we need to get clear on the values we hold dear, the boundaries we would like to create, and the rhythm of home, work and life that would create balance for ourselves.

To do this . . .

> **the 'big ASK' we need to make of ourselves is: 'Who and what really matters most to me . . . and what am I doing to protect them?'**

When we take time to identify and articulate our values and make space in our schedules to live them out in our daily routines, we develop a real sense of purpose, freedom and vitality which show up in our approach to work, life and love.

Getting ready to make better ASKs

Sadly, many relationships still break down as a result of expectations that are assumed as common and never voiced. If you've been following the journey so far, hopefully you'll now see that understanding different cultural assumptions and other ingrained belief systems is a key part of recognizing where we each stand and where others are coming from. It's what helps us pause before reacting in disrespect, get better at 'thinking the best' about other people's intentions and have better conversations around potentially tricky, difficult or sensitive topics.

Getting clear on what we value allows us to make better ASKs of ourselves in terms of our availability and the things we commit to. It also allows us to make better ASKs of our bosses / colleagues, and of our partners and/or families – because now we know what really matters most to us. Equally, it allows us to be more open to other people's perspective and more respectful of what matters most to them. By learning to ASK, rather than assume, we create the foundation for developing authenticity in our relationships and build mutual trust and respect.

The next step is for each of us to clarify our own values and the boundaries we would like to create so we can ask for what we need in order to build quality relationships around us. This is what we will address in the following two chapters. Chapter 10 provides practical models and techniques to help you clarify what is really important to you, create healthy boundaries and make space in your schedule for the people and things that matter. In chapter 11 we'll help you pull this all together to make better ASKs of yourself and the people around you and have effective, courageous conversations when necessary.

Time for Reflection

Key Takeaways

- The three key underlying assumptions that cripple courageous conversations around a more sustainable work-life balance are:

  ◦ that we must keep all matters personal out of our professional lives,

  ◦ that roles and responsibilities in the home are set, and

  ◦ that life is a never-ending treadmill and the best we can hope to achieve is squeezing things into snatched pockets of time.

- We need to challenge these underlying assumptions in order to develop more creative, sustainable approaches to work and life, especially given the global impact of COVID and trends toward increased working-from-home.

- We need to get better at valuing our values and create healthy boundaries for ourselves – no one else will!

Building Your Understanding

1. Which of the three assumptions do you find the most difficult to challenge?

2. If you were able to, who would you ask for more support and/or to renegotiate roles?

3. What do you need to ask for to have a more sustainable approach to work and life in the New or Future Normal?

4. What assumptions could block you from making the necessary 'big ASKs'?

Taking Personal Action

- Write a paragraph on the ideal work-life balance you would like to create. What would it take to make that happen?

- Write a list of the things you would like to be different – the support you would like and the roles you would like to negotiate.

- Spend some time thinking about how you would make the ASK of those around you. Hold on to the list until you have completed the next two chapters.

Chapter Ten

Clarifying and protecting
what matters most

'No one can respect the boundaries you don't set.'

Now that we have spoken much about some of the things that drive our behavior and the need to identify our core values, how do we figure out what's really important to us? This is not something that most of us tend to pause much to think about on a regular basis – except perhaps for New Year's resolutions!

But how can we ask for what we need, to be *on purpose* with our life or to create a sustainable work-life balance, if we don't know what we're working toward? And how can we as individuals be 'aligned' with organizational values if we struggle to articulate our own? Also, how can we ask for support at work or help at home if we're not clear on what needs our priority attention?

It seems a bit obvious, but how will we ever measure 'success' in our lives, if we don't first take the time to clarify, at least in our own minds, the people and things that for us, make it all worthwhile?

In this chapter, we offer a few strategies for identifying and/or clarifying your values and creating healthy boundaries in order to live to your values. In the next chapter we go one step further to help you design a template schedule that makes space for the things you value, establishes healthy boundaries and enables you to create the life balance you desire. We also share strategies for having courageous conversations to ask for the support you need at work and at home to help manage these boundaries effectively. Habit #3 is a chunky one (four chapters), but by the end you will be equipped to ask and discuss rather than assume and stereotype, live to your values, and build relationships based on mutual trust and respect. So, let's dive in . . .

Identifying your values

Being clear on our values and the balance of life we want to live allows us to say YES without hesitation to the right things in the right season, and NO without guilt – even to good things, if they're not right for now. Pay attention to this. This is a 'must do' in order to reduce stress and live your best, authentic life.

Different strategies help different people and there are many great books offering useful suggestions. Below, we share three strategies that we have found particularly helpful in provoking soul searching around the things that really matter to most people. Spending time working through these questions using the 'Value Your Values' worksheet in the Appendices will help you uncover what drives you at the core and the things that will make you feel purposeful and fulfilled in life.

1. What 'grates' on the inside?

There are generally two kinds of 'gratings' on the inside that we can experience. One is the emotional discomfort that comes when you are on the edge of pushing outside your comfort zone – meaning you are about to develop a new level of skill / experience and perhaps feeling a bit anxious or fearful about getting it wrong. That's a good grating. Growth is about to happen and of course as most of us already know, in the words of Coaching Practice Leader Will Linssen, 'There is no growth in the Comfort Zone and no comfort in the Growth Zone.'[59] That grating will always happen and is just a signal that you are about to 'level up'! The best way to deal with that is just to prepare as best as possible, then push through.

The other kind of grating is more like a warning light that must be heeded. This kind of grating is the emotional discomfort that comes when a core value is compromised or contradicted.

> So many of us live a life on the outside that contradicts our values on the inside. 'Gratings' help us know when the balance is off.

The 'grating' is that sinking feeling that washes over you when the very things you hold dear have not been lived out on this occasion, or series of occasions. If you run a business from home, or work from home, you might be able to relate to the 'gratings' on the inside when the balance feels wrong between being under pressure with work and being available for the family. If you are anything like us, the 'gratings' show up as feelings of guilt and disappointment from being irritable and unpleasant with each interruption from our loved ones, from working evenings and weekends, and from always expecting to be understood because 'we are doing it all for the family'. Falling into this rut every now and again is understandable, but as a long-term strategy this could quickly become the catalyst for relationship breakdown on many levels.

When we are each clear in our own head what's OK and what's not – what helps us work toward our own values and goals and what grates against them – we *gain* respect for our own boundaries and we *give* respect to other people's boundaries. So many of us could reduce the stress in our lives by discovering and living happily in the intersection between what works for others and what works for us. Except we need to know what works for us first.

A classic example is in arranging appointments with bosses or important clients. There is a voice in our head that generally says we should jump at whatever they suggest because 'the client comes first, and the boss is always right'. However, if we are already clear on the dates / times we want to ring-fence for family activities, school runs, personal appointments or other reasons important to us and we are able to be proactive about suggesting dates that work, more often than not we can find a date that is mutually convenient. That way we can turn up to work events with no regrets and 'play full on' because we know the other aspects of life that are important to us are on track to get their due attention as well. But if we don't value our values and end up going with whatever works for other people, we will keep compromising on our values. And that grates . . . and causes stress levels to soar.

Ever found yourself getting upset with people when it's not something they did or said but something you said yes to when you really should have said no?

Pay attention to the gratings . . . they are the warning lights that indicate the need to create or recreate healthy boundaries.

This is one of the big lessons we learned in managing the constant tension between making a living and making a life, doing the stuff that earns the money and doing what it takes to be 'fully present' parents with our teenagers. The 'gratings' forced us to have a better conversation about our own values and create healthy boundaries as Andrea explains:

Jon and I both value working hard and delivering to deadlines . . . and we both value home life and time with our kids. But four years ago, when we started running our latest business together, and this time from home, we needed to learn to give each other space to live out our values differently and recognize when our own personal balance was off.

Thanks to Jon's brilliant natural follow-through we stay on task and are able to focus and deliver more things than I would do on my own because he keeps working out the detail long after I get bored and have lost the will. And I have learnt to value that immensely.

However, given Jon's Lion-Beaver personality tendencies (as we discussed in chapter 5), on a day-to-day basis his default is to let himself be driven more by his 'to do' list than his values – unless they are intentionally brought to the surface. To create the right balance, one of the great habits Jon has developed is to diarize what he will do each week to be present as husband and as father in a meaningful way to each of us. Given his very strong task focus, he has developed this practical way to live his priorities, recognizing that without that kind of visual reminder he could easily get lost in his own world of 'getting things done'!

However, whenever we're working on a big project with a looming deadline, there is no cut-off time for Jon until the job gets done. It wouldn't bother him to have the children fend for themselves for a while – which means they would typically end up eating cereal, instant noodles and chocolate, and regulating their own screen time and homework. Heaven for them but serious 'gratings' against values for me.

I am happy for Jon to continue burning the midnight oil while I attend to home life, but I really kick back when he calls me to look at something 'for two minutes' then suddenly we get engrossed and two hours whizz by with both of us poring over some document while the kids are left in free fall – dinner is late, bedtime is late, and for me it feels like life at home descends into chaos. Once in a while is OK, but it really grates when I start to feel that despite all the career choices to work from home to be with the children, I was merely passing time with them around me but not spending time doing meaningful things with them – 'because we were working for the family'. Aaargh!!!

Being present as a mum is a very important value for me. It took seven long years and a whole lot of trauma and heartache to have our first child and now that we are blessed with not one but two miracles, as much as possible I wanted to be present and do it right. My enduring goal has been to be physically and emotionally present, having a strong influence in their lives, helping them to become people of strong faith and character, and guiding them through the maze of values and beliefs in their teen years as young black youth in Britain.

While Jon and I share the value of 'being fully present as parents' the way we interpret being 'present' is different, and we had to learn to understand and respect that. Part of the way I interpret being present is to be fully available when the kids come home. I want to have dinner ready on time, be present to get 'the low down' on what happened at school, listen and look for all the clues in their eyes and tone of voice to indicate if there is a problem or not, make sure homework doesn't get rushed in preference for YouTube or Netflix and get them to bed on time.

Until we understood and valued each other's perspective, we kept having arguments which often escalated to boiling point in a heartbeat — a big clue that a major value was being compromised. Often in those moments, my 'Chimp' would respond to Jon before my more measured self, because it grated on the inside of me at a gut level. Beyond the frustration of feeling sucked into something I didn't plan to be doing at that time, at a deeper level, I felt like I was failing as a parent . . . an emotionally absent, bad mother.

We would end up arguing over superficial things like who was working 'harder' and who had to cook the dinner, but the real problem was that my core value of being physically present was being compromised and provoking a gut reaction in me, while the core value of pushing through the detail and getting the job done was being compromised, creating frustrations for Jon. Sometimes it takes a while to uncover what's driving the responses, but the presence of the 'Chimp' is a good indication that there is a core value or need being ignored.

There is nothing more contradictory than working hard on workshops to help others build great relationships in the midst of having a beast of an argument at home. And the irony is never lost on our children, who are always very quick to hold us accountable! In so many ways we <u>have</u> to practice what we preach!!!

Jon soon learned that I would happily get back to things after bedtime for the kids if we had to, but in general those hours between school pickup and bedtime were not for long work conversations. In my view, multitasking during those times was seriously overrated. To be able to give my best to my family, as much as possible, I chose to be unavailable for work at those times.

An easy shortcut to identifying your values is to pay attention to the 'gratings' on the inside . . . and watch for when the 'Chimp' turns up!

2. When exactly is 'one day'?

Another way to find out what you really value is to ask yourself the question – when exactly is the 'one day' that you will do 'the thing' that you've promised yourself you'll do? What is 'the thing' you really want to get done before you kick back into retirement or at least live life at a more relaxed pace?

Here is a quick exercise – let's assume we each have eight decades of life (more please, God!). Subtract the last decade to allow the option to kick back and take life at a slower pace or be forced to do so if health fails, so now that leaves seven decades.

Then subtract the number of decades you have lived so far. How many decades do you have left?

For example, if you are 45 you are well into your fifth decade. That leaves another two decades to do what you want to do in life. Now ask yourself that question again – when exactly are you going to do the things you said you would do 'one day'?

Doing this exercise ourselves a few years ago brought the dreams and plans we had for our lives into sharp focus – having both at the time just passed the 50-year marker. We both came to the point of realizing that the one thing we would regret the most was doing nothing with the dreams we had for making relationship education more accessible, knowing the difference this content has made in our own lives. In the context of the number of decades left, the killer question that got us in the gut was this – *If not now, when?*

So, our challenge to you is 'What is the dream you dare not speak?' That is a big clue on what you value, but it takes real courage to actually voice it. Be careful who you share it with though – not many people have the courage to pursue theirs and are likely to be quick to kill yours too, if you give them the chance.

The reality is that if we are not focused on the thing that we say we'll do *one day*, another decade could easily pass before we get it together. Asking that question helps us zoom in on the things that we really value ... because the clock is ticking.

Another take on asking this question is ...

If you were given six months to live, how would you spend it?

You may be surprised at the reaction and thoughts this question evokes in you. Like a bolt of lightning from nowhere, this question provoked clarity and a real sense of urgency in us around the need to start writing, although we were engrossed in other careers. Suddenly there was this overwhelming drive to pass on what we had learned about building quality relationships through online courses and workshops and books, so that we could leave a legacy for our children and others to benefit. Today, four years later, 4 Habits Consulting and Soulmates Academy Foundation are both established and provide relationship education through multiple platforms to organizations, communities, couples and individuals.

Sometimes if we are quiet enough in our conscious mind, we can hear the real longings of our hearts to do the things we were meant to do. If you find yourself feeling unsettled about life, maybe one season is coming to an end and another is about to begin. It's time to get quiet and still. That's when we can discover core values we didn't even realize we had.

3. The 8 Fs Framework

A third way that works well for those more logical / framework minded like Jon is the 8 Fs Framework he likes to use.

Over the years, a number of authors have developed very helpful tools for prioritizing life. Zig Ziglar came up with his 'wheel of life'[60] and Batz and Schmidt talk about 7 Fs.[61] Jon first came across 5 Fs in a coaching session with business growth coach Verne Harnish. In his brilliant book *Scaling Up: How a Few Companies Make it . . . and Why the Rest Don't,*[62] Harnish credits the 5 Fs for what mattered most to those near the end of their life, in the order listed, to veteran private wealth advisor James Hansberger. Loving the 5 Fs but feeling like they didn't go quite far enough for him, Jon expanded them into his own version of 8 Fs which he uses to this day to map out and prioritize his yearly, monthly, weekly and sometimes even daily activities. Essentially, the 8 Fs provide a structured approach for thinking about what matters most, both now and in the future, by thinking about eight key areas and creating healthy boundaries around them.

So, what are the 8 Fs?

FAITH – It makes sense to start with FAITH only because it is often faith, or the absence of it, that determines how people deal with major life issues like loss, illness, death and grieving. Indeed, numerous surveys revealed a resurgence of faith in the wake of COVID-19, as many confronted both their own mortality and those of loved ones. Faith also often guides decisions about use of resources like time and money, and influences the set of our moral compass.

To be clear, this is not a judgement call on whether or not you should have faith. Rather it's a call to make a conscious decision about what you believe in sooner rather than later, if anything. For us, our shared Christian faith has been the bedrock that has held us firm and pulling together on the same side through many painful seasons in our lives.

If faith is important to you, not only is it vital to be clear where you stand on it, you must also make space in your schedule for it. Our recommendation to you would be, if you have a faith, be a student of it, because that will have a strong influence on your values, as well as how you prioritize and make decisions in life.

FAMILY – Quality relationships with our nearest and dearest nurture us to be physically, emotionally and mentally healthy so we can turn up as our best selves in all aspects of life. But quality relationships don't happen automatically – they need time, investment and intentionality. They are cultivated on purpose. Family includes relationships with a spouse or partner, children or any others who live with you at home, as well as with parents, siblings and wider family relations. It's easy to pass time around each other, but it takes effort to invest in nurturing the relationship, creating memories together and strengthening emotional connections. Time and distance can also get in the way of staying connected with wider family members unless we are intentional about keeping in touch.

Here is the point, if we want to enjoy quality family relationships both now and in the future, we have to invest in them by making space in our schedule 'to be present' – whether physically or virtually.

FRIENDS – Similarly, we need to be intentional about nurturing the friendships we want to survive into our old age. Who would you like to sit and reminisce with when you're old and gray . . . and in a rocking chair? Or who would you like to go on holidays with when you're retired, or when the children have flown the nest? And if you don't have any ideal long-term friendships currently, where could you find new ones? Either way, how will you strengthen and maintain your ideal friendships to make sure they exist in your 'golden' years?

Whether it's an annual holiday together, a monthly catch-up visit, a weekly call, regular nights out or some other version of staying in touch, relationships need to be fed for them to last. *Absence* and *silence* often create doubt, anxiety and misunderstanding which means friendships can be eroded without a single word. In the busy lives we lead, weeks, months and years can pass without being in touch. Being intentional about the friendships we want to preserve requires us to draw healthy boundaries around the time in our schedule to invest in those friendships consistently.

FITNESS – It's been said that by the age of 50 we each have the body we deserve (ouch!). Sometimes, it's not so much a weight problem as it is a planning and scheduling problem. If you're like us, when we don't anticipate the busy periods, we eat on the run, eat late, eat rubbish, get less sleep and live on caffeine and sugar. Less sleep leads to weight gain around the middle and after 40, anything to do with sugar and carbs seems to go straight to the waistline. Oh . . . and by the way, each large glass of red wine is basically a 'liquid cream cake' (check the calorie count if you're struggling to believe that!). We've learned that one the hard way!

But in addition to helping our body parts resist the pull of gravity, FITNESS is also about 1) being physically able to do the things you dream about doing in the future, and 2) helping prevent the onset of heart failure, high blood pressure, diabetes, osteoporosis and the like. So much of our health is linked to what we consume and our exercise habits – or lack of them. One of the things we would definitely tell our younger selves is to develop a health and fitness regime from early on and stick with it!

FINANCES – Most of us have been around the block long enough to know that money isn't the most important thing in life. But as American author, salesman and motivational speaker Zig Ziglar so aptly put it: *'it's reasonably close to oxygen on the "gotta have it" scale!'*[63]

A helpful way to think of FINANCES is as the 'fuel' to make your dreams and goals around all the other Fs come alive.

For many of us a big part of this comes from having a job or career. For all of us finances *should* include plans for having a meaningful income when you no longer want to, or are able to, work (your pension, retirement income, 401K). Now that we're all generally living longer, we each need to make provisions to ensure that we can continue to enjoy a decent lifestyle in 'retirement'. Predictions of a retirement crisis where people aged 65 and over are 'either dead or dead broke' and needing to work longer into their old age are already coming true.[64]

For some, finances will also include plans for additional sources of income too – property, investment, own business, etc.

And if you stop to think about it, clarifying values and goals around finances should be something that women in particular take seriously as they, statistically, tend to outlive their partners. Yet often (at least in western society) many women have tended not to be as involved in financial decisions around pensions, savings and investment for the future. It's important that we each take responsibility for at least knowing what's going on with the family finances if we are to avoid ending up with a nasty surprise about our financial circumstances later in life, or while grieving the loss of a loved one. When working with couples, we recommend they discuss and make joint decisions around values and priorities for the future, and if finances are not a strength for either or both, that they take a course or two. We recommend you do likewise. The quality of your future life may well depend on it.

FULFILMENT – What makes your heart sing? FULFILMENT is about pursuing the things that inspire you in life and make it all worthwhile. If time and money were no object, what would you do? Some of your responses to the questions around identifying your values will help you uncover the things that make you feel like you are living your best life. Would you like to start your dream business, travel the world, learn to play a musical instrument, learn a foreign language, run a marathon? The journey of a thousand miles begins with the first step.

We had no idea what shape a business in 'relationship education' would take, but 25 years ago we started with home-group discussions which developed into evening and weekend seminars which have now grown into a consulting business, a registered charity, a TEDx Talk with well over 1.9 million views, courses that have benefitted thousands of people, and now this book! As journalist and best-selling author Malcolm Gladwell identified in his brilliant book *Outliers: The Story of Success*, 'the magic number for true expertise: ten thousand hours'.[65] The key is to make space in your schedule for it, ring-fence the time to dedicate to it, and start. Before you know it, you will have done your 10,000 hours.

FOUNDATION – This is about the life contributions you choose to make, the legacy you set out to leave or the causes or charities you choose to support. It's about a purpose that is bigger than you that moves you to do something beyond looking out for your own comfort. Sometimes we're moved by the pain, injustice, suffering, or lack we see around us and feel compelled to make a difference. It could be making a difference in the lives of loved ones around you, your community, or on a grander scale something that impacts the whole world.

A great question to ask to help identify your FOUNDATION is 'What breaks your heart?' Or what do you notice and wish someone, somewhere would do something about? Maybe that someone is you. It doesn't have to be grand. It could be simply volunteering to serve in a foodbank, a soup kitchen, or in a local place of worship. It could be going on a holiday project to build houses in a developing country.

Somehow, for many of us, giving back and helping others less fortunate creates a real sense of purpose and foundation in our lives. It makes us feel more human, brings all of life into perspective and challenges us to discover and live on a higher level. And as we have learned, defending space in our schedule to make lasting contributions to other people's lives also helps make us happier, more grateful and more content with life. But we could end up missing out on these benefits if we don't create boundaries around the time to do it, because the hectic pace we live at leaves no room in the margins unless we put them there.

FUN – Apart from the obvious, FUN is about doing the things that inspire us, activities we enjoy, things that bring light and laughter to our world and help create lasting memories with loved ones. For some personalities more than others (especially Otters!) having fun things to look forward to – travelling, exploring, spa days, 'afternoon teas', etc. – helps keep them motivated and focused through 'less fun but necessary' work times. For Beaver-type personalities, this framework helps them remember to 'come up for air' every now and again. They thrive when they do but left to them, fun may not feature on their 'to do' list. Recognizing this, Jon added the FUN category as the eighth F to give himself permission to indulge in it from time to time!

The real beauty of the 8 Fs Framework is that it helps us be intentional with our time, allowing us to invest our days rather than squander them. Here's how Jon brings them to life in his diary . . .

> Maybe it's just me, but I find I very quickly forget to do the things I know I should be doing on a regular basis to achieve the things I want most out of life. And the problem isn't that these are generally hard things to do. I know they're important – heck on the relationships front, often it's things that we teach! – so I know that I'll benefit in the long-term. It's just that life tends to take over and some things inevitably slip off the radar. So, I figured out a long while ago, that I needed a mechanism to nudge me every now and again.

> In the early years I tried the New Year's Resolutions thing, but typically just ended up re-enforcing the early drop out statistics. For years I would goal-set every New Year's Eve. But before long, the goals would be a dim, distant thing of the past.

> Then I came across the 5 Fs . . . and over the years expanded them into 8 Fs that work better for me.

So now, at the end of each year rather than setting Resolutions, I spend time thinking about what I could be doing to strengthen my FAITH, improve relationships with my FAMILY and FRIENDS (and remind myself of some of the tips that we teach that I've forgotten to implement recently!), and take care of my health and FITNESS. I also take some time to think about what would spell FULFILMENT for me, how I would like to give back (FOUNDATION) in the year ahead, and maybe even what would make for a really FUN holiday this year!

With those in mind, the next step is to get them into my diary.

Now I already have a very detailed diary management system which works for me (don't judge me, I'm a Beaver!). I'm partial to using a Moleskin notebook (sized somewhere between A4 and A5), and I draw lines in it to create my ideal diary system – a bit laborious I know, but I'm yet to come across something out there that meets my precise need. Once the lines are drawn, I end up with a week-to-a-page diary with a bit of clear writing space down the left-hand side.

Before each week begins, typically on a Sunday evening, I spend a bit of time thinking about how I would like the week ahead to go and transfer any important appointments from my electronic calendar into the paper version of my diary.

Then comes the interesting bit.

I write down each of the 8 Fs as headings down the left-hand column space – literally, Faith, Family, Friends, Fitness, Finances, Fulfilment, Foundation, Fun. And then I think, what do I want to do this week, that aligns with my FAITH goals for the year? Oh yes, this year I wanted to memorize 52 wise verses – one-a-week. What's my verse for this week? And then, in the FAMILY category, what can I do to show love to Andrea this week? Oh yes, I haven't actually _told_ her how much she means to me in the last few weeks – time I pick that one up again. Before you get the wrong idea, of course, I've _shown_ my love for her lots of times through all the things I do for her (that comes naturally to me), but as we'll discuss in chapter 13, showing love by 'doing things' and communicating love 'verbally' are two different things . . . and I know Andrea hears love loudest when she is told (which doesn't come so naturally to me, so I really do benefit from this nudging system!).

And what can I do with each of the kids this week to keep our relationship strong? Let's make time to go for a bike-ride with my youngest this week . . . and let's carve out some time to just sit and chat with my eldest this week. And so on. You get the point. The 8 Fs force me, each week, to think about what's most important to me and write down something practical to do about each of them. And of course, some weeks I write them down and never get to them, but at least I have a record of where I've 'fallen off the wagon' and can re-double my efforts the following week – because as a super-Beaver I never move on to the next page until everything has either been completed or carried forward. Again, don't judge me!

These three strategies: What 'grates' on the inside?, When exactly is 'one day'?, and the 8 Fs Framework, have been huge in helping us identify and clarify our values and the people and things most important to us. With those clear, we are then better able to decide how we commit to things in our schedule, and the boundaries that we create to achieve the life balance we desire. Hopefully they will resonate with you and help you identify your own values, so that you too can create healthy boundaries around the things that matter most to you.

Creating healthy boundaries that serve you

The more clarity you have around your values and priorities, the easier it becomes to set healthy boundaries and ask for what you want.

To a great extent, we all give people permission to treat us with respect or not, based on the boundaries and the standards we set for ourselves. As a simple example, just think about how you feel when you enter someone's home. If everything is pristine and in order, you may feel obliged to take your shoes off, sit upright and straighten the cushions when you get up. If, on the other hand, the environment is more relaxed (or messy!), you tend to be less worried about any mess you might be making. Equally, if someone is very organized with their diary, always on time in booking appointments, prepared for meetings and very focused on the objective, you too tend to put more effort into preparation for meetings with them.

By and large, we all set the standards for our relationships and how we expect to be treated, by the standards we set for ourselves. Unclear values can leave you vulnerable to anyone and anything. As we have witnessed time and again over the years working in this space, it's almost impossible for a relationship to be successful if both parties don't value who they are, what they bring to the party and where their boundaries lie around the things that matter most to them.

No one can respect the boundaries you don't set.

And if you don't set them, your health, wellbeing and relationships will suffer as a result. Period.

People will presume on your time and you will let them, but it will likely cause stress and resentment. You can even end up resenting people who have their own boundaries set when you don't. For example, you may judge others for stopping work at a certain time to be with their family while you feel stuck with unfinished tasks, simply because you had no cut-off time yourself and resentfully, ended up picking up the slack. If you don't create and respect your boundaries around time and availability, no one else will.

No one can respect the boundaries you don't set

The 4 Habits

Depending on your personality type, you may also be at risk of having your agenda overridden by others (for example, more Lion-type personalities), but clarity around your values helps you respond with more wisdom to other people's demands.

The great news is that as you put the right boundaries in place, it becomes easier to find the courage to ask for what you need from those around you in order to create a lifestyle that is consistent with your values. The better you get at creating healthy boundaries, the more sustainable the life balance you create for yourself.

The reality is, there can be no balance without healthy boundaries.

Five key boundaries for a P-E-A-C-E-ful life

Creating healthy boundaries helps us defend the time and space to live out our values and push back on demands for our time and attention when appropriate. This allows us the chance to respect other aspects of life (the 8 Fs) that help us replenish our energy, feed our souls and nurture our important relationships. When we create healthy boundaries ourselves, we also develop more empathy and respect for other people's boundaries which allows us to make better ASKs of those around us.

Importantly, boundaries will be different for different people.

For example, some people need a complete escape from everything that reminds them of work in order to be replenished which means the current 24/7, 'always on' culture is a source of ongoing stress for them. However, numerous surveys have shown that millennials and later generations seem to be more comfortable with blurred boundaries and expect to live far more integrated lives. But while they might not be stressed by being 'always on', they too are likely to get stressed by being busy without being purposeful. As the pace of life continues to pick up for us all, we can't think of a time when it was more urgent for us all to learn how to lead ourselves well by staying focused on the things that matter in the midst of the noise and clamor of all things digital.

We have found the following five key boundaries to be pivotal for managing mental, emotional and physical wellbeing and for nurturing relationships, especially where they are impacted by the invasion of work on home. When we honor these boundaries, we create PEACE inside and out, and the 'mental space' to work and live well.

Prioritize the morning routine – For most of us, what we do first thing in the morning sets the tone and pace for the day. What we choose to think about, listen to, watch or read influences our thoughts and level of anxiety for better or for worse. Once you think of it like that, it's clear that it's better to spend the first hour of your day focusing on things that uplift and inspire, rather than letting the cares and troubles of the world into your headspace (unrelenting news or social media updates, spring to mind!). We have found this to be invaluable and couldn't recommend it more highly.

If you're a parent, you might find like us that early in the morning before the household wakes up, means your 'parent antennae' – the automatic listening out for the sounds from your children to decipher if they are happily occupied, getting up to mischief or getting into danger – can be turned right down, with one less thing to compete for your attention.

Owning the first part of the morning means you can direct your day to the things that are your true priorities before the demands of the world command your attention through the chimes, pings, emails and alerts of technology, pulling you into OPAs – Other People's Agendas. This is also a time for feeding your soul, lifting your spirits and seizing the day. You could use the time for praying, meditating, reading words of inspiration or keeping a gratitude journal. Despite our attempts to live on the 'high octane' of incessant activity, our souls long for that quiet place of restoration and peace. Cognitive neuroscientist Dr Caroline Leaf talks about the importance of daily moments of meditation or day-dreaming. In her book *Switch on Your Brain*, Dr Leaf states: 'Regular meditators – by this I mean those who have adopted a disciplined and focused, reflecting thought life in which they bring all thoughts into captivity – show that . . . their brain is more active, growing more branches and integrating and linking thoughts, which translates as increased intelligence and wisdom and that wonderful feeling of peace. God also throws in some additional benefits such as increased immune and cardiovascular health.'[66] Positive mental health and wellbeing are often to be found in those quiet moments of reflection ahead of the noise of the day.

The overriding principle though is this – develop boundaries that guard your thoughts . . . and you will guard your peace.

Establish a clear schedule of work 'focus time' and availability – Stress and tension usually come from undiscussed assumptions and unmet expectations. Agreeing times for focused work, meetings, home pressure points or time with family, is vital for managing expectations and reducing tensions both at home and at work. This means when it's time to work you can work 'full on' and not worry about other things screaming for your attention because they will all have their moment. Within this focused time, concentrate on things that really matter rather than being distracted by non-income producing activity like sorting paperwork . . . again. As author and business philosopher Jim Rohn says, in any business 'there are a half-dozen things that make 80% of the difference . . . A half-dozen things'.[67] When it's time to work, focus on those half-dozen things as a priority.

For us the half-dozen include research, writing courses or articles, business development and presenting on client workshops. You will know the key tasks in your role that deliver the greatest results, and the amount of time and effort they require. As much as possible, choose the times when you are at your peak concentration, especially for things that need big chunks of creative focus. Scheduling time for focused work also means you don't have to panic about upcoming big projects and make huge demands on the patience of the people around you, if you know time is also scheduled in for them.

And remember, 'START time' is as important as 'STOP time' to prevent work bleeding into home and vice versa. If you work from home and are lucky enough to have a home office or other dedicated space, close the door as you leave when you're done for the day. If you're not so fortunate, get a box or use a cupboard to pack away the implements of work and create mental space – especially if you have to work from your bedroom.

For some people changing clothes also helps to separate work life from home life – even if it is from one set of jogging bottoms to another! The point is to work with focus in work time but to create the mental space to be 'fully present' and give equal respect to the time for family and home. As American Christian missionary Jim Elliot,[68] in his short life concluded, 'wherever you are, *be all there*'. Which leads us neatly on to the next point.

Arrange regular one-on-one time for your key relationships – Having a great relationship with a significant other can be a key resource for maintaining resilience and a sense of wellbeing. Stress sucks the oxygen out of relationships, quality time together helps to put it back in. Regular one-on-one time is essential to keep relationships alive, mutually supportive and emotionally connected. But it doesn't happen automatically. And don't be fooled into thinking that merely passing time together is enough – it's easy to pass time together in the same physical space with no emotional connection. Whether the key relationship is with partners, children, parents or close friends, schedule the time together, and put the effort in to make it special. Time together that you defend.

This is such an important point, it's worth pausing for a moment here to expand on the idea. 'Date nights' (or days!) together is a *must do* for any couple wanting to build a strong marriage or partnership. Ring-fencing time in the diary to share moments of undivided attention is one of the greatest investments for future-proofing any long-term couple relationship. This is a discipline that has served us well over the years.

> *When our children were little, we had date nights in to avoid the need for constant babysitting arrangements, but we had a clear routine. The children would get their favorite dinner – spaghetti bolognese – so they would eat well without drama, have a fun bath-time and bedtime stories with lights out at 7:30pm. We looked forward to date night and so did they!*

> *Once the kids were tucked into bed, we would bring out the wine, candles, mood lighting, takeaway (usually Chinese or Indian) and enjoy one-on-one time together. It was in those moments that we would finally get to finish conversations started earlier that week, watch a movie, cuddle . . . and do anything else that came naturally! Now that they're older, we can enjoy date nights out, but we still often do date nights in, and have taught our children to respect the importance of time alone for Mummy and Daddy.*

Please pay attention to this crucial point – the most important relationship for family stability is the relationship between the parents. When the parental relationship is strong, everybody thrives – parents and children. When the relationship between parents is weak or broken, everybody suffers . . . and children suffer the most. Research shows that where things get so bad in the relationship that parents split in the early years there is an increased chance of mental health issues when children hit their teens.[68] The research went on to show that this tends to show up in boys as behavioral issues and in girls as emotional issues. Predictions were that half the children born in the UK in 2019 will experience parental separation by the time they sit their school-leaving exams (GCSEs) at age 16. Putting clear boundaries around the time to invest in couple relationships is not just a lovely romantic idea. It's vital for building strong, long-lasting relationships . . . and where children are involved, it can be a determining factor in the mental health of future generations.

Creating healthy boundaries around relationships with our children is also vital. World-renowned leadership coach and pastor, Andy Stanley, shares how despite the pressure and expectations people generally have of *pastors' kids* or *preachers' kids*, probably the most important goal he and his wife Sandra set was that they would parent in such a way that their children would still *want to* come home and hang out with them long after they had to.[69] That resonated strongly with the type of relationships we desired with our kids and so we adopted that as our goal as well.

Making space in the diary for one-on-one time with our children helps create the long-term relationships we desire. When our children were little, we could take them wherever we wanted to go, or wherever we wanted them to be. As they got older and developed independent interests, however, we found ourselves having to go where they were and learn to share their interests if we wanted to stay emotionally connected with them. And the transition happened much quicker than we might have thought!

In the one-on-one time, be careful to spend the time doing and saying the things that build connection and encouragement, demonstrating that you have their backs (rather than constantly being on their backs!). During the pandemic we had great fun as a family playing cards and board games, completing a 1,000-piece Marvel puzzle – and then starting from zero and going through and watching the entire Marvel series! We spent time learning the games they enjoyed and making time for the family activities they wanted to do. Minecraft, anyone?

Carve out 'Me' time – When the pressure is on, many of us forget, or sacrifice making time to look after our own physical and mental health. But we can't give what we don't have. This is why in aircraft emergencies we're advised to put on our own oxygen masks, before helping others. Making time to do the things that refuel you and help you keep your sense of humor – exercise, hobbies, movies, beauty treatments, quiet reading time and so on – is not necessarily a luxury or mere selfish indulgence.

Taking care of yourself and looking after your own needs can be a vital part of the strategy for maintaining personal resilience and wellbeing, especially through times of stress and uncertainty. And once you are in a better place mentally and emotionally, it's so much easier to make deposits into the Emotional Bank Accounts of the people around you.

If you don't already, it's worth thinking about having a day each week where you unplug from the world, switch off the usual routines of work and take time to reset and recharge. This is particularly important if you work from home where every day looks and feels the same and one day just blends into the next. Understandably, this idea of a day of rest contradicts the busyness culture where so many of us feel unproductive if we stop for even a moment. We kid ourselves that the world will stop turning if we do. Good news – the world will keep spinning without us and we will be better off for it. Slowing down at regular intervals allows us to be even more switched on and productive when we go back to it. Busyness is not the problem *per se* – everybody is busy. But we will only add to our stress levels if we don't develop a healthy rhythm of work and recovery time in our cycle of busyness.

And as a bonus, taking time to refuel also helps us be more enjoyable to be around – a better person in every sense of the word. It makes us predictably pleasant instead of hassled or frazzled . . .

While we are on the topic, it's worth practicing speaking kindly to yourself and giving yourself a break when things don't go to plan. There's a whole world of stress out there beating on you – no need to beat up on yourself as well.

Carving out 'me time' is about enjoying the things that make your heart sing, keep you optimistic and remind you that despite it all, life is worth living.

Engage with your support network – In the busyness of life, it is easy for conversations to be reduced to functional discussions around who needs to do what when, without really connecting with people in meaningful ways. One thing that stood out for many people through the COVID pandemic experience was the importance of staying connected with the people who matter most to them. Young or old, with family or isolated, it's fair to say everyone experienced their own version of COVID stress. And people learned to play their part in looking after each other's mental health by making time to check in on loved ones, be their support, and build a support network around themselves.

Those who lived on their own were particularly impacted in this regard. The learning – if you live on your own, it's important to be deliberate about booking time to connect with the people who matter to you. And try not to feel put out if you find you're the one having to reach out most of the time – chances are you have more free time than those in busy households.

Of course, while technology can be a great deterrent to relationships when we use it inappropriately, it has also proven to be a force for good in connecting with people across the miles. Many of us have come to be totally familiar with the likes of FaceTime, Zoom, Microsoft Teams, Google Meet and other video-based technologies as a result of life under lockdown.

In a Future Normal in which distance and time apart continue to feature, for relationships to thrive, it's important that we find creative ways to use these technologies to ensure casual conversations continue, to share laughs, and to maintain involvement in the detail of each other's lives.

Now, while being busy is almost inevitable in our 24/7 digital world, it doesn't have to be overwhelmingly so. But long-term success is unlikely to come from simply trying to find new and different ways to juggle between home, work and life. In our experience what makes the most difference is developing a new mindset and learning to choose the 'right thing' to be busy doing at any moment in time.

> **In the busyness that has become our culture, success comes from finding your own rhythm of 'sprint and recovery' or 'work, rest and play' in a way that keeps you energized and fully present for the people and things that matter most to you in life.**

Identifying and putting boundaries around the relationships and things that are important to you and defending the space – physically, mentally and emotionally – to attend to these priorities in the rhythm that works for you, is what will help you enjoy PEACE on the inside as well as around you.

Once the key boundaries are in place, the next step is to develop a schedule based on those values that will help you live out the life balance you desire and make space for developing quality relationships. That's the focus for the next section, but before we go there, let's have a quick look at a couple of practical ways to free up more time for the important and get rid of things that we don't want and/or things that consume our time unnecessarily.

Getting clear on what you *don't* want

Clarifying what you *don't* want in your life is sometimes as important as clarifying what you do. It helps you really zoom in on the heart of your truth, and eliminate other things that might try to piggyback and squeeze their way in.

So, let's look at some tips to shave off the passengers!

Do, Delegate or Dump?

Being clear on what we don't want involves recognizing the things that only you can DO versus what you can DELEGATE or DUMP.

Only *you*, for example, can be the particular spouse or partner that you are to your spouse or partner. Equally, only you can be the mother or father you desire to be to your child(ren). Others could fill the role, but it wouldn't be the same as you doing it. Only you can do the things you know you need to do to live a life of no regrets – like looking after your health, spending time with ageing parents or relatives and pursuing things on your 'bucket list'. These are all the people and things that generally don't scream for your attention and can be postponed, but they can also be lost with devastating consequences to you.

This is where being very clear on your values and the things that are important to you will help you lead yourself better. Make time in the diary to *do* and *be* the things that only you can do and be and think about delegating or dumping the rest. The more disciplined you are about prioritizing your time toward the people and activities that matter – and not postponing them – the more you can live 'ahead of the curve' and not be stressed out by always playing catch up or firefighting avoidable emergencies. You've probably heard the saying – 'Isn't it funny how we can't find 30 minutes a day to exercise but we can find a week to be in hospital!'

Many of you will be familiar with the 'Eisenhower matrix' of 'urgent' versus 'important' tasks made famous by Stephen Covey in his globally acclaimed book *The 7 Habits of Highly Effective People*.[70] Rather than repeat that information here, we will share some specifics that we have found really helpful around Do, Delegate and Dump:

- *Do* **leave margin in your schedule and resist the temptation to fill 'white space' in your diary.** If your diary is too crammed, you will always be hurrying. But as author John Mark Comer points out in his brilliant book on *The Ruthless Elimination of Hurry*,[71] hurry and love are incompatible. We are never at our best self in our relationships when we're in a hurry – and our loved ones bear the brunt of what comes out under pressure.

- *Do* **create meal plans for one or two weeks at a time and shop online when you can, unless you genuinely get refueled by wandering the supermarket aisles** – personally, we resisted this one for a while but have now wholly submitted to the discipline. This cuts down on the number of decisions and stress over what's for breakfast, lunch and dinner and allows you to save money because you buy what you eat and eat what you buy. In our household we have to cater for severe allergies to dairy, nuts, eggs and shellfish, plus one vegan and one who doesn't eat pork. Thinking ahead made a huge difference when we (Andrea!) finally stopped resisting the idea of this level of detail and structure. You will discover less stress around mealtimes and get more people sharing the load because the question of 'what's for dinner?' is already answered. Not only does this save time, but it also saves relationships!

- *Do* **what you can to restrict your errands / chores to one day to minimize 'breaking up' several days.** It's amazing how easy it is to waste time by constantly popping out to do errands. Just a bit of thought into organizing errands together – like a trip to the post office together with a trip to the pharmacy or doctor or before a school run or after the gym, etc. – can free up bigger chunks of time for concentrated work or more space for leisure time in your diary. Same for organizing a day of online meetings and leaving clear days for projects that demand longer thinking time.

- *Delegate* **by getting both inside and outside help, where possible.** Share tasks at home and, if you can, hire help for the stuff that is necessary but doesn't have to be necessarily done by you (ironing, anyone?). If you live with family, enlist them in fitting stuff into the nooks and crannies of life to free up time to do meaningful things together. As a family, we fold laundry while watching a movie together, and empty the dishwasher, washing machine or dryer while in the kitchen cooking. If you need to multitask, do it around the things that don't deserve 'prime thinking time'. And definitely try and restrict multitasking to *things* rather than *people*.

- *Dump* **stuff that just wastes your time and adds no value** – like many of the updates and forwards on social media. Some of that stuff can indeed be 'good', but as Jim Collins points out in his fascinating book *From Good to Great*, 'Good is the enemy of great.'[72] Spending time on good, often keeps us from going after great.

Your list of chores, activities and routines will be different to ours, but the point is to be intentional about where your time goes and develop routines that keep chores and 'to-dos' from dominating your day. That way you can have more time to invest in the people and things that really matter most to you.

Time for Reflection

Key Takeaways

- Investing the time to clarify our values helps us become intentional about designing and living the life we choose on purpose.

- When we get clear on our values, we can create healthy boundaries around the people and things that matter to us and develop a schedule based on living out our values.

- Three helpful strategies for identifying what matters most to you are:

  ○ Think about what 'grates' on the inside.

  ○ Think about when exactly is 'one day'.

  ○ Use the 8 Fs Framework.

- Once you've identified what's most important to you, it's time to set boundaries around them to ring-fence and protect them. Remember no one can respect the boundaries you don't set.

- For help setting boundaries, put in place the five key boundaries for a P-E-A-C-E-ful life:

  ○ P-rioritize the morning routine

  ○ E-stablish a clear schedule of work 'focus time' and availability

- ◦ A-rrange regular one-on-one time for your key relationships

- ◦ C-arve out 'Me' time

- ◦ E-ngage with your support network

- In clarifying what's important to you, remember to also identify what you *don't* want.

Building Your Understanding

1. Which strategy for clarifying your values resonates most strongly with you?

2. What boundaries do you think you need to create or recreate?

3. What *don't* you want in your relationships going forward?

Taking Personal Action

1. Using whichever of the three strategies resonates most strongly with you (or another one, if you already have something you're comfortable with), take some time to think about what matters most to you (people and things). Write down your thoughts somewhere where you will be able to see them regularly.

2. Take some time to think also about what you *don't* want going forward. Write it / them down.

3. Think about if / how the P-E-A-C-E-ful approach might help you with your boundary setting.

4. Using the worksheet in the Appendices, continue making a note of the things you plan to STOP / START / CONTINUE / CHANGE including at least one thing to help develop Habit #3: ASK, don't assume.

Chapter Eleven

The art of ASKing well

*'Knowing what your ideal schedule looks like will help
you make better ASKs of the people around you.'*

Clarifying the things that matter most to you and creating healthy boundaries around them is like putting the foundation, walls, roofs and other structures in place for building a solid house. The next step is to create the experience you desire inside 'your house' by designing a schedule that 1) gives the appropriate space to the people and things that matter most, 2) respects the boundaries you created, and 3) supports you in living out your values in your daily, weekly and monthly routines. As with building a house though, success comes from finishing the project – just identifying your core values and boundaries is not enough. It's important to put pen to paper and design the schedule that fits your values into real-life commitments so that you can then be intentional about living them out in practice.

Knowing what your ideal schedule looks like will help you make better ASKs of the people around you.

Designing your ideal template for life

You've no doubt heard it said, 'our diaries and our bank statements reflect our *priorities*'. Well, probably the more accurate statement is, they reflect the priorities we're living out, and not necessarily the ones we hold dear. And that, for many, is the beginning of stress – especially where we find ourselves in a routine that is *not* how we really want to live life. Success comes from recognizing that and taking action.

In our experience though, many fall at this hurdle because they have bought into the following couple of myths:

1. I don't have time to plan

This is often the most problematic mindset to confront. It's so easy to get caught by the deception that we don't have enough time to plan because, of course, planning takes time and many of us are already living time-poor lives as it is. The reality though, is that failing to plan is planning to fail.

Here is the truth – we do have enough time. We each get 168 hours every week – 24 hours a day, 7 days a week – no extra time for good behavior. Even if we work a 50-hour or 70-hour week and sleep for 8 hours a night (yes, it is possible!), that still leaves us between 40 and 60 hours to eat, socialize and do 'stuff'. That's almost a whole other working week each week! Where does that time go? 'The stuff' of life will always expand to fill the time available. Our job is to harness that time and use it for our advantage.

Admittedly, it might mean having a long hard look at how you use your day and making different choices around the times you get up and go to bed. This can be painful but necessary – as we discovered. But as a result, we've learned to be early risers. Getting up early (5:00-5:30am!) is a habit that serves us well, especially when it's supported by a habit of getting to bed before 10:00pm. On a good day, by 9:00am our souls are centered through our individual quiet time, breakfast is done, the kids are at school, we've done our exercise, the house is tidy, the laundry is on, dinner is organized and we can focus on crunching through the key deliverables on the work agenda before the evening routine kicks in. When it works, it's like clockwork – pun intended! Even if we fall off the wagon a few times – like during the school holidays – we get things going again because rising early is a habit that serves us individually and benefits the whole household. It also helps keep our minds and emotions at peace.

2. I'd rather just go with the flow

The second myth is around feeling constrained by structure and preferring to do things when we are 'in the mood'. This is deception, not a strategy for success. In nature, things tend toward chaos. That's why people don't cruise to become debt-free or eat whatever they want and achieve great fitness or reach the pinnacle of their career by accident. It's also why most of us don't automatically end up with great long-term relationships without effort. Scheduling your time and attention to invest in the things you value and then honoring that schedule are key disciplines to keep you on the path to success. It was what caused Zig Ziglar to say: *'If you do what you need to do when you need to do it, then the day will come when you can do what you want to do when you want to do it'.*[73]

We would encourage you – *make the time* and be disciplined and *on purpose*.

Life balance isn't something that exists outside of us, it's something that we have to create for ourselves based on the things we decide to include in our life simultaneously.

The great thing is that we *can* take control of our lives and decide what gets into our diary and what doesn't. And when it does, it can be beautiful. If you're still wavering though, here's a quick overview of why you won't regret taking the time and energy required to push through and complete the exercise.

Why scheduling based on values works . . .

'To do' lists are never ending. There is always something to do and there will always be things that get rolled to the next day, week, month, year. The question is how to choose which things get done or rolled, given that visually, a simple list gives equal weighting to each item. Scheduling based on values will allow you to make better ASKs of yourself and of those around you, so that you can live out a more sustainable work-life balance. In practical terms, it will help you put 'First things first' à la Stephen Covey.[74] Here are four reasons why scheduling based on values delivers results:

1. *Scheduling based on values helps you design* your *ideal balance*

   A schedule based on values will help you prioritize, starting with the most important things and fitting the other things around them, rather than having unimportant activities consume time that would be better spent focused on meaningful work and involvement. For those of us at work, big chunks of the day will be consumed by work commitments and so it's easy to fall into the reactive cycle of work tasks followed by home tasks, then rinse and repeat. Even for those of us with more flexibility over our time, it's easy to end up stressed and frustrated, trying to juggle everything all at once and living permanently in fire-fighting mode. Generally, the challenge isn't about our willingness or ability to work hard. The real challenge is in overcoming the sense of overwhelm in trying to fit everything into an already 'jam-packed' schedule. Success comes from learning to prioritize the things that are really important, instead of being at the mercy of a never-ending list of all the things screaming for attention at equal volume, despite not having equal importance.

2. Scheduling based on values helps you be 'fully present' in the moment

By starting with the important chunks like work time, time with partner, time with children, time for exercise and so on, remarkably, the noise of things screaming for your attention is silenced.

Peace comes from knowing that everything that matters is catered for somewhere in the plan. This offers you the gift of living with deep attention and focus – in your work and in your relationships. It also means your partner and family can be more supportive of the things that take you away from them because they know their time is protected and is coming. In our experience, the mental peace and fulfilment that comes from being able to be 'fully present in the moment' are usually reason enough to schedule based on values.

3. Scheduling based on values helps you make better decisions and reduce stress

When we become intentional about our values, priorities and the balance of life we want to create, we become more realistic about the demands we place on ourselves. Scheduling based on values helps you know with clarity, what you can say *yes* to because it fits with your values and what you must say *no* to, as good as it is, because it isn't a priority in this season of life.

Your values-based schedule becomes your guide for making better decisions. Firstly, it eliminates the mental load of having to make daily / weekly decisions about when you need to get certain things done because they already have allocated times in the schedule. Secondly, it highlights when you are available to commit to things like appointments and meetings. And thirdly, it allows you to make better choices around what it will 'cost' you when you have to shift things.

We have found, having a rhythm for how we live and work around the people and things that matter most to us also helps prevent us overcommitting ourselves or placing the family under unnecessary stress. Here are a couple of examples of what's worked for us:

We have found that blocking out 6:30-7:30 first thing in the morning on weekdays instantly eliminates the debate in our heads about whether or not to exercise today and when.

At the other end of the day, being present and available for the evening routine with our children is important to us so, as much as possible, no calls get booked during school pick-up time, or dinner time.

Daytime we are available for meetings and workshop delivery so it's an easy yes when they fit inside school drop-off and pick-up times. Tuesdays and Thursdays are generally the days for connecting with / following-up with clients, so these are the days we propose in order to contain the amount of travel and not eat into the focus time for doing concentrated work on other days.

Thursday evening is our date night, so it is ring-fenced and blocked off in both our diaries. If anyone wants to book something on a Thursday evening the answer is an easy no – unless it's significant in which case we reschedule date night for another time that week to ensure we don't lose our one-on-one time together.

On a Friday night our teens want to just hibernate and have their own downtime after a long week, so inviting people round for dinner where they're expected to be there typically provoked groans and frustration. As such, now we tend to use Friday evenings for our own catching up with friends and socializing.

We have also learnt the importance of quiet times together with no agenda so we can just connect and refuel as a family. Our faith is important to us so on Sundays we do the early service at church and spend the rest of the day chilling with no commitments or time pressures. In the past we used to say yes to things on impulse (especially Andrea, the resident Otter!) wherever there was 'white space' in the diary. This would put the family on a relentless treadmill of activity which, although fun at times, was creating mental, emotional and physical exhaustion for all of us. Now we have learned to respect our own boundaries and check in with each other before making any such commitments.

4. **Scheduling based on values helps you know when you've missed the mark and fix it**

Inevitably there will be crises or crunch times that throw your schedule off balance. Scheduling based on values helps you know what has to be shifted and what you need to do to get things back on track again. It helps you know which 'balls' to drop when something has to give. Some balls will bounce – like social outings with casual friends, laundry, cleaning – but some balls will break if dropped too often – like health and important relationships.

Given the nature of the work we do, every now and again preparation for a new workshop or delivery to a local community group means we end up working late into the night or through the weekend. Inevitably it means having to shift some things – maybe our Thursday evening date night, maybe being available for hanging out with the young people, definitely the cleaning and house chores! Those times tend to drain Emotional Bank Accounts all round and . . . to be honest they can result in us being a bit impatient and short-tempered with each other.

What keeps us sane in those moments is knowing that the disruption will only be for a limited time and that we can look forward to getting back to our schedule before long. And sometimes to make things extra special we'll plan a family pajama day, a weekend away, or even just us going off as a couple to the movies in the middle of a workday! We find that by intentionally arranging events and activities that replenish our Emotional Bank Accounts, life gets back into balance again soon.

Scheduling based on values will help you manage key activities, nurture relationships and create the dynamic balance of life you desire in a way that planning based on 'to do' lists never will. It allows you to get ahead of the curve and be proactive about managing your availability rather than just reacting to the demands placed on you by OPAs: Other People's Agendas.

Importantly, this can help you manage upwards (your boss) and outwards (people around you) by anticipating demands on your time to minimize moments of panic and emergency, especially when working with others who are not as forward thinking in their approach.

Designing your own template – a practical guide

If you already have a planning system that works for you and helps you achieve the balance you desire based on what really matters most to you – great! Just skip past this section to the next one. However, if you'd like to check out something new and different, we're confident you won't be disappointed.

Yes, it's going to take a bit of work and the process might feel a bit overwhelming at the start. We get that. We've been there. But real gold awaits you on the other side of doing this properly. As author and business philosopher Jim Rohn said, '*We must all suffer from one of two pains: the pain of discipline or the pain of regret. The difference is discipline weighs ounces while regret weighs tons.'*[75] Scheduling based on values helps us make better ASKs of ourselves and provides a practical way for ensuring we avoid the pain of regret.

And if planning and structure are not natural strengths or interests of yours, take heart. Where Jon took to this like a duck to water, Andrea used to feel planning was an attempt to kill her spirit and put her in a straight-jacket! That is, until she learned that spontaneity is fun but not a great life strategy.

We figured if Andrea could learn to plan in detail like this, any and every one can, so we thought it might help to let her share how she did it (and continues to do it!)

One of the strategies I found very useful in developing this skill was to create a visual, high-level 'template' of a schedule for my ideal week, making space for key responsibilities as well as everyone and everything I valued. No surprises given my flare for creativity and fun, that I use colored pens a lot to draw healthy, visible boundaries.

For me, nothing beats seeing the week mapped out in living color and having a general template to use in making decisions day by day and week on week. It works because the template helps me see the general structure of the week at a glance – where all the important work activities that need to be done will have their moment for attention; the gaps where I can squeeze in chores and other 'stuff' that need to get done so they don't consume prime time; and where real moments of connection with the people who matter most are ring-fenced so I can have something fun to look forward to and that will allow us to create memories together.

We've included an example of one of Andrea's actual templates in the Appendices so you can see exactly how it works for her. We've also included a template you can use to develop your own.

We couldn't encourage you more strongly to make an appointment with yourself and invest the time to develop your own template schedule. This simple process will help you identify where a few changes and tweaks could reduce stress and overwhelm, increase peace and harmony and bring your real-life experience into alignment with the life you really want to live. Importantly, it will also empower you to make better ASKs of those around you and renegotiate availability and priorities where necessary.

Just start. Before you know it, planning based on real priorities will become your new habit. Your life of better balance and fulfilment awaits.

> *Tip: If it helps, feel free to adopt Andrea's carrot-and-stick approach to getting it done. Planning was such a struggle for her that she had to make it more fun. Her commitment to the two or three hours it typically takes would feel less of a burden when she could do it sat in one of her favorite cafés or hotel lounges, be uplifted and inspired by their beautiful surroundings, and be served copious cups of tea while getting the job done!*

Will life work to the schedule every week? Absolutely not. And the template schedule itself will need to be updated regularly – for us, it changes about every three months. It will likely take a few attempts, but by getting started and getting it wrong, you will learn how to get it right for you in a way that has you living out your values and priorities with a more sustainable work-life balance. The rewards of making the time to think about this are powerful.

Making better ASKs (of those around you)

Being clear on WHAT to ask for, and knowing what your ideal schedule looks like, will help you make better ASKs of the people around you.

Below are a couple of examples of how this approach has helped us make better ASKs.

Making better ASKs of your boss(es) / colleagues

Of course, the real world of work means that sometimes the convergence of appointments and other commitments will kick life out of balance for a bit. Like in any business there are times when deadlines must be met, and schedules need to be abandoned. Being clear up-front on values and priorities though, is what can help you manage the imbalance so that it is short-lived rather than a way of life – which is never sustainable.

As Andrea experienced first-hand, the life of a management consultant with one of the Big Four global consultancies often placed huge demands on personal time and time away from home. Being clear on her values and priorities was what empowered her on numerous occasions to make better ASKs of her boss. Here's one example from the early days . . .

> *Living and working away in Japan for a year meant that we didn't get to see family and friends often, so every visit was treasured. Jon's mum and dad were due to visit that summer and we were counting down the days. Finally, the week of their arrival came, and they were scheduled to land on the Friday. That Monday my boss called me into his office and proudly confirmed that I had just been assigned to a client delivery project in Seoul, South Korea. Now this was a really big deal, because working in Japan without being able to speak Japanese meant I was working on research and thought-leadership pieces that could be done in English and translated, but not on 'proper' client-facing work. In their words I was 'functionally illiterate'! However, this client project was being done in English – so it was hugely important that I took it. But doing so would mean that instead of two weeks with my in-laws I would only get the weekends. To make matters worse, I had no annual leave available.*

I was clear on the expectations of the consulting industry I had signed up to as a career but also clear on my values. And being clear, I was able to make a better ASK. I said yes, I would go on the project, but boldly asked for the day-off on the Friday (despite not having annual leave) to greet them at the airport and have a long weekend with them before going. And against standard HR policy at the time, my boss said yes and made it happen.

Also, knowing the project was going to be months long with weekly travel to Seoul, my boss and I also negotiated that I would travel back on flights that allowed me to be in Tokyo early Friday afternoons and not travel out until Monday morning.

Recognizing the pressures work would be placing on our relationship, Jon and I made the commitment to ring-fence Saturdays in general as our downtime at home with no visits, meetings and appointments – just us. Shopping, errands, meeting up with friends would be done on Sundays when we were going out for church anyway. We outsourced the cleaning and ironing so that we didn't have to spend our limited time together doing housework. This was before the days of technology like FaceTime or Zoom calls, so we knew prioritizing time to invest in our relationship when we were together was vital to help us stay emotionally connected through the weeks and months ahead.

Having a schedule that reflects your values means that you will be able to make better ASKs of your boss(es), team leads and colleagues rather than bottle resentment or feelings of being unsupported or taken for granted.

Making better ASKs of those at home

Likewise, being clear on our values, priorities and ideal schedule has also helped us make better ASKs of our loved ones at home. As we discussed earlier, sometimes it will be asking for their patience and trust through times of intense work delivery, with the assurance that a time is coming soon where we will redress the balance and have time for them. Other times it will be asking for them to take on more tasks and responsibilities to help share the load of household chores. And other times still it might simply be asking for their support for you to pursue a course or hobby that means you are going to be absent or unavailable when they might otherwise expect you to be around. The clearer we are on what we are working toward and how the family will be impacted, the more specific we can be in asking for help, negotiating changes to the schedule and getting willing support to make things work all round. Here are a couple of examples of how having an ideal schedule helped us make better ASKs:

As entrepreneurs running our own business, we know just how easy it is to pass time around each other without being 'present'. We also know how easy it would be to let the entire summer pass by with us working and our children being left doing their own thing. But to help us live out the value of being present as parents, during school holidays, we have learned to modify the schedule (and meetings and deliverables) to start early and work through to mid-afternoon while the kids sleep-in. That way we are available for fun family activities and outings late afternoon / evening, or just for spontaneous conversations with them (with teenagers you have to take it when you get it!). We also include a handful of what we call 'well days' (as opposed to sick days) where we all just lounge around in pajamas and enjoy a guilt-free day together of having nothing to do and all day to do it in!

Being intentional about what we commit to do through scheduling based on values has become such a part of our approach as a family, that now we even create schedules for our holidays. Now before you tell us to get a life . . . let us explain! We know it sounds counter-intuitive, but what we learned by doing it is that this is the best way to get the most out of holidays together and create the memories we each desire on purpose. At the start of the holiday, we ask everyone to write down their list of what they want to have achieved, experienced and enjoyed by the end of the holiday and we then get one of our Beavers (typically Jon) to come up with a schedule that accommodates as many of everybody's desires as possible. And where the magic works is that not only do activities and excursions get scheduled in, but so also do chill times by the pool, time for family games, times for catch-up conversations, etc. We're yet to have someone complain it didn't work for them – and with an extended family of up to 14 when we get together, we think that's saying something!

Whether it's with relationships at home or at work, having a template schedule in place will help you be on purpose about achieving the things that matter most to you, no question.

Where the conversation is likely to be a tricky one to have though, we recommend you adopt what we call the C-A-L-M approach, which we cover in the next section.

The C-A-L-M way to have courageous conversations

As we've said before, one of the main benefits of identifying our core values, creating healthy boundaries and designing a template of our ideal weekly schedule / balance is that we become armed with the information and the conviction we need to make the required 'big ASKs' of those around us to make things smoother in our relationships. Being clear on the life we want to lead, helps us become clear on the help we need from others to make things work better.

But then comes the time for us to actually make the 'big ASKs' and that can feel scary.

The thought of having these conversations can make us feel vulnerable and exposed. Often, they make us confront underlying emotions and assumptions, and the thought of challenging them – in ourselves or in others – can leave us feeling rather uncomfortable or troubled. These feelings of discomfort in ourselves along with anxiety about the possible reactions from the other person make these conversations feel difficult, requiring courage to face them. Thus, the name 'courageous conversations'.

In their book *Difficult Conversations: How to Discuss What Matters Most,*[76] authors Stone, Patton and Heen point out that, at those times, there are actually three conversations going on in our heads – the 'what happened' conversation, the 'feelings' conversation and the 'identity' conversation. Meaning the issue as I see it, the emotions provoked in me, and how the situation makes me feel about myself.

> *Using the challenge Andrea had around roles and responsibilities at home as an example, the 'what happened' conversation was that (in her head) the family were seeing the chores and choosing not to be supportive; the 'feelings conversation' was around emotions of frustration, overwhelm and being taken for granted; and the 'identity conversation' was around questioning her value as a mother and wife because her assumption was that good mothers and wives take charge of these chores themselves.*

Learning to process these conversations in your own head and anticipating that the person you are in discussion with will be having similar head conversations themselves, will help you be prepared and more effective in having these courageous conversations.

Of course, all that we have discussed so far around The 4 Habits® for successful relationships is vital equipping for doing courageous conversations well! However, here are four specific strategies to help you prepare for and make these 'big ASKs' using the acronym C-A-L-M to help you remember them. The first two strategies are about preparing well in advance of the conversation. The second two strategies are about doing the conversation well.

C – Clarify the goal

The first thing to do in preparing for a courageous conversation is to be clear on the goal.

Beyond the things that are frustrating and irritating, what do you want? What does good look like? More help with meals, laundry, changing work hours, days or responsibilities? Getting a promotion or challenging disappointing feedback from a performance review? Think beyond the frustrations to decide what outcome you would like and keep that as the focus during the conversation.

Being clear on the goal is your key to navigating through the emotions and counter-arguments that can easily derail the conversation.

This is where taking the time to clarify values, ideal schedules, and the ideal balance you are working toward will pay dividends, because they will give you a strong 'why' for the ASK and the courage to pursue it. In deciding on the goal, think about what you need and also what you can offer to support others. Where can you be flexible to help them be able to meet your 'big ASK'? What sacrifices are you willing to make so everyone can win? There will always be sacrifices – being clear on your goals will help you choose the right ones.

Being clear on the goal also means you can make your 'ASKs' simply and succinctly without criticism or accusation. This helps prevent overwhelming people you care about with a flood of words and emotions that become too much to process in tricky conversations.

Importantly, being clear on the goal also includes being clear on who you want to be in the process. How do you want to be experienced during the conversation? Setting this goal and holding that thought throughout will help you pre-program your automatic responses to be more measured and in control. It will also allow you to think through back up strategies in case the other person's 'Chimp' starts to run riot.

To help give the best chance for a great conversation that stays focused on the goal, choose a time and place when people and emotions are at their best. The H-A-L-T acronym is a good pulse check on timing – avoid times when either party is Hungry, Angry, Lonely or Tired.

One of the concerns often raised by workshop participants is *'What if we ask and they say no?'* This is one of the lingering fears that often stops people even broaching the subject of 'big ASKs' in the first place. But not making the ASK is guaranteeing a 'no' without even trying. Asking opens the possibility for a positive outcome. In a very real way, if you don't ask, you don't get. Being clear on the goal helps you to ask with confidence and to ask well. If the answer is no, or the response is very negative, or both(!), the goal doesn't necessarily change but you might need to rethink how to achieve it – even if that means revisiting the conversation at a later date with more ideas on how to make it happen.

A – Assume the best

The second thing to do in preparing for courageous conversations is to 'assume the best'. Courageous conversations are most likely to succeed when we start with the assumption that intentions are good on both sides, there is commitment to the relationship and that those involved are both willing and able to emerge from the conversation stronger for it. Without the context of commitment to the relationship, courageous conversations can be just brutal without a cause.

As we discussed in Habit #2, quite often in conflict situations, our default tendency is to assume our understanding of the situation is 'right' and that others are against us. Now, of course, we're not suggesting that you be naïve about this – sometimes people will have ill intent toward you, like when office politics are at play. However, even there, just in case you're wrong, we would still recommend that you assume the best in your approach but be wise in preparing for the worst. Assuming the best will allow you to leave the door open for a different perspective on the situation and even the slim chance that intentions were good.

We spoke earlier about the neurological impact of thinking the best or thinking the worst on our brains. When we assume the worst, we produce cortisol, our 'fight or flight' hormone, which isolates cells, short-circuits rational thinking and sends us into 'Chimp' survival mode. Our hearts race, our breathing becomes shallow and rapid, our muscles tense, lighter skin tones turn red. Those we are in conversation with will notice the changes and often mirror the same state of tension – which is why things can escalate into unhelpful situations very quickly.

Assuming the best releases our happy hormone serotonin which helps us stay optimistic and positive in our approach. Through a series of chemical reactions, this hormone helps create a connection between neighboring nerve cells and literally develops a positive 'train of thought', to help us think more creatively about possible solutions. This ability in the brain to create a positive train of thought is one reason why you can go to bed wrestling with a problem and wake up in the morning with the answer. The brain continues making these neural connections and pathways toward finding a solution as you think creatively and positively about possible outcomes.

One strategy to help with assuming the best is to move from a mindset of trying to allocate blame to reframing the issue. Instead of viewing the situation as negative and personal, reframe it as an opportunity to understand each other better and find creative solutions that work both sides. One way to put this into practice is to ask yourself 'What's good about this situation / relationship / person?'

> There's a story told of a salesman who messed up at work and lost a key client. Everyone expected the boss to hit the roof and fire him on the spot. To everyone's surprise and curiosity, the boss didn't say a word, went to his desk and started writing. When he finished, he went and spoke with the salesman, reviewed what had gone wrong and discussed how it would have to be compensated for. But contrary to what everyone expected, the salesman didn't get fired. As it turns out, despite the boss's fury, he made himself sit down and write a list of all the good the salesman had done for the company, which tempered how he turned up to address the mess up.

Assuming the best gives you a much healthier starting point for having a courageous conversation. It helps put you in the mindset to genuinely ask and discuss, instead of attack, complain or grumble. This means you are more likely to get a positive response than provoke a defensive one so that you can address issues from the same side, especially with the people who matter to you.

L – Listen to understand

In any conversation, but especially in a courageous one, a key strategy to implement for successful outcomes is to listen for understanding. Relationships get tested when things get tough. It's easy to be friendly and supportive when everything is plain sailing, but friendships and relationships get tested when our expectations are unmet, when we disappoint each other and

260 | The 4 Habits of all Successful Relationships

when we turn up 'ugly'. And we each have the potential to do that, especially where core values are being challenged. As we covered in chapter 7, these are the moments where we must listen for understanding not defense. It's worth saying it again – using the time the other person is talking just to reload and wait on a pause to get your point across is *not* listening. Remember *their* feelings and views are as legitimate as yours.

> **Courageous conversations are not about changing the other person but about genuinely hearing their story, sharing your story and problem solving together.**

We'll expand on the art of listening in chapter 13 and share a strategy for listening well. In the meantime, think about how you would like to be treated in a tense or conflict situation. The truth is most of us want to feel validated by at least being given the chance to share our story and be genuinely heard. Doing the same for others helps relieve at least some of the stress and tension.

M – Manage emotions

The final pillar of the C-A-L-M strategy is to be intentional about *managing emotions* during the conversation.

For many of us, the challenge with emotions is that we resist acknowledging them for as long as we possibly can, and then when we do, we try to justify how we're feeling through logical reasoning. So, for example, if we feel disappointed or angry, we try to discuss the facts that led to those feelings (e.g. the dishes are left piled up in the sink, again!) but our emotions leak out all over the conversation in judgement and character attacks ('you're so lazy and selfish, always taking me for granted and assuming I'll clean up after you!'). And this could be happening on both sides. That sabotages genuine listening and provokes a downward spiral of attack, defense and counter-attack.

Despite growing awareness of the importance of emotional intelligence and emotions as a valid source of data, far too many of us still struggle to talk about emotions. This is a big part of the reason why these conversations are so difficult. We are simultaneously trying to have a rational conversation while fighting to keep a lid on our own anger, upset, frustration and challenges to our self-worth. At the same time, we're also trying to deal with anxiety about how the other person might be responding emotionally as well.

The key is to acknowledge and address each of the bubbling cauldrons of emotion desperate for your attention.

Call them (the emotions) by name and evaluate what they are trying to tell you. Show yourself empathy for feeling them and then focus on the ASK you want to make.

With the best will in the world, you're only ever going to have control over your own emotions. However, by staying in control you can help the other person mirror your attempts to keep the conversation healthy. Here are a few suggestions that we have found particularly helpful over the years:

1. **Own your own feelings** – by using 'I' language rather than 'you' language – saying things like 'I was frustrated when' instead of 'you made me angry when'. Also, as much as possible, try to avoid using inflammatory words that exaggerate things (saying things like 'you always') or delivering threats through ultimatums (saying things like 'you need to do this or else ...').

2. **Affirm the other person as an individual** – even if you disagree with their behavior. This is about separating the issue from people's identity and sense of self-worth

– critiquing the *performance* not the *performer*. Andrea loves to share a great example of this that she witnessed in her team marketing business.

> *One of my mentors had a great style for managing emotions on both sides when addressing tricky issues – like if someone was lacking integrity or discretion or breaking trust in the team in some way. She would always address the issue head on but preface the conversation with her commitment. So, she would start with a statement like – 'I'm going to share something that will hit you between the eyes, but I'm here for you to pick you up and I know we will get through it'. Basically, what she was saying was 'watch out, this truth is going to sting but it doesn't change my commitment to you and my confidence that we will get through this together'.*

The simple truth – people 'hear better' when they feel affirmed, validated and respected. More on that when we look at Habit #4.

3. **Have a mantra** – it could be something you say to yourself when the temperature starts to rise – like 'this too will pass' or 'will it matter tomorrow?' Or it could be simply noticing when your body is moving into a heightened state of tension and stress, and then breathing, counting to 10 backwards and come back to the present by focusing on your goal and the behaviors you decided you would demonstrate through the process (remember your Ground Rules and Anger Management Strategy?).

In our experience, the above strategies will help you stay open to listening and finding positive ways forwards. But don't be disheartened if the conversation goes off the rails – where emotions go deep it might take a few goes to get it right. If things start to escalate, give yourself permission to create space or time out by going to get a coffee for example, but don't leave the other person hanging – agree when you'll come back to the conversation.

Practicing the above principles and techniques will help you make 'big ASKs' more successfully and build your SKILL in making Habit #3: ASK, don't assume, a natural part of your behavior in all your relationships.

Moving from assuming to ASKing

As we have learned first-hand, once you're clear on what's most important to you, and you're able to align your schedule with your life goals, you feel empowered to live life fully present and engaged. Moving from assuming to ASKing frees you from OPA's and OPO's – other people's agendas and other people's opinions. You know what you're about and have your own voice.

This is what allows you to create healthy relationships around you rather than unhealthy connections and dependencies. Sometimes you will have to challenge assumptions, prejudices and stereotypes that are no longer valid – in yourself and in others. Sometimes you will have to have courageous conversations around tough, deep-seated issues in order to develop deeper, more meaningful relationships of trust and respect. The better you become at ASKing rather than assuming, the more you are able to live authentically – making healthier choices about how to interact with the people around you and put healthier boundaries in place.

The more you can GET understanding of the core values and beliefs that drive your behaviors (and those of the people around you), the more you can BE understanding of other people's expectations and the more effectively you can manage your own.

But there is no shortcut. You have to go through the discipline of articulating your own values and life balance, and support those around you to do the same. Because when we get it wrong and trample on their values, or they trample on ours, you both end up making instant, huge withdrawals from Emotional Bank Accounts. Without clarity on values, you will feel the negative effects but might not understand why. And if you do that too often, you will ultimately kill the WILL to make the relationship work.

So, be patient with yourself and others, but keep talking and having courageous conversations until you get the balance that supports your wellbeing and productivity for the long haul. Mastering the art of ASKing well will allow you to draw closer to living the life you desire more of the time. It will make all of life breathe easier and help you know at the end of the day that you're climbing the 'right' ladder leaning against the 'right' wall.

Time for Reflection

Key Takeaways

- Investing the time to clarify our values helps us become intentional about designing and living the life we choose on purpose.

- When we get clear on our values, we can create healthy boundaries around the people and things that matter most to us, and develop a schedule to help us live out our values.

- We can have C-A-L-M courageous conversations around the things that matter when necessary by adopting the following strategy – **C**larifying goals, **A**ssuming the best, **L**istening to understand and **M**anaging emotions.

- Developing Habit #3: ASK, don't assume means learning *how* to make better ASKs of the people around us – and ourselves – so that we can build relationships of mutual trust and respect.

Building Your Understanding

1. Who do you need to have a courageous conversation with in order to make a Big ASK?

2. What is your goal?

3. What is your strategy for managing emotions – yours and theirs?

Taking Personal Action

1. If you haven't done so already, use the template worksheet in the Appendices to create the template schedule for your own ideal week. As you do so, start creating a list of the things you want to delegate or dump.

2. Ready to have some courageous conversations? Look back at the list you developed in chapter 9. If you are ready, choose a good time and invite (note we've deliberately used the word *invite* – don't make it feel like it's an instruction to them!) the relevant people to meet with you to discuss the support and/ or renegotiation of roles and responsibilities that will help you create a more sustainable work-life balance. If necessary, talk it over and practice with a friend first to build your confidence.

3. Using the worksheet in the Appendices, continue making a note of the things you plan to STOP / START / CONTINUE / CHANGE including at least one thing to help develop Habit #3: ASK, don't assume.

Habit #4

CONNECT, before you correct

Chapter Twelve

Connection and Belonging

*'We are relational beings at the core,
wired for connection.'*

Wired for connection

In the mid-1900s, Abraham Maslow, one of the fathers of modern-day psychology, identified a hierarchy of human needs for psychological health.[77] In it, he suggested, once our basic needs for food, shelter and security are met, our next most important need as human beings is for love and belonging, which we seek to satisfy through meaningful relationships. A number of studies have since gone on to show that this fundamental need for connection and belonging is so strong that it impacts our ability to achieve our potential in life.

Indeed, back in the late 1980s, long before wellbeing was a 'thing' as it is today, psychologist Professor Carol Ryff of the University of Wisconsin-Madison went on to demonstrate that relationships and connection are also vital for psychological health through her research on what it meant to live a good life. Based on a multidimensional investigation across medical science, philosophy and psychology, in 1989 Ryff developed her six-factor model for psychological wellbeing, contentment and happiness. This was one of the first thoroughly researched models of psychological wellbeing, and it continues to be used as a relevant and respected model for understanding wellbeing today. Unsurprisingly, *positive relationships with others* emerged as one of the six key factors, along with self-acceptance, autonomy, environmental mastery, purpose in life, and personal growth.[78] The jury was in ...

Our ability to connect with people and build warmth, trust and intimacy in our relationships is vital to our psychological health and wellbeing.

Despite the wealth of knowledge underscoring its importance however, it seems this need for human connection has been relegated to last place in our quest for progress in life. Longer work hours, longer travel times (as people move further afield to find jobs) and the shift from generational families to nuclear families or living in isolation, have all served to reduce the number and quality of human connections we are able to foster. And this has slowly been breaking us apart on the inside.

In January 2018, UK Prime Minister Theresa May appointed a 'Minister for Loneliness' to the Cabinet to address the increasing issue of loneliness and isolation. One might be forgiven for expecting the main target population to be the elderly but in fact, the data reveals that the epicenter for loneliness in the nation was and continues to be amongst the 16- to 24-year-olds – despite them being the most technologically savvy and electronically connected generation. That government appointment was swiftly followed by the appointment of a 'Minister for Suicide Prevention' in October 2018, with responsibility for addressing the increasing prevalence of suicide – again highest in the 16- to 24-year-old cohort – the group creating most cause for concern over increasing mental health issues.[79] This is echoed in the UNICEF report on teenage mental health. According to their data 'up to one in five adolescents will experience a mental disorder each year and self-harm is the third leading cause of death for adolescents'.[80]

Paradoxically, it would appear that the more technologically advanced our modern societies become, spanning time and space and making the world more geographically connected, the more disconnected we become as people. It has become abundantly clear that just being around each other, physically present or tethered through technology, is not sufficient for creating emotional connection or meaningful relationships. In fact, the busyness and distractions of technology have made the need to be intentional about building relationships and connection even more essential. Yet somehow, we've never made this a particular priority – as individuals, as organizations, or as societies. In our modern lives of hype and speed, we've become much more focused on self-centered transactions (what can I get?) rather than on relationships (what can I give?). We spend more time telling people where they fall short and need to improve but feel awkward communicating how much we love, value and appreciate them as they are.

The impact of COVID-19

The COVID-19 pandemic took us back to basics. As the world stood vulnerable and exposed to the deadly virus, many of us rediscovered in an instant the power and resilience that comes from connecting human-to-human in caring, compassionate and meaningful ways. As the pandemic shook the foundations of everything we thought important, we were reminded that what mattered most to each of us was the health and safety of the important people in our lives and our ability to stay connected with them. Pictures of high-end branded leather goods developing mold in empty department stores told a powerful story. It was apparent that in the fierce battle for survival against the pandemic, nobody cared about 'stuff'. All the things people used to clamor for in life and exhaust themselves trying to achieve quickly became insignificant, in the context of keeping lives and loved ones alive and healthy. Relationships mattered again.

This time we used technology to connect in meaningful ways. Whether located together or connecting over distance, as families or organizational teams, we drew emotional strength and comfort from each other as we confronted our fears together and lifted each other's spirits.

In our family we used Zoom, WhatsApp and FaceTime calls to keep in touch and give mutual support with family, friends and colleagues all over the world. The technology helped us support each other through tough times and also allowed us to keep the fun alive. We held online birthday celebrations, learned a family dance together with a professional choreographer and just kept each other company and enjoyed casual conversation – like hanging out together as we wrapped Christmas presents, despite being separated by the Atlantic Ocean.

Some of the hardest battles people faced in the pandemic were around being isolated from loved ones and having to depend on others to be their proxy of emotional support as loved ones breathed their last breath. Much of the mental health concern – especially in the teenage and young adult population – was not because of the lack of entertainment or information, but due to feelings of isolation and lack of human connection. The pandemic forced us to rediscover the simple truth of humanity:

We are relational beings at the core, wired for connection.

Through the multitude of webinars and workshops we ran over the course of the year, the message came through time and time again – building strong, connected relationships is not just a feel-good, 'nice to have' option, it's vital for our very wellbeing and survival. This is why learning to develop Habit #4: CONNECT, before you correct, is fundamental for building great relationships. It's about developing the SKILL to build great rapport, warmth and connection in relationships by being more intentional about communicating love, value and appreciation in meaningful ways, instead of always being poised with 'constructive feedback'. It's about prioritizing genuine connections with people above the need to correct them.

The pandemic highlighted the simple reality that we need meaningful connection for relationships to flourish. Without that sense of connection and belonging – a need which is hard-wired in each of us – relationships will disintegrate. As the saying goes, 'people go where they feel welcomed but stay where they feel valued'. And that's as true with work relationships as it is at home. Importantly, as well as motivating people to stay in the relationship, communicating value, appreciation and love in meaningful ways are also vital for fostering healthy thinking and mental wellbeing in the individuals we care about.

Healthy emotional connections lead to healthy thinking

Meaningful relationships with genuine human-to-human connections help create the emotional health we all need to deal with the challenges and negative experiences in life. In addition to dealing with tragedies which affect us all, daily life can feel like a battlefield of sustained attacks on our mind and mental health. From the critical voice inside our heads, to the bombardment of social media marketing 'perfection', to the harsh realities of inequity, racism and injustice, our self-confidence and self-esteem are constantly being undermined.

The love, value and appreciation communicated to us by the people who matter in our lives help keep our confidence high and our thoughts positive as we combat these daily attacks on our sense of self. Building genuine connections and a sense of belonging in relationships are crucial for developing the mental stamina to reject the thoughts that could otherwise destroy us. The stronger our sense of self through connection and belonging, the more we are empowered to consciously reboot and choose a new mental script when the world around us treats us in emotionally crippling ways.

Nowhere is this more relevant than it is for our young people, who have become the most emotionally vulnerable generation.

274 | The 4 Habits of all Successful Relationships

One of the keys to helping build their resilience and mental health is to stay emotionally connected with them through the teen years. This is one compelling reason for getting better at relationships as parents and couples. Teens need their parents to be emotionally resilient and connected at a time when their own emotions and behavior can be the most challenging. This is such an important point that if you have (or will have) teens yourself or spend any amount of time interacting with young people, it's worth taking a couple of minutes to share a high-level summary of what goes on in the teen brain and why 'connecting *before* correcting' is especially important in those relationships.

The teen brain under construction

As anyone who's ever lived or worked with teens would agree, the teenage years can be volatile! Have you ever had one of those moments when you say something to a teen that you think is completely innocent and simple, only to meet with raging anger or floods of tears?

> We've been blindsided by responses which seem to come from nowhere. A simple question like 'Do you want baked beans on toast for breakfast?' could produce angry or tearful responses – 'Why on earth would I want that?', or 'You just don't understand me, do you?', or 'Why don't you ever listen?'

In the middle of feeling stunned, or disrespected, what you say next determines the level of stress and emotional disconnection in the relationship for hours . . . or maybe even days. And if you get it wrong repeatedly, it could affect the relationship for years, creating distance and sometimes premature departure from the family home.

Here's what's really going on. Psychological research has shown that while our brains have generally reached their maximum physical size by age 14 (in boys, 11 in girls), fairly major structural development and reorganization continues through to our mid- to late-twenties, with further smaller changes continuing throughout life. As one writer put it, what that means is 'The brain of a teenager is undergoing massive restructuring – a bit like a house being rewired'.[81] It turns out, as their bodies grow and mature, teenage brains are literally under construction too!

Much of the 'construction work' is being done in the frontal lobe – the part of the brain dedicated to reasoning. With the frontal lobe basically out of action, teens are forced to do more thinking with the limbic system – the part of the brain normally responsible for emotions. As we discussed in chapter 6, the limbic includes our 'fight, flight or freeze' center which is wired for self-preservation and comes out fighting at the least sense of threat or danger. This is why sometimes teens do things that provoke the response from us 'What on earth were you . . . thinking?!' And now you know – they really weren't thinking rationally at all.

And that's why seemingly simple, innocuous comments and conversations can quickly descend into anger, tears or both. It's also why teen emotions can turn up in such extremes – elated or depressed, 'full of beans' or exhausted. Add to that the fact that the internet allows them to be such an informed generation – they can sound so knowledgeable and oftentimes know more than us about stuff – that we get tricked into thinking they are sufficiently equipped to have adult conversations. But they are not. Without wishing to patronize them, the reality is that thanks to Alexa, Siri and Google, they are informed and up-to-date about a whole lot of things that sadly their brains are not yet ready to process fully. If you can get them to agree to that statement though, you've done exceptionally well!

In this phase of being part adult, part child, they can easily feel misunderstood or overwhelmed and many times words and attitudes come tumbling out wrong in ways that surprise and frighten them. And often they don't know how to come back from that. But this is where being able to remain constant in affirming their value and worth as individuals even when they are getting some things wrong becomes vitally important. We have found that sometimes we have to give ourselves a 'time-out' so that we don't end up throwing our own tantrum and creating real hurt, anger and distance in the relationship.

Lessons for successful parenting

Developing our own Relational Intelligence and our ability to stay constant and consistent in communicating value and appreciation even when someone gets 'ugly' is crucial for developing strong emotional connections. And this is not just for relationships with teens – adults can challenge us in similar ways too, especially when we expect more from their age and level of seniority / experience.

The challenge is that most of us have more urgency around telling people in general – and our kids in particular – where they need to improve rather than making sure we create and maintain an emotional connection with them. As 26th American President Theodore Roosevelt Jr., leader of the reform movement in his day, is reputed to have said: *'People don't care how much you know, until they know how much you care.'*

Genuine connection earns you the permission to have a voice of relevance and influence in someone's life.

This helps explain why some managers struggle with effective feedback sessions – constructive feedback around performance tends to land flat where there is no sense of care and connection.

But for us, the message really came alive in the area of parenting. Focusing on maintaining strong emotional connections (through communicating value) has been one of the most important lessons in our parenting journey – especially through the teen years and into young adulthood – as Andrea shares below . . .

It's so easy to get into a cycle of constant 'telling off' with our teens – the state of their room, their version of time keeping, money choices they're making – I'm sure we are not alone in this! As parents we all have the good intention of one day delivering our teens as trustworthy adults into the working world.

But overdosing on the corrections at a time when they are already questioning their self-worth can be crippling . . . so we have learned (and continue to learn) to choose our battles.

Most times we get it right, sometimes we get it wrong and sometimes we have to have the courage to stand our ground and say 'no', trusting that the connection is stronger than the disappointment – even through the sting of hearing 'I can't wait till I'm at university and I won't have to do what you say anymore!' As if . . .

More than ever, what teenagers need is the assurance of their parent figures being there as their 'predictably safe space' – willing to forgive and help them get back on track – while they go through these emotionally confusing years. It's about intentionally building the connection and through that, maintaining a stronger voice of influence in their lives than their peers or the pull of social media and the internet.

And although we have used teens as the example, we have found that the message is powerfully relevant for the entire age spectrum. Strong relationships are built through developing great rapport and emotional connection, which creates an environment where people feel safe, free to be themselves and accepted, loved and valued for who they are, not just what they do. This is the foundation of *psychological safety* – the absence of interpersonal fear.

Lack of strong emotional connections also sit at the heart of the challenges of achieving genuine inclusion and belonging being faced in the corporate world and in society – more on that in chapters 15 and 16. But this is the power of Habit #4. By developing the SKILL to build strong connections with the people around us, we help to anchor them in their self-esteem and sense of belonging so they can bring the best of who they are to our relationships with them and still feel safe when they get things wrong, as we all do from time to time. By tilting the balance toward communicating love, value and appreciation, we arm them with the positive emotions and resilience to counter the things that would otherwise tear them down.

So, the question then is what creates emotional connection? To answer this, let's return to the concept of the Emotional Bank Account for a moment.

Connection through deposits in the Emotional Bank Account

As we covered back in chapter 1, when someone says or does something that lands well with us, it becomes a deposit in our Emotional Bank Account. And as long as nothing happens to completely drain our Emotional Bank Account, the more deposits there are, the more open we are to engaging in the relationship and creating good rapport and connection.

But what's really interesting is that, for all our individual uniqueness as human beings, there is a very common and consistent theme that runs through the things that we all need if we are to feel valued, respected and appreciated.

One of the small-group exercises we use in our workshops to make this point is around identifying the things that 'land' as deposits in people's Emotional Bank Accounts – by discussing what makes them *feel respected* and what makes them *feel disrespected*.

Without fail, participants' responses around what makes them feel valued and respected include some version of:

- My ideas are acknowledged, and opinions are considered

- I am listened to

- I am invited to contribute

- I am approached for help

- I am given praise / recognition for what I do

- I am treated the same as everyone else

- I am given feedback

- I am made to feel like I count

In most cases, feelings of being unvalued or disrespected were created by the reverse actions, with the following specifics mentioned:

- I am talked over / interrupted

- I am not listened to / heard

- My requests are not taken seriously

- My ideas / suggestions are ignored

- I receive unconstructive feedback

- They don't respect my boundaries

- I am micromanaged / not trusted to do things

- I feel like I am being insulted on purpose

- I don't get praise

- My manager has no time for me

The first observation from these lists is that you don't need special education or a degree to do the things that communicate value and respect. But you do need to be intentional. Doing more of the things that make people feel valued and respected consistently, is what will help you build strong rapport and connection – with adults and with children.

Equally unsurprising, the second observation is that there is a prevalent theme around the need to be genuinely listened to / heard / given a voice, in order to feel valued and respected. The simple truth is that we all feel validated through being heard and listened to, and share the same frustration and crippling sense of exclusion when we are not heard. (And if listening is on your list of key SKILLs to develop, look out for the model we'll be sharing in the next chapter.)

For the third observation – and this is where things stop being so obvious – it turns out that the specific ways in which people feel valued and respected can be different for each individual. By the same token negative things also impact people differently – for example 'I don't get praise' was the worst for some, whereas for others it was 'my manager has no time for me'. This is a crucial theme to explore because developing genuine connection means learning how to communicate value and appreciation in ways that are specific and meaningful to each individual. We will cover that more in the next chapter when we discuss the 5 Love Languages and the 5 Languages of Appreciation.

Before moving on to practical ways to connect with each individual though, it's worth taking a look at where far too many of us have been going wrong.

Where we've been getting it wrong . . .

While it might seem like an exercise in semantics, a big part of failed connection in relationships comes down to the false assumption that Recognition and Appreciation are one and the same thing. They are not.

The distinction is probably more obvious in a work context, so let's start there – although it is often confused there too.

Recognition and Appreciation share the same intent – to communicate a positive message to the recipient. However, they achieve different results because they come at it from different view-points:

- Recognition is about acknowledging a job well done.

- Appreciation, on the other hand, is about valuing a person for who they are.

Going further, recognition is both conditional and backward looking. You only get it if you have done a good job. It is also a limited resource conveyed by a restricted group. You can quickly see how recognizing *everyone* would water down the effect, and that the recognition can only really come from 'the powers that be'.

Appreciation, on the other hand, is unconditional and time independent. You get it because you're a great person (and that's not likely to change) regardless of your recent performance. And the really great news is that your receiving it doesn't mean someone else has to miss out – everyone can be appreciated at the same time and by anyone, without it watering down the effect.

Where relationships are concerned though, the impact is different – recognition feeds ego, whereas appreciation feeds self-esteem.

Societies, companies, and families that have focused more on recognition than appreciation tend to end up with a culture of worth based on what people *do* rather than who they *are* – and a spirit of competition and one-upmanship that often goes with that. The danger of course, is that by focusing on value based on 'production', we undermine people's resilience and ability to bounce back from the blows of life that reduce what they can do, or when they do wrong, or when others seem more successful than them.

For long-term successful relationships, it's vital that we understand the difference between *recognition* and *appreciation*, and work to build self-confidence and self-esteem in the people who matter to us.

And we do that by letting them know we value and appreciate them for who they are, rather than for what they did or achieved.

In one corporate survey around employee engagement, 51 percent of managers felt they were doing a good job of recognizing their people. But when their team members were surveyed, only 17 percent said they felt valued and appreciated.[82] That is, over half of the managers thought they were doing well, but less than 1 in 5 of the employees agreed. Not great!

When it comes to communicating value and appreciation, the big question we all should be asking is not 'Do you appreciate the people around you?', but 'Do *they* feel appreciated?'

Understanding this can be the difference between employees staying or leaving jobs, partners staying or leaving couple relationships, or children having strong self-esteem or being left feeling vulnerable to attention from the wrong crowd.

Showing appreciation and recognition in meaningful ways to the significant people around us is a powerful way of making huge deposits in their Emotional Bank Account. It's also vital for fostering healthy thinking and maintaining positive emotional health.

And remember, *not* showing appreciation over time can be as unhealthy as showing disrespect, because it can trigger the same negative thoughts and downward emotional spiral.

Most organizations tend to talk about showing appreciation and recognition as a means of motivating employees to work but getting them right has the potential to do so much more than that. Leaving people feeling appreciated also has the power to foster and encourage strong emotional health which, these days, is a matter of life and death.

However, we can't show appreciation in a meaningful way unless we know people specifically and identify what makes them 'tick'. That will be the focus for the next chapter.

Time for Reflection

Key Takeaways

- Us human beings are 'wired' for connection and thrive on developing meaningful relationships.

- When we *feel* valued, loved and like we belong, we are empowered to be the best version of ourselves and achieve our true potential.

- We need to become more intentional about connecting with people than correcting them.

- Recognition is about a job well done; appreciation is valuing who you are.

Building Your Understanding

1. Who do you need to invest more time connecting with, so they know how much they are loved, valued and appreciated?

2. Who can you connect with more to help them ward off feelings of loneliness, isolation and negative thoughts?

3. Who do you need to connect with to deal with your own feelings of loneliness, isolation and negative thoughts?

4. Where do you need to redress the balance and do more connecting than correcting?

5. How will this understanding of the difference between recognition and appreciation influence how you communicate value going forward?

Taking Personal Action

Connect with someone you enjoy spending time with and/ or haven't been in touch with for a while – make a call, arrange a meet-up or virtual coffee time . . . and just enjoy building warmth and connection.

Chapter Thirteen

Getting better at connecting

'Giving attention says "you matter" in neon lights.'

Way back in chapter 2, we shared Sanjay and Deepti's story. As a quick reminder, Sanjay was the guy who said:

I know I need to get better at communicating. I just don't know what to do.

As we shared with him, to get better at 'communication', he was going to have to learn The 4 Habits®. The journey to success would definitely involve him learning to minimize the unintentional withdrawals he kept making from Deepti's Emotional Bank Account, and developing habits that made deposits on purpose.

In this section, we will explain two practical models that we shared with Sanjay, that you too can roll out any time you want to make deposits on purpose. The first is showing respect through implementing the principles of listening well. The second is communicating love, value and appreciation in practical ways that are specific and meaningful to each individual.

Both models will allow you to be on purpose about developing deeper, richer, more meaningful relationships with warmth, rapport and emotional connection. Both will help you develop the SKILL to make Habit #4: CONNECT before you correct, your default behavior.

Listening with both E-A-R-S!

If you've been following through chapter by chapter, by now you'll be fully aware that although we are each 'wired' differently and feel valued and appreciated in different ways, some things are core to the human experience. The need to be treated with dignity and respect is one of them. Anything less can be soul destroying.

And as the feedback from any number of workshops we have run confirms, one of the main ways in which many of us fail to treat people with the dignity and respect they would like, is that we don't listen well. On the flip side, when we take the time to *genuinely listen* to people, we leave them feeling heard, validated and like they matter. Intuitively most of us get that, but sometimes in the middle of a conversation or heated debate, it seems we forget the fundamentals.

Whether you believe we were designed or we evolved to be this way, the ratio of two ears and one mouth seems deliberate. Our experience is that success in relationships comes from engaging them in that 2:1 ratio! We developed the E-A-R-S acronym to help us anchor the principles of good listening and as a useful *aide-memoire* for listening well in the moment – listening with both E-A-R-S as it were! We hope you find it as helpful as we have.

E – Empathy

As we started discussing in chapter 7, many of us are guilty of poor listening. If we're being honest, often we're only really listening for a pause to get our voice heard rather than listening with genuine care and empathy to understand what is actually being said. Our tone, body language and reactions betray the fact that we have already passed judgement and are just biding time to give our verdict. Empathy is the ability to understand and relate to what people are going through and genuinely engage in their story, *without judgement*.

At its core, empathy is about really listening to what is being said *and* to the emotions behind that. We spoke earlier (in chapter 11) about the importance of being proactive in *managing emotions* as part of the C-A-L-M strategy for having courageous conversations. Showing empathy is very helpful there. It's about letting the moment be about the other person, their opinions and concerns, not about you – which is quite often very tough. It's not about excusing behavior, but it is about walking in another person's shoes, and treating them with care, knowing this could be your story.

One thing most of us can do better at in our relationships, is to develop real empathy by listening with genuine care for how people are experiencing things.

Being willing to share your own vulnerability is another important aspect of empathy. In our experience, people are more willing to open up and talk heart-to-heart when we share our own stories of times we had similar experiences, fears or concerns we have had, or even when we got things wrong. The truth is we all have challenges and make mistakes and go through 'stuff'. Being willing to share those moments with others going through the similar challenges builds a bridge of connection. As Brené Brown, research professor, podcast host and author of five number-one *New York Times* bestselling books on the topics of courage, vulnerability, shame and empathy, puts it 'vulnerability is the birthplace of connection'.[83] The more we share of our inner world – our thoughts and feelings and dreams – as appropriate – the more connected we feel with each other.

A – Attention

Often, all most of us really want is to 'feel heard' fully without judgement or interruptions. Many arguments could be short-lived if people *felt* truly heard.

The reality though, is that in the busyness of life, time is a precious commodity and our default is to short-circuit conversations with poor listening habits. In our rush to get on to the next thing, heavily influenced by our presumptions about our own opinions being 'right', many of us jump to conclusions quickly, based on our own biases, experiences and interpretations of what we *think* we have heard – and then offer solutions prematurely. On top of that, the very distracted world that we live in makes it all too easy to succumb to the ping of a text message, or other alert, on our various electronic devices.

Yet, few things communicate value and appreciation as powerfully as 'being fully present' and 'giving undivided attention', even if just for a few minutes. Giving attention says 'you matter' in neon lights. And if you genuinely can't give your attention at the moment, a caring approach would be to agree to get back to them at a time in the not-too-distant future by saying something like – 'this is really important and I want to hear more, can we discuss it for five minutes now and then have a proper chat about it at . . .' then set a time and stick to it.

One of the most memorable experiences we have of the power of listening well came from a workshop activity we ran, where participants worked in pairs to practice their listening skills. For the activity, one person spoke for 10 minutes with the other person listening, using encouragers like nods and 'mmhmms' but without interruption, and then swapping roles.

The exercise was simple enough, but the feedback proved it was hugely impactful. Those describing their experience of being 'the listener' often reported how they felt challenged not to jump in with their own story and opinion, to resist the urge to 'reload' and give a response, and to stay focused on the other person for the whole 10 minutes. This ability to focus in and just listen is an art to rediscover in itself. There was a notable sense of pleasure around the experience of being listened to. One manager in particular was visibly holding back the tears. She described how valued and significant she felt, just by having the luxury of someone listening to her share her story, uninterrupted, for 10 whole minutes.

The simple conclusion – we each have the power to connect with people in far more meaningful ways just by developing our ability to give undivided attention.

Listening with attention works because it allows you to take the spotlight off yourself for a moment and shine it on someone else. Without any words being used, that simple act delivers the powerful message – 'I see you, not just your physical presence but the essence of who you are . . . and you matter.'

Of course, paying attention involves great body language like facing the person, uncrossing arms and making eye contact. However, the caveat is that cultural or other differences might influence what great body language looks like and of course, there is no shortcut for knowing what lands well with each individual. Numerous research studies have concluded that women in general prefer being face-to-face with eye contact while men prefer being side-by-side, because full-on face contact feels confrontational.[84] Again, while there will always be exceptions, the key point to bear in mind is that different people might need different body language to feel at ease and ready to engage on a deeper level.

The other point about body language is to look for congruence between what is being said (actual words), how it is being said (tone and volume) and the body language on display. As you know, if someone says 'I'm fine' with crossed arms and a brusque tone, without a doubt they are feeling anything but fine! When words and body language contradict each other, body language will speak more truth than the actual words. To help keep the focus and attention on the other person and listen to what is being said, it's helpful to use encouragers like nodding to signal to them to keep going, verbal cues like 'mmhmm', 'yes . . .' or 'tell me more' often work well.

Asking questions for clarification or expansion such as 'meaning . . . ?' or 'help me understand . . .' are also useful practices to get to the core of the issue. In his book *The Coaching Habit*,[85] author Michael Bungay Stanier identifies seven great questions for running effective coaching sessions. We have found his second question 'And what else . . . ?' is a brilliant way of making space to help people unpack *the issue behind the issue*. Quite often the things said first are not the things people really want to talk about. They are just the issues that are easier to voice without feeling too vulnerable. Asking 'And what else . . . ?' what Stanier calls the *AWE* question, helps create the space and encouragement for deeper issues to be voiced. But you can only get to that level of connection if you give your full attention to everything being communicated through both verbal and non-verbal cues.

In so many ways, we listen with our eyes as well as our ears.

R – Respect

We've said it before, but the point remains – most people are super alert to disrespect. Respect is one of those words that is hard to define but is powerfully recognized and experienced in the moment, based on the way we are being treated. When we are treated with respect, we generally feel elevated and affirmed. When we are treated with disrespect, we often feel crushed and invalidated, and it can provoke intense anger.

Listening with respect communicates to others that they have a right to their own thoughts and opinions, even if you don't share them.

Listening with respect means saying *yes* to someone as a person even when you're saying *no* to their ideas.

It also means giving them the right to make mistakes, because we all make mistakes. This is a fine but necessary line to tread in general, but especially so with teens for the reasons we outlined in the previous chapter.

One of the ways we implemented listening with respect in our household was to implement the strategy of a 'safe chair', especially when our children were young. Anyone sitting on that chair could express exactly how they felt and say anything they wanted to say without fear of being in trouble for being rude or disrespectful. This was also a practical way of not interrupting or cutting across them when they were struggling to express their feelings.

Now that they are older and better able to stand their own ground, the physical chair isn't used anymore but the expectation of being able to be fully heard and not interrupted is still there. This requires a lot of patience from us at times, especially when it feels like a never-ending monologue, but the opportunity this creates for genuine connection and getting to the heart of the matter makes it worthwhile. Does it work like clockwork every time? No. But by overcoming the temptation to patronize, belittle or berate in those times, time and again we have literally watched tensions drain and openness build through them feeling validated and heard as a result of our decision to listen with respect.

S – Summarize

A good habit to form as part of developing strong listening skills is to listen with the intent of being able to summarize and play back what you have heard.

This is not about interpreting, responding, solving or giving your opinion on what has been said. It is simply saying what you have heard in your own words to confirm that you have heard and understood the issue *as they see it*, as simply and succinctly as possible. Only then are you qualified to give an informed response. Sometimes, no response is needed at all. Sometimes all that is needed is the reassurance of being heard, respected, cared for and validated through genuine listening. Many arguments dissolve at this stage because people recognize a clear misunderstanding of words and/or intent.

Another great coaching question from Stanier's *The Coaching Habit* to ask at this point is 'How can I help . . . ?' Rather than trying to take on the world and solve everybody's issues, this question allows you to empower people to say what they want and need, and to discuss how you can help make that happen.

Now, for many of us, learning to genuinely listen with empathy, attention and respect, and to summarize before offering our opinion, takes unlearning old habits and learning these new behaviors. But in order to build real rapport, connection and feelings of value and appreciation in relationships, these are the skills not just to learn, but to master.

As we said at the opening of this chapter, to build connection, in addition to listening well, we also need to become proactive in saying and doing the things that communicate value, appreciation and love to the people around us in specific ways that mean something to each of them. One of the most powerful models we have seen for learning to build strong emotional connection is the concept of the 5 Languages of Appreciation (in the workplace), or the 5 Love Languages (in the home). The concept is so powerful that we highly recommend you take the time to get and read at least one of the books, but meanwhile, here's a quick overview.

Building Connection *on purpose*

The concept of *The 5 Love Languages*[86] was developed by Dr Gary Chapman almost three decades ago and continues to have a profound impact on the level of warmth and connection created in relationships across the globe. In 2011, together with Paul White, he developed the corporate version – *The 5 Languages of Appreciation in the Workplace*[87] – but, for the most part, the principles are the same.[88]

The key point is this – we all feel most loved / valued / special / appreciated in one or more of five different ways. When others 'speak' our Love Language to us, interactions land very well and major deposits are made in our Emotional Bank Account. This is a simple but powerful concept which provides very practical ways for being intentional about connecting with people and communicating love, value and appreciation in ways that are meaningful to them.

Building connection and warmth in relationships is very much about understanding what lands powerfully for each individual. In our workshop exercises, quite often one person will mention some version of feeling valued and respected when someone says 'thank you' while another comments that saying thank you *too often* sounds patronizing and for them, has the reverse effect. How is it possible that two people can view the same thing so differently? The answer lies in understanding the 5 Languages of Love / Appreciation.

We highly recommend that you get hold of one of Gary Chapman's books and check out his website www.the5lovelanguages.com to complete an online assessment and discover your own Love / Appreciation Language. Meanwhile, from a 30,000 ft view, they look like this . . .

- **Words of Affirmation** – For some people, words are literally the wind beneath their wings. They feel most loved, valued or appreciated when they receive *verbal praise* and compliments. In the workshops we run, these are the people who say they feel valued and appreciated when others say 'thank you' for something they've done, or when they are being complimented and recognized for their contribution.

- **Acts of Service** – Then there's a group of people for whom actions definitely speak louder than words. Chapman describes their Love Language as Acts of Service. These people feel really special when you *do things* for them out of appreciation, but not out of duty – like rolling up your sleeves and coming alongside a colleague who is working late to meet a deadline, or jumping in to help your partner do a task or chore that they're responsible for. For them, verbal encouragement just won't do it, and might even sound patronizing. These people feel loved when you actually DO thoughtful things for them.

- **Quality Time** – For others Love and Appreciation are spelt: T-I-M-E. True, to some degree, we all value and enjoy spending time with people we like, but for Quality Time people, *undivided attention* is love's loudest language. Being 'fully present' and undistracted by phone, laptop or other technology is super important for people who have Quality Time as their primary Love / Appreciation Language. As much as possible, never cancel a meeting with a Quality Time person and if you do need to cancel, be sure to rebook straight away. As with all the Love / Appreciation Languages, doing the reverse means you risk delivering a much more powerful *negative* message than you might imagine.

- **Gifts** – Then there are some people who feel most valued or appreciated when they receive a gift from you. Be careful not to confuse this with consumerism – this has nothing to do with the value of the gift. It could be that you simply picked a flower for them or picked up a cup of their favorite brew of coffee on your way to meet them. For them, the gift is a *tangible expression* of your love, appreciation or value.

- **Physical Touch** – For others still, physical touch is their most powerful Love / Appreciation Language. These are the natural huggers among us, and they tend to gesticulate a lot. While speaking with you, a Touch person might touch you on the arm, or if they're seated next to you on the knee or the thigh . . . but to be clear, this has absolutely nothing to do with sexual touch! In a work context, these will be the people who will want to high-five, or fist-bump or pat on the back to mark success. It goes without saying that this language is potentially the most problematic to get right in a work context . . . but don't lose the humanity. The fact that it can be tricky to show, doesn't negate the importance of Touch as a powerful and essential language for communicating value and appreciation to some people, even in the workplace.

The challenge is we generally only speak our own language(s), so when we come across someone who speaks a different language, we struggle to communicate love, value and appreciation in a way that lands powerfully with them. If you remember back to our workshop delegates' lists on feeling respected and disrespected in the previous chapter, there were comments around feeling respected when given praise, recognition and feedback and feeling disrespected when there was no praise or managers had no time. These are classic examples of how important it is to speak the specific language of appreciation that means something to each individual. Not understanding their language of appreciation means that efforts go unnoticed, and people are left feeling unvalued, unappreciated and disrespected to some degree.

Learning what speaks love and appreciation the loudest to each person – your team member, your boss, partner, child, parents, friends – helps to build emotional connection on purpose with minimum effort and prevents people being hurt or emotionally closed because they don't feel valued or appreciated in the way *they* need to experience it the most.

As Chapman points out, one key way to know someone's Love Language is simply to observe what they do. If they give lots of praise, they are probably most alert to Words of Affirmation; if they are doers, they probably feel most valued through Acts of Service and so on. But this also explains how we can emotionally 'miss' each other as couples, families, friends or colleagues. Basically, we exhaust ourselves trying to communicate love, value and appreciation in a way that means something to us . . . but often doesn't even register on their radar. In other words, when their Love Language is in our 'blind spot', all our efforts, though well intentioned, disappear down a 'black hole'.

Building Connection in practice

Understanding the principles of the Love and Appreciation Languages provides powerful and practical ways for making deposits in Emotional Bank Accounts and building warmth and connection in relationships.

> *As if it was meant to teach us this lesson first-hand, we have all five of the Love Languages covered in our family! Andrea is very much a Words person, closely followed by Touch. Jon is big on Quality Time and Acts of Service. Our eldest definitely has Gifts as his primary Love Language and our youngest is Quality Time and Touch. Knowing this helps us be creative and consistent in showing love and reinforcing the message of value and appreciation to each other.*

We have found five important ways to implement this understanding of Love Languages and share some stories below to help bring them alive:

1. Create memorable experiences and bonding times

> *Understanding Love Languages has helped us make special occasions really special for each person as well as prompted us with ideas of how to show love spontaneously 'just because'. For example, knowing that both Quality Time and Acts of Service are important to Jon, to help make his birthday celebrations during COVID-19 lockdown a memorable experience, we created our own home-baked scones, brownies and sandwiches and delivered a 'champagne afternoon tea' family experience in our dining room. Knowing Kind Words are the key to Andrea's heart, Jon makes sure that any gift on a special occasion is accompanied by a purposefully selected card with appropriate words and includes his own words as well. Every now and again he surprises her with a love note stuck on her computer, in the car, on the bathroom mirror and so on just*

to bring a smile and make deposits in her Emotional Bank Account on purpose.

This knowledge also helps us be deliberate about creating moments of bonding time. Consistent with the Love Language of Gifts, our eldest just loves shopping and browsing in stores. Instead of fussing, asking 'How much longer?' and rushing him in frustration, we now know what to expect and as much as possible make any trip to a store with him – even the supermarket – more of an experience, with time to browse the aisles, get a coffee and enjoy the moment together. In addition to the bonding time, it creates a real opportunity for meaningful heart-to-heart conversations – rare moments to be engineered and grasped to stay connected with university students. Our youngest generally prefers to be home playing on the computer, but offering to be involved in anything he is doing – like helping him brush our pet guinea pigs and clean their cage – magically opens up some very 'interesting' conversations about what is going on in his teenage world! It's about connecting, not just conversing.

2. Redress the balance in the Emotional Bank Account

Sometimes we need to lean heavily on each other for support and understanding, which over sustained periods can drain Emotional Bank Accounts. For example, working in high-pressure jobs which involve being away a lot through long hours and/or travel as Jon and I did at different times, often meant that we missed home events and needed the other person to pick up our slack. With the best will in the world and despite understanding the logic, this can still be emotionally draining and make huge withdrawals from the Emotional Bank Account of the person covering for you. However, being intentional about speaking their Love Language can help you feed their Emotional Bank Account both remotely and when you are back home. For example, one couple we know – where the husband is on the road 80 percent of the time – have developed a habit of scheduling in time for unhurried video calls at the end of the day to keep each other company and catch up on the day's events – just like they would do if they were sat in the kitchen together. Their Love Languages are Words and Quality Time so making the effort to 'speak' their Love Languages despite the distance helps keep them warm and connected, combatting the strain distance and travel placed on their relationship. They also make a habit of carving out alone-time as a couple when the husband is home, often disappearing for the weekend at short notice. This helps make deposits that counteract the inevitable strain on relationships caused by extended periods apart.

It works in the office as well. If you haven't been around much and your colleague has had to bear the load in your absence, just pausing to show appreciation in a meaningful way to them will make a world of difference and pour credit into their Emotional Bank Account. Without doing things that make them feel valued and appreciated, the imbalance can cause them to feel unappreciated and taken for granted. When this happens, it is not uncommon for people to hide behind excuses and logical reasons for not being able to help out when the real issue is that their Emotional Bank Account has been drained. Taking the time to communicate value to someone through speaking their Love Language can help redress the 'balance' in their Emotional Bank Account, smooth many knots in the relationship and help things get back on track.

3. Avoid unintentional hurt

One example that comes straight to mind was when Andrea asked Jon to help find an earpiece for hands-free calling in the car. Here's the story as Andrea recounts it . . .

I asked Jon to help me find a good earpiece to be able to use my phone hands-free in the car because the laws were about to change. The car I was driving was already about 16 years old and soon to be replaced, and the in-car system no longer worked. It never dawned on me that there was anything special going on when Jon said the car needed to go into the garage one day, because he usually takes care of all things mechanical in our household. When he got back, he asked me to come out to the car to have a look at something. As I climbed in, I noticed a satin red ribbon across the center console and a brand-new 'all singing, all dancing' in-car system installed and ready to connect with my phone!

Now, had I not understood Love Languages . . . and that Acts of Service was one of the ways Jon says 'I love you', I could have gotten this badly wrong. My head was saying, 'What's the point! This system probably cost more than the car itself and isn't worth the money! All I wanted was a simple earpiece.' But my heart heard him saying 'I love you' in a Language very powerful to him. Thankfully, this knowledge helped guide my response from the heart rather than the head. As a result, we were both able to enjoy the giving and receiving of the 'I love you' message through Acts of Service. Had I not understood what was going on though, the outcome could have been very different. I would have been frustrated by finances and he would have been deeply hurt by rejected shows of affection.

Over the years we've also learned how *not* valuing a Love Language, just because it felt foreign to us, could create huge hurt and disappointment.

From when our eldest was about three or four years old, whenever either of us was going out without him, he would hurriedly grab a piece of paper and draw a heart or something, or pick up some other small random object around the house, and give it to us to keep to remember him until we got back home. We recognized that for him, a tangible gift was his way to show love and appreciation but never thought to make a fuss over gifts for him.

We learnt the hard way that ignoring requests on a birthday or Christmas 'wish list' goes deep, because it says to Gifts people that you didn't care enough about them to get something that mattered. For a long time, Gifts remained in our 'blind spot' and we told him off for being too materialistic and ungrateful, provoking even more tears and upset. We got it so wrong! Finally, in a much delayed 'aha moment', we recognized that Gifts was as valid and crucial a Love Language for him as, say, Quality Time and Touch were for us. His sense of self-worth, value and appreciation is fed through these tangible expressions of love and we were denying him these moments of feeling really special by ignoring the lists so that we could 'surprise him'. Understanding this has helped us avoid unnecessary hurt and stay connected with each other, especially through the teen years.

We've seen people have real breakthroughs from years of pain caused by misunderstanding through finally understanding this concept.

We attended a marriage retreat years ago, where the 5 Love Languages model was being shared. As we discussed the impact of positive words for people whose Love Language was Words of Affirmation, an older gentleman (looked to be in his eighties) got up and moved to the back of the room. As it turns out, that day he finally realized how his stubbornness around cards meant he had been depriving his wife of feeling loved in a way that mattered to her – for decades. He had always moaned whenever he saw her buying special occasion cards for friends and family, as he maintained cards were an unnecessary expense and just clever marketing from card companies to get us all to spend more money! He had banned her from getting him any and had himself stopped getting her birthday and anniversary cards, let alone Mother's Day, Christmas and Easter! That evening, for the first time, he understood that Words meant as much to his wife as Acts of Service meant to him ... and that not buying cards had left her feeling unloved all those years. They silently wept together at the back of the room in a private moment of expressing regret and forgiveness, and no doubt found deeper emotional connection through this new-found understanding of Love Languages.

4. Interpret frustrations

Often, we struggle to talk about our emotions but understanding Love Languages can help us interpret frustrations, especially unusual levels of frustration about something that seemed minor, as it was with Jon and mobile phones.

It seemed like every time the family headed out on a long drive with me (Jon) behind the wheel, Andrea would use the opportunity to catch up on calls or messages, send a few emails and maybe have a look through social media, thinking that was efficient use of the car journey. I found myself getting really frustrated and making comments about her being on the phone but not wanting to make a scene of it. It took a few goes before I was able to articulate how it made me feel, but somehow, I managed to find the words that made her realize that her constantly being on the phone or laptop made me feel ignored and that everyone else in the world was more important to her than me. I knew that was the furthest thing from her mind but that's how it felt, and I resented it. You can just imagine the horror on her face as she finally realized how hugely undermining her behavior had been to me. Now, as a family we have adopted a 'no phones' policy as much as possible in the car. As a result, we have enjoyed many great and sometimes very informative conversations on car journeys – discovering things we might otherwise never have heard from our young people!

This is how we can miss each other emotionally by simply not recognizing each other's Love or Appreciation Language. And this is as true in the work context at it is in the home.

James, a friend of ours, shared how confused and upset he was about a conversation with a colleague he was mentoring. Turned out his colleague was feeling deeply offended because in his eyes, James kept turning up late for their meetings or cancelling them. He complained bitterly that he did not feel James' support. For his part, James had always communicated ahead of time if he was going to be late and always offered an alternative date if he had to cancel. On multiple occasions he had explained how 'crazy busy' his diary was at the time. So, James was shocked that his colleague felt that way because he felt he had been deliberate about finding ways to show his commitment and support. For example, he had invited this colleague to join him on various conferences to help give him exposure, while also supporting a whole range of funding requests for training and development to demonstrate commitment to his career development. The more James thought about it, the angrier he became. In his mind, 'he' should be the one feeling offended because this other chap had never once come to say thank you for all his support!

They both had very different views on what being a mentor meant and had each started cooling off in the relationship as a result of what they perceived as repeated withdrawals from each of their Emotional Bank Accounts. The reality is, despite good intentions, all James' efforts were going down a black hole. His colleague felt most valued and appreciated through Quality Time, but James had been guilty of expecting his colleague to appreciate all the 'Gifts' James was focused on giving. Understanding Appreciation Languages gave them the chance to have a meaningful conversation about how each person's behavior was landing with the other, recognize how they were both emotionally missing the mark and restore their friendship and connection.

5. Drain tensions

You can also use the Love Languages to drain tension and re-establish positive emotional connections. Andrea recounts a 'lightbulb' experience she had with our youngest . . .

Back in the days when our youngest had just started school, the long days initially overwhelmed him. By the time Friday afternoon rolled around he would often be so tired that he would end up in floods of tears on the car journey home. Sometimes we would be stuck on the motorway and I would not be able to do much to comfort him as he sat strapped into his car seat in the back.

But one day, in a moment of inspiration while he was crying his little heart out, I gently asked if he wanted to hold my hand. You could almost see the conflict going on in his head. On one hand he wanted to stay angry because he was so frustrated, but on the other hand you could see him really wanting the comfort from holding hands, since Physical Touch is his primary Love Language. I just gently reached back and held my hand out (thank God for automatic gearboxes!) and after a few moments he reached for it and held on tight! You could literally feel the tension and frustration drain away from him and in no time, he was fast asleep. Amazing!

Then it dawned on me – I am exactly the same! Jon knows that when I am upset, usually all I need is a gentle hug to calm down. The funny thing is it works even when I am upset with him! I might resist it at first, but for me, gentle loving Touch is pure magic. Eventually I give in and my anger drains away, opening up the connection and the space to talk about what happened.

We have learnt that speaking each other's Love Languages regularly helps us maintain strong, positive balances in our Emotional Bank Accounts. Whenever things get frustrating or tense between us, speaking each other's Love Language with care also helps reduce tensions, open the door to better conversations, restore emotional connection and get the relationship back on track.

Importantly, this is not about manipulation – people will see through you and always know the heart behind your actions. Speaking Love or Appreciation Languages must be done with the right intentions, otherwise it will backfire and break trust. However, done with care and wisdom, speaking Love Languages can build real warmth and connection in relationships and prevent unintentional hurt.

Equally important is the fact that not speaking Love or Appreciation Languages leaves an emotional void.

Not speaking Love or Appreciation Languages to the people you care about leaves them vulnerable to others who do, and can leave them looking to get their emotional needs met in all the wrong places.

This helps explain why in a home situation, partners can start to be attracted to others who speak their Love Language, ticking the box on a deep emotional need for them and potentially leading to inappropriate emotional connections or affairs. It also helps explain what we mentioned before – people leave bosses, not companies, often through the frustration of not being made to feel valued or appreciated.

Making a habit of 'building connection' really should be a part of everyone's daily living.

Making a habit of CONNECTing before we correct

Perhaps it's a sign of the pressures of modern-day life, but for whatever reason, the harsh reality is that far too many of us have become experts at pointing fingers, casting blame and offering 'constructive criticism' of what other people do. But we are not so good at balancing criticism with making people feel valued, appreciated and loved in a consistent and intentional manner. However, building connection and a sense of belonging is a fundamental need in all of us, so we must learn to do it well in order to build confidence and self-esteem in the people we care about and enjoy deeper, richer, more meaningful relationships.

Just listening and genuinely wanting to hear someone's story – their thoughts, feelings, pain – without judging and criticizing, is a great place to start. When you help people feel validated, heard and cared for, they are far more likely to be open to your story and your input on what needs to change, if anything.

You only earn the right to correct, when you have genuinely connected.

Understanding Love / Appreciation Languages and making the effort to 'speak' the relevant language *on a regular basis* to the people you care about at home or work will feed their Emotional Bank Account, boost their self-esteem and ensure they feel valued and appreciated. You can instantly increase the level of warmth and connection in any relationship, by taking the time to understand and make a habit of speaking Love or Appreciation in ways meaningful to them. This is true for everyone in general and for teens in particular.

To really connect emotionally with teens, we have found it helps to focus on building their self-esteem by letting them know we take pleasure in each of them as a person (no matter how frustrated we might get at some of their behaviors!) and by taking the time to connect heart-to-heart often.

More connected than the internet!

As a final word on the subject of connection, a while ago we asked our young ones what practical suggestions they would give for establishing strong emotional connections. They identified four things which have worked really well for us, and out of them came what we now refer to as the four principles for staying 'more connected than the internet' with your kids:

1. **Have routines of time together** – like mealtimes, especially at dinner, where we all put away phones so we can talk and connect.

2. **Don't force the relationship** – pull rather than push. For example, don't ban phones or video games if you find those things getting in the way of time together. Instead, find ways to make them want to be around you – like a game or activity you both enjoy.

3. **Listen well when they are ready to talk** – recognize that teens feel judged easily and try to handle problems themselves so as not to feel criticized. Ask about things in a way that makes them feel supported and coached rather than just pointing out where they did things wrong.

4. **Speak their Love Language(s) – often**!

In fairness, much of this wisdom is as appropriate to relationships with adults as it is with teens. The more we invest in doing the things that create a sense of emotional connection and belonging, the more we can enjoy quality relationships where people feel loved and valued and have enough 'emotional buffer' to deal with inevitable challenges in the relationship and/or in life. This is the real power of developing Habit #4: CONNECT, before you correct.

Time for Reflection

Key Takeaways

- Habit #4: CONNECT, before you correct – is about developing the social skills to build warmth, connection and good rapport in relationships by learning to communicate value, appreciation and/or love in meaningful ways.

- Listening well is vital for building rapport and connection. The E-A-R-S acronym provides a useful model for implementing the principles of good listening.

- Understanding and 'speaking' Love or Appreciation Language(s) is a powerful and practical technique for communicating love, value and appreciation in meaningful ways and making huge deposits in the Emotional Bank Accounts of the people you care about.

Building Your Understanding

1. Which of the principles in the E-A-R-S model do you need to focus on improving?

2. What do you think your Love / Appreciation Language(s) is(are)?

3. Think of someone very close to you – is their Love / Appreciation Language the same as yours?

4. Who might you have been ignoring because of your 'blind spot'?

5. Where might you have been pouring attention down a 'black hole'?

6. How could this understanding of Love or Appreciation Languages help explain and/or diffuse tension in a relationship currently?

Going Deeper

1. How can this understanding of Love and Appreciation Languages help you create new relationships with people very different to you?

2. How can you use this information to stay connected with people who are physically separated from you / remote?

Taking Personal Action

1. What are your Love Languages? We recommend you complete the online exercise at www.5lovelanguages. com (FREE at the time of going to print).

2. What are the Love Languages of those closest to you? If you are able to, ask them to complete their own profile online too.

3. Practice listening with both E-A-R-S with a friend. Using a timer, take turns telling your story for 10 minutes, while the other person practices listening with **E**mpathy, **A**ttention, **R**espect and the intention to **S**ummarize.

4. Using the worksheet in the Appendices, continue making a note of the things you plan to STOP / START / CONTINUE / CHANGE, including at least one thing to help develop Habit #4: CONNECT, before you correct.

PART C

Taking Responsibility

'The price of greatness is responsibility.'

Winston Churchill[89]

Chapter Fourteen

Taking responsibility for yourself

'We first make our habits,
and then our habits make us.'

John Dryden[90]

Even before the pandemic, increased automation, Artificial Intelligence and the emerging 'gig economy' were heralding a new approach to work, life and balance – what some have referred to as the Fourth Industrial Revolution. As the world recovers from the biggest global pandemic in living history, we have an opportunity to redefine life in more purposeful and meaningful ways for a better 'Future Normal'.

The key message throughout this book has been that you can and must take personal responsibility for building your own Relational Intelligence – how you 'turn up' to and behave in relationships, especially relationships that matter to you. Hopefully, we've shown you how investing the time to make The 4 Habits® become your own natural habits will help equip you with the skills to have better conversations and achieve better outcomes in all your relationships. We also hope you've seen how these fundamental habits can provide practical ways to strengthen both personal and work relationships, whether 'up close and personal' or long distance and help you improve your emotional health, wellbeing and productivity. As you consider how to redesign your life balance for 'Future Normal', we trust these habits will give you the confidence and skill to ASK for what you need to make life work, so that you can better manage the intersection of work, home and life.

But don't miss the point – where you are now does not have to dictate where you end up. To a great extent, you get to choose what happens next. You certainly get to choose who you become through the habits you decide to form.

As John Dryden famously said: 'We first make our habits, then our habits make us.'

Learning and understanding The 4 Habits® as we have covered in detail, is the first step. Then comes practicing and practicing, and revisiting and practicing again and again, until the habits become your natural, default response. Building successful relationships with others is an ongoing process of learning about yourself and others, practicing helpful skills and techniques and changing your behavior from habits that damage relationships to habits that strengthen them. The beauty of developing great habits is that they reduce the need for debate and decision-making and will set you on course for great outcomes in life.

If you've been doing the exercises at the end of each chapter, well done! Now is the time to round up all the notes you've made – we'll help you review them. If you haven't don't worry, we'll help you go through them and write down your thoughts in this section.

What will it take?

Like training for a marathon, improving your relationships on purpose is about setting believable goals, taking small simple steps, working through the pain of developing muscle, maybe even falling over but picking yourself up and trying again. Perhaps it will be getting it wrong in an argument, learning more, trying again. Perhaps it will be undoing years of other bad habits, before more helpful ones take their place. Either way, it will be an ongoing process of learning about yourself and the people you relate to, practicing helpful skills and techniques and ultimately changing your behavior. Sometimes you will get it right, sometimes you will get it wrong. Sometimes it will feel like hard work with no reward, sometimes it will feel simply amazing.

But step-by-step, with consistent effort, it will transform your relationships.

And it will transform you.

So, who do you want *to be* in your key relationships? How do you want to 'show up' in life to the people who matter to you?

As one young lady said at the end of a keynote speech we delivered: *'I'm definitely going to put the effort in to learn The 4 Habits® now, so that when I meet Mr Right, I will already be Mrs Right.'* In a nutshell she expressed the heart of one of our charitable mission statements – to equip people to do 'single' well so that they can do 'couple' better too. And the vision is to help as many as possible do so as early as possible – by making resources available free at the point of access in schools, colleges, universities and local communities. Incidentally, if that vision resonates with you, do get in touch with our UK registered charity, Soulmates Academy Foundation.[91]

Meanwhile, at a more personal level, what could developing The 4 Habits® mean for you?

You now know that being proactive about building Relational Intelligence means being equipped with both SKILL and WILL ahead of inevitable challenges, which will allow you to 'turn up' to relationships better, have better conversations and achieve better outcomes. Practicing Habits #1 and #2 will help you minimize withdrawals from Emotional Bank Accounts and learn to get along better with each other. And practicing Habits #3 and #4 will help you increase deposits into Emotional Bank Accounts and develop the buffer to have *courageous conversations* around tricky subjects allowing you to create deeper, more emotionally connected relationships of mutual trust and respect.

The rewards are unquestionably there for the taking . . . but the taking will take effort.

Are you ready to run your relationships marathon?

Developing your very own Personal Action Plan

In this section, we're going to help you bring together everything you've learned so far into your own personal strategy for change and develop a clear plan of action for building your '4 Habits muscles'.

If you decide you want to improve, but don't develop a clear plan for doing things differently, you are at risk of falling into the definition of insanity – doing the same things and expecting a different result! Remember the movie *Groundhog Day*[92] where TV weatherman Phil Connors (Bill Murray) was stuck in the cycle of repeating the exact same day – same conversations and same outcomes – every single day?! Too many of us live that experience in our relationships. A plan of action will get you into momentum for better relationships, better conversations and better outcomes.

Stop Doing / Start Doing / Continue / Change

By now, hopefully you've found one or two things that resonated particularly strongly – things that if you did nothing else you would implement, turn to regularly, and seek to reference in all your relationships going forwards.

Hopefully, you've been using the worksheet in the Appendices (or a notebook) to capture thoughts around:

- things you want to STOP doing because they are not helpful,

- things you want to START doing that you have not been doing before,

- things you are already doing but would now like to adjust or CHANGE in some way, and/or

- things that you are already doing that are working well that you want to CONTINUE doing on purpose.

One suggestion would be to look over those lists and condense the key thoughts to three or four things in total that you will commit to implementing. Pausing to give thought to the overall lessons you have learned so far and capturing them in this way will help you be intentional about investing in and managing the relationships that are most important to you. These are the 'quick wins' that can start to make an instant difference in the warmth and quality of the key relationships around you.

Creating healthy boundaries

One of the things we would urge you to start doing if you haven't already is to clarify your values, create healthy boundaries and make space in your schedule for the things that really matter to you. This is the easiest thing to postpone because generally we are all so time poor. But nothing will change and you won't be able to respond in a healthy way to the 'asks' of others – or even the ask of yourself – if you do *not* have healthy boundaries around the people and things that are really important to you in life.

We guarantee that if you take the time to do this now you will find you have more hours in the day than you realized and more than enough time to do the things that are truly important to you.

If now is simply not the right time for you, book an appointment with yourself for a couple of hours over the next few days, weeks, months even – but get this done. Doing it will instantly reduce stress and leave you feeling more in control. And importantly, you will have begun the journey to creating healthier relationships, starting with your relationship with yourself.

Thereafter, making a habit of scheduling based on your values will help you prioritize things so that you end every day / week / month / year feeling like you've achieved most, if not all, of the *really* important things without compromising your values. Don't worry about getting it right first time – it's far more important to get it going and learn on the job. Revisit chapters 9, 10 and 11 for the detail of how to do this, if necessary, and follow the step-by-step instructions in the Appendices to create your schedule based on *your very own* values rather than your *to do* list.

The 4 Habits Experience Model revisited

In chapter 3 we introduced The 4 Habits Experience Model and explained how your level of SKILL and WILL can describe and predict what you are likely to be experiencing in any given relationship. You may have identified key relationships and where they are positioned in the model already, or you may want to give that some thought now. This gives you a starting point for articulating what you are experiencing and what you might want to do about it.

Here are some questions to reflect on as you put your action plan together:

1. Is there a particular relationship you want to work on? If so, which one?

2. Where would you position that relationship on The 4 Habits Experience Model? Why?

3. Which of the habits do you think will help you get started on improving the balance in Emotional Bank Accounts (yours and theirs) and move the relationship closer to mutual satisfaction?

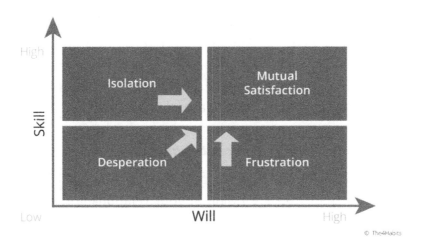

© The4Habits

Once you have decided which relationship to work on and which Habit will deliver the most impact first, revisit the Habit in the relevant chapter if you need to. Maybe read through them again with that relationship in mind, giving more thought to the reflections and exercises at the end. As you practice the tools and techniques shared and refine your understanding, you will notice a shift in the way you approach issues and a change in your behavior toward habits that strengthen rather than damage the relationship. Don't get frustrated if you get it wrong sometimes. It took years to develop your current habits so don't expect that you're going to be able to change them overnight. Keep going. Remember, as English theologian and historian Thomas Fuller once pointed out, the darkest hour is just before the dawn.[93]

Building Relational Intelligence for life

Getting started and making immediate change is one level of becoming more Relationally Intelligent, but like anything that truly matters, success will come from setting yourself up with the mindset of life-long learning, getting better and better with time.

To progress on this journey to better relationships in life, it helps to do some honest introspection on how you are being experienced in all your work and home relationships, how consistent you are being in your behaviors and where you may need to change your behaviors from habits that damage relationships to habits that strengthen them. In other words, you need to conduct a relational audit.

Conducting your very own relational audit

You will likely already have a gut sense of how well (or not so well) you think you are doing in your relationships, but others may view things differently.

At one level you could ask some basic questions to assess where you are in each relationship and how consistently you are being experienced.

You could take the Habits at face value and ask yourself:

- Which people / groups do you tend to criticize more than others?

- Who do you need to be more careful and less crushing with?

- Where are there unchecked assumptions and biases that need courageous conversations?

- Who do you need to invest more time in making stronger connections with?

You can also go deeper with this and assess where all your most important relationships have ended up in The 4 Habits Experience Model based on SKILL and WILL. Taking an honest look at your level of SKILL in living out the Habits and the impact that has had on WILL in each relationship will help explain why you might be experiencing what you're now experiencing in certain relationships. Useful questions for assessing where you are include:

1. How aware are you of the impact of your behavior on other people?

2. How easy is it for you to recognize and embrace differences you observe between yourself and others?

3. How well do you think you manage disagreements and conflict in your relationships with key family / colleagues?

4. How often do you make time for key family members / colleagues to just connect and catch up?

5. How well do you listen to and understand the needs of your key family members / colleagues?

6. How confident are you in your ability to have courageous conversations with key family members / colleagues, discussing sensitive topics that need to be aired but could get intense?

7. On average, how would you rate the level of trust and respect in your relationships with key family members / colleagues?

8. How well do you know the specific things that communicate value and appreciation to your key family members / colleagues?

The more honest you are with these questions, the more clarity you will have on where you need to focus efforts on the habits you want to develop and improve as part of your ongoing personal growth and development. These are questions that you can revisit over time to celebrate how you have improved and take the learning to another level.

Accountability partners

There is a wise old saying that . . .

Two are better than one, because they have a good reward for their toil. For if they fall, one will lift up his fellow; but woe to him who is alone when he falls and has not another to lift him up.[94]

Holding yourself accountable for developing stronger Relational Intelligence is a great start, but if you can get someone to come alongside and help you, so much the better.

Who could you ask to be your accountability partner to help you stay on track with your own personal development? Ideally this would be someone (or a small group of 'someones'!) who is also committed to developing their own Relational Intelligence so that you could learn together and give each other mutual support and encouragement. However, it could also just be someone you respect and are able to be open and vulnerable with, so that they can encourage you in your own goals – as well as challenge you when necessary.

Scheduling regular reviews

It's an old cliché: 'What gets measured gets done.' Scholars debate over who actually said it – some of the more famous names in the hat include W. Edwards Deming (the statistician behind the sampling techniques still used today by the U.S. Census Department and Bureau of Labor Statistics), Peter Drucker (the Austrian management consultant, educator and author often referred to as 'the founder of modern management'), scientist Lord Kelvin and even mathematician and Renaissance astronomer Rheticus. Either way, the message is clear – the act of measuring something allows you to keep an eye both on the goal and progress toward it. Setting up a schedule of regular reviews at the frequency that works for you – weekly, bi-weekly, monthly, quarterly – will help you take stock of how far you have come, so you are encouraged about progress and stay motivated to keep going.

While it's fresh in your mind, why not get your diary out now and put some review dates in?

Keep going!

And if you're feeling discouraged having experienced a string of disastrous relationships, we want to encourage you that you can still become the person who builds strong, mutually supportive relationships on purpose.

> **Wherever you are in your relationships you can become intentional and proactive about building, or rebuilding, great relationships at work, at home, in life.**

We all invest in things we want to last – houses, careers, pensions. It's time to put your relationships on the radar and get better at doing them well.

As you put this knowledge into practice, before you know it, you will find yourself acting and reacting more like the person you desire to be and making The 4 Habits® your default response.

And as you anchor yourself in great, meaningful relationships, you get to turn up to life as the best version of you – fully engaged, full of energy, fully on purpose, fully you – and equipped to help those around you to achieve the same.

Now THAT, is worth getting out of bed for!

Making an impact

Making the change in your own world is worth the effort . . . but you can also become a catalyst for the change you want to see in the world, by starting right where you are.

Sometimes it's easy to feel overwhelmed by problems in the world that feel so much bigger than us – broken homes, poverty, inequalities and injustice – but we can create that ripple effect by improving the quality of our relationships in our own circle of influence. When we each take personal responsibility for how we show up and behave, we become better friends, better partners, better colleagues, better parents ... better people to be around.

You can make an impact right where you are.

If you'd like to make an impact on the people around you, in the final two chapters, we share some thoughts on how The 4 Habits® can help you be a better leader in the corporate world and a better contributor to society, simply by getting better at doing relationships well.

One by one, we can turn the tide on broken relationships ...

Chapter Fifteen

Taking responsibility as a leader

'Strong results come from strong relationships
both at work and at home.'

Our message throughout the book has been that as individuals, we must each take personal responsibility for how we turn up and behave in our interactions with the people around us, and that we can do that by developing habits that help us do relationships well. That remains the central point. However, as life under COVID-19 lockdown laid bare, there is a whole lot more that leaders and organizations can be doing to support their people on the journey to improved relationships . . . and when they do everyone benefits.

The changing context of leadership

The experience of the pandemic provoked a coming together of wellbeing and productivity in unprecedented ways. Managers and team leads were left with no choice but to step up in their ability to nurture relationships long distance, maintain productivity and support wellbeing, while managing their own personal circumstances. Team members had to learn to embrace new ways of collaborating and covering for each other while maintaining healthy personal relationships and healthy boundaries around home life and self-care. For many, this meant demonstrating new levels of Relational Intelligence and having conversations that had previously felt outside their remit . . . and comfort zone.

Quality workplace relationships have long been established as pillars of strategic organizational priorities such as employee engagement, teamwork and client relationship management. From the boardroom to the shopfloor, from team leads and individual contributors through to clients and external suppliers, overall organizational success has always been dependent on the quality of the relationships that exist at each level. However, as the lines between home and work continue to be blurred, it has become more evident that employee resilience, mental health and wellbeing are also dependent on people's abilities to build strong, supportive relationships around them both at work *and* at home.

In a very real way, helping everyone do relationships well has become the pivotal behavior change required for organizational success.

Relying on social capital built in the office environment has brought us thus far. But the trends suggest that going forward, organizations need to become more intentional about developing and modelling cultures of relationships that foster cohesion across remote teams to achieve a singularity of purpose. In the Future Normal it appears that, more than ever, the quality of people's relationships will be the glue that holds teams and companies together allowing them to work effectively across difference and distance to achieve outstanding results.

At the same time, the convergence of work and home life under pandemic lockdown made the link between personal home relationships, mental health and individual performance very direct and visible. The cycle of work pressures impacting home relationships and home pressures impacting workplace performance finally came into the spotlight, and as the 'Relationship Breakdown and the Workplace' research study (we spoke about this in chapter 9) confirmed, the two are inextricably linked. Literally weeks before the first wave of national lockdowns swept across the globe, the data confirmed that neither employers nor employees themselves had clear strategies for building strong relationship capability and reducing the likelihood of personal relationship breakdown.

The evidence is clear – strong results come from strong relationships both at work and at home. But for the most part, 'learning to do relationships well' remains the missing piece of the puzzle in professional development and in strategic conversations around employee resilience, engagement and performance.

Redefining what good leadership looks like

As leadership guru John Maxwell aptly put it, *'A leader is one who knows the way, goes the way, and shows the way.'*[95] This mantra will undoubtedly have been playing on the mind of many a great leader as they grappled with figuring out what the post-pandemic Future Normal would look like.

Many leaders will have become acutely aware of the increased importance of nurturing relationships but will have been challenged to find ways to do so in a world heavily biased toward making sense of things through analyzing data and information. The challenge has become recognizing and rewarding performance that delivers results through building great relationships, creating inclusive environments and promoting emotional wellbeing. This is not a new challenge, but a challenge of new strategic importance. Successful leaders of the future will now need to get better at doing both. *And*, not *or*. The recent uproar and subsequent resignation of the UK Chairman of KPMG,[96] the Big Four consultancy, because he told his people to 'stop moaning' about the pandemic confirms this shift.

As a recent research study out of Case Western Reserve University put it, success in the future will require that good leaders get better at using *both* their neural networks.[97] Where we have been historically good at using the *analytic networks* in our brains to stay on top of the logical, rational pathway to successful outcomes, we need to get better at harnessing our *empathic networks* – those parts of our brains that allow us to process more qualitative data and relate to and connect with those around us on an emotional level. And what's even more interesting coming out of the research is that because the two networks actually work as opposing forces – one literally suppresses the other when it is activated – success will come from learning not only how to effectively use both neural networks, but also from learning how to switch seamlessly between them, as required.

Putting that in the context of the challenges of the day, for many, successful leadership will come from bolstering their Relational Intelligence and also learning how to switch between using that and more hard-nosed, data-driven conventional business thinking to drive decisions.

While specific frameworks and metrics to achieve the more empathic side of things are yet to be embraced and enhanced, the challenges of the times around mental health, employee engagement and inclusion, suggest they will remain a priority focus until effectively addressed. And with 'poor relationships' being the common thread running through them all, the case for improving your own Relational Intelligence as a leader, along with the Relational Intelligence of all the people in your sphere of influence, has never been stronger.

It's time for Relational Intelligence to become a key part of professional and leadership development.

The 4 Habits® for better leadership

If you are an organizational leader, the good news is that you already have in your hands the tools you need to progress your own journey to stronger Relational Intelligence. The 4

Habits® offer practical approaches to help everyone achieve the relationship-centered behavior changes required for navigating the future world of work.

To help leaders remember, and practice implementing, The 4 Habits® as they go about their daily business, we developed an acronym aptly called K-A-R-E.[98] This will help you keep the focus and attention on creating and managing your very own micro-environment of performance and wellbeing through building strong relationships with the people around you.

In practice, The 4 Habits® for Better Leadership look like this . . .

K-now your team

A-ddress conflict immediately

R-enegotiate priorities, availability and expectations

E-ngage and encourage as individuals

Know your team

Knowing your team is about getting better at relating to each individual rather than just following company prescribed procedures and protocols. Of course, this demands getting better at understanding and working with their individual differences, which is the essence of Habit #1: BE CURIOUS, not critical. The more you understand about each individual, both in terms of their strength of contribution and their circumstances, the better you will become at nurturing relationships through their different life-stages (single, parent of young children, 'squeezed-middle' looking after parents and children, empty-nesters, serious illness and bereaved, etc.), thereby fostering an environment of great performance and supporting wellbeing.

Meaningful one-on-one relationships with each individual also create the context for more effective execution of key management responsibilities around delegation, feedback and performance reviews. These benefits ripple through to talent development, career progression and retention, including better retention of under-represented groups like women, blacks and LGBTQ+.

Increasingly, organizations are waking up to the fact that a more diverse workforce is not just good for social and moral currency – it's also good for bottom-line business. However, the presence of diversity does not guarantee the results. Lasting results come from genuine inclusion that creates a sense of belonging and empowers people to bring their authentic self to make a positive impact. Ultimately, inclusion (or the lack of it) is experienced in one-on-one relationships. The more leaders model building strong relationships across difference, the more people feel valued, respected, like they belong, and empowered to make their best contributions to organizational goals.

There is no shortcut for investing the time to know your team as individuals, but the rewards are worth their weight in gold. Inclusive organizations consistently outperform the competition.

Address conflict immediately

Today's increased remote, virtual team-working environment presents significant challenges to employee communication and interactions. The social cues that we normally pick up from being face-to-face with each other – especially through body language – are not that easy to spot on camera, and even less easy to spot when people choose to be *off* camera! For some people, video technology creates a false environment where they're tempted to 'perform' or feel awkward or self-conscious, and not be their true selves. For others, time and distance fuel anxiety about deterioration in relationships and FOMO[99] given the absence of casual office conversation and 'water cooler moments' to help stay 'in the know'.

As we discussed in Habit #2, for many of us, our default responses in conflict situations can damage rather than strengthen relationships . . . and in a world of increased working across distance, the challenges tend to be amplified. How leaders and managers handle conflict ultimately creates the culture for how conflict is addressed in the team. So, to get the best from your teams especially in a remote working context, it's essential to foster a culture of 'thinking the best'. In every situation (at least until proven otherwise), assume intentions are good, and seek to clarify any misunderstandings quickly. And if things are tense or can be misinterpreted, lead by example, pick up the phone and talk about it. Don't leave anything to fester and, as we all already know (though sometimes are not so diligent about implementing), be super careful with written words in emails or texts because they can all too easily be misinterpreted.

It's also worth bearing in mind that as a leader, your positional authority tends to make conflict situations with you feel worse. So, if you need to say something that could be challenging or difficult to hear, say it softly albeit without diluting the message.

Perhaps unsurprisingly, forgiveness is not a word we use much in the corporate world these days, but it wouldn't hurt if we all got better at forgiving others, forgiving ourselves and moving on. Allowing words and actions that show kindness and compassion in your leadership style and the way you model treating others, especially in conflict situations, will serve you well.

Renegotiate priorities, availability and expectations

As many learned first-hand through life under lockdown, working from home is not just about relocating work to a different environment and replicating the same hours, or level of availability and productivity. Working from home often involves working around real-life commitments, relationships and responsibilities at home. However, as we discussed in chapter 9, many feel unable to have open, honest conversations about their home circumstances. Consequently, they try to juggle life and loved ones around their perception of office expectations and live with a pressure cooker of emotions including resentment and guilt. Totally unsustainable.

Until the world gets better at talking about these issues, the onus is very much on leaders to bring the conversation into the room and renegotiate workloads, deadlines, availability for meetings, etc., based on both corporate priorities *and* individual capacity and strengths. Sometimes this means reassigning work and responsibilities across the team, which in itself demands a new level of team synergy and strong relationships across the team.

One very practical way of renegotiating priorities and expectations is modelling how to create healthy boundaries around availability, to ensure time for personal priorities and importantly for self-care. Under lockdown, some companies implemented ideas like a 'meeting-free' afternoon or an afternoon off every week for personal time to show care and support for their employees, many of whom had been working extended hours.

Creating healthy boundaries is important for everyone but doubly so for team leaders dealing with the challenges of holding down their own home situation while managing and supporting teams. As a leader, the pace you set will generally be the pace team members assume you expect them to follow. It's not about the rules and processes in place, but the leadership behaviors on display. So, if you're working long days which spill over into the weekends, it's likely team members will feel pressured to do the same, regardless of how different their circumstances might be. They will also be looking to you for cues on how to maintain balance and wellbeing – but you can't give what you don't have.

It's helpful for leaders to model being human and vulnerable by sharing some of their own situation and challenge, so people feel they have permission to be real. Something as simple as how you respond to interruptions from a child or a pet during a video call while working from home for example, will signal to people that it is OK to be human and set expectations that they do not need to stress when 'real life' happens. Rather than get tense, bring the moment into the room and take the opportunity to get to know your colleagues – and their partner, kids, dogs, cats – a little bit more!

The more people feel supported, the stronger their engagement and willingness to go the extra mile to overcome obstacles and make things happen. It's about managing their Emotional Bank Account well. There has never been a more urgent need for leaders to get better at human connection.

If you get this wrong, people will feel violated and disengage. Worse yet, you will likely leave them feeling broken physically, emotionally and/or mentally.

But don't be fooled – this needs to be more than just tinkering at the edges with new regulations. Getting it right involves a change in leadership mindset, culture and values. It's about creating the right relationships and inclusive environment so that people feel safe to talk honestly about their own priorities and values, encouraged to make room in their schedule for the people and things that matter to them (partner, children, exercise, hobbies, rest!!) and empowered to push back against things that challenge these boundaries.

Strong relationships help create a psychologically safe environment – meaning an environment where there is no interpersonal fear – where people feel able to be open and honest about what they need to make work and life work. This is vital for maintaining both wellbeing and productivity. As a leader, this might mean having conversations about things you have never had to discuss before like anxiety and mental health issues or difficulties in home relationships. Investing in your own Relational Intelligence is vital to creating those trusting relationships that support better conversations to help people clear the 'mental space' to focus, stay emotionally resilient and stay connected with the team.

For many organizations, this will involve a culture shift through deliberate investment in creating more Relationally Intelligent leaders, delivered as a core part of their leadership development strategy for success in the new landscape. However, regardless of the corporate culture or approach, you can take responsibility for starting where you are to create your own inclusive, psychologically safe micro-environment.

Engage and encourage as individuals

Whether in-office or via remote connection, how people feel treated by their team lead or boss will have a strong influence on how they view their entire organizational experience.

A friend shared how he was quietly disengaging from his firm during the pandemic. Despite the risk of exposure to the virus, his boss had insisted that he was present in the office, commuting one hour each way – to spend the day on Zoom calls. Worse still, not once did his boss or any of the other executive team members ask about his personal circumstances and how he had been coping with the pandemic – NOT ONCE! Every conversation was focused on work and results, with the undertone that he needed to justify and be grateful for the salary he was receiving, where others had been laid off. Sadly, he was not alone in that experience.

The pandemic revealed what felt like a particularly uncaring strain in our friend's boss, but the reality is that his mindset probably existed before. It's clear that a huge part of the successful leader's role comes from engaging and encouraging their people, and as we discussed in Habit #4, unless we do that, we leave people vulnerable to external approaches. It will be very interesting to see if we experience any spikes in the job transfer market once things return to some semblance of normalcy and people feel more confident to change jobs.

Some companies had already caught the vision of the world being one big global marketplace and have developed the work cultures and environment to benefit from it. In a world where remote-working is perfectly normal, talented people can access opportunities everywhere and can be more discerning about the type of company they want to work for. Importantly, this is not just in terms of the jobs and career progression on offer, but the distinguishing qualities of values, purpose and culture.

More than ever, the lived experience of culture through relationships and one-on-one interactions will make or break engagement and commitment to leaders and the organizations they represent. For great talent, the world is literally their oyster.

For long-term successful outcomes, leaders and organizations will need to be intentional about encoding and replicating the behaviors that create their winning culture and consistent, positive employee experiences, even in virtual and remote environments. Beyond just acknowledging their physical presence, or tolerating their diversity representation, this is about intentionally including people, so they feel like they genuinely belong and have found their 'tribe'. It's about engaging with, supporting and encouraging people as individuals. This is particularly important for the retention of new recruits joining remote teams. Typically, they will have no real experience of the organizational culture outside of their team interactions. Strong relationships will help them build the internal support network they need to anchor them in the new role.

As remote a possibility as it might seem though, the ultimate cost of *not* engaging people and building strong relationships – especially strong personal relationships in a remote working context – is loss of lives.

On August 13, 2019, The Guardian newspaper reported a surge in suicide attempts at Hinkley Point C,[100] Britain's under construction nuclear power station plant and, at the time, the UK's biggest construction project since the Second World War. Apparently, there were 10 suicide attempts in the first four months of 2019 and, worse still, at least two workers connected with the project had taken their lives since construction started in earnest in 2016.

At the same time, they also reported a rise in the number of people off sick with stress, anxiety and depression, and an increase in workers suffering from mental distress. The main causes of the distress, the report concluded 'appear to be loneliness, relationship breakdown and the struggle of being sometimes hundreds of miles away from family'.

The really sad thing is that poor mental health is not new news in the construction industry. According to the same article, the construction industry suffers suicide rates at more than three times the national average for men (more than 85 percent of construction workers are male) with contributing factors including bullying, homesickness and isolation.

It seems, the more virtual and remote the work environment becomes, the more crucial it is that leaders engage with and encourage employees in meaningful ways and create a culture of mutual support across the team.

'Three checks' for increased engagement and encouragement

To help leaders get better at building engagement and encouragement with team members on a practical level, we came up with the 'three checks' mantra for increased engagement and encouragement – *Check-in* and *Check-up*, before you *Check-off*:

1. Check-in on how colleagues are REALLY doing.

It seems most of us are programmed to say everything is 'fine' whenever we get asked about our welfare. We are fine and everything is OK. It takes a trusting relationship and unrushed time to get to understand how people are doing, really.

To help build trust, it's important to take the time to get to know the names of any loved ones (even pets!) so you can ask about them specifically – in a caring non-intrusive kind of way. Making allowance for time to have these conversations without feeling pressed to move on will help develop the relationship for more authentic, honest, open conversations. This could be including a 'check-in' time on the agenda of group meetings where everyone gets one minute to share what's on their hearts and minds so they can support each other through the week. It could be an informal check-in, like creating a virtual 'water cooler' moment in an unplanned one-on-one conversation before or after a team call where you encourage people to share what's happening in *their* world and how they're really feeling.

Some companies have formalized a rhythm of checking in with people – like once a day for a quick catch-up, once a week for discussing projects and deadlines, and once a month for a longer conversation. However, as we discussed in Habit #1, different people will have different preferences and tolerance for the level of frequency of keeping in touch, so talk about it with them to get the level of support right. It's also good to discuss and create your own team rituals for connecting and engaging emotionally with each other. This insight into 'real life' can really help everyone 'be team' for each other, spot opportunities to give support where needed and help manage everyone's inclusion so people feel cared for. For some teams it works to have Friday afternoon drinks where they kick back and only talk about life, not work. Another team we worked with implemented a 'coffee roulette', randomly picking names from a hat to arrange one-on-one coffee socials to meet more people across the organization. The point is to think creatively about ways and rhythms of keeping in touch with everyone on a personal level and keeping everyone connected.

2. Check-up on progress with any personal circumstances and issues they might have shared with you.

The more you get to know people and the concerns in their lives, the more you can follow up with care and compassion. Listen well to any comments, hints and hesitations they may give around issues they may be dealing with themselves or in their families. Both things said and not said can give real clues, but you will only hear it if you listen with the intent of offering genuine support in an unhurried conversation. Sometimes it is worth scheduling a call just for this.

3. Ensure you have genuinely Checked-in and Checked-up on progress with any non-work concerns they had BEFORE you Check-off the to-do list of tasks and deadlines.

A few months into lockdown, one manager complained that he was not getting any of the work on his desk done because he was spending so much time listening to people off-load their concerns. We had to gently remind him that especially in seasons of challenge and uncertainty, the job of the leader is to help people get the mental space and clarity they need to work well *and* be well. Spreadsheets won't feel uncared for and neglected – but people will. Employees generally know how to do their jobs and for the most part want to create that sense of accomplishment from getting tasks done and meeting deadlines. Often, they just need a listening ear and compassion to help them move forward. And once projects and goals are completed, remember to show appreciation in a way that is meaningful to them (Habit #4 style) – like virtual high-fives, giving them a moment in the spotlight with the team, an email, a card, one-on-one time, and so on.

Once considered 'the softer issues', it is now becoming increasingly clear that empathy, compassion and a focus on employee wellbeing deliver hard, direct and visible positive bottom-line impact. Key to unlocking potential, innovation and engagement is to ensure that employees feel cared for and supported in the things that matter to them. Get this wrong and the reverse is true. People will end up feeling disengaged and resentful. More than that, you risk losing it all – productivity, relationships, wellbeing, employees. Knowing how to manage emotions and relationships has never been a more crucial skill for leaders.

What can organizations do?

The question many organizations then ask is: 'How can we get involved without crossing personal / professional boundaries?'

We have found that including interventions as a natural part of professional learning and development processes helps organizations reach their goals of wellbeing and performance whilst also supporting home relationships and work-life balance. Interestingly, we have also found that asking the right questions even in a group setting often opens up a flood of dialogue – it's clear that people want to talk about challenges in relationship space and are just looking for permission to discuss them in a work context and get support in handling them well.

Five key areas of focus for corporate audiences are:

- **Improving Strategic Alignment amongst Board / Executive Team** – Executive coaching to strengthen relationships amongst the senior leaders, create alignment of goals and priorities and develop clarity of direction. This is especially important in smaller co-founder, couple-run and family-run businesses where strategic direction rests solely with a small group of leaders and relationship breakdown can derail the entire business.

- **Developing Relationally Intelligent Leaders and Role Models** – Helping leaders develop the skills and habits to lead with more empathy and compassion, build relationships of trust and respect, and model behaviors that foster employee wellbeing, engagement, performance and retention.

- **Building Social Health and Wellbeing in the Remote / Hybrid Workforce** – Equipping everyone across the organization with the relational skills to stay connected and resilient by: strengthening relationships at work and home, having courageous conversations where necessary, creating healthy boundaries and designing a more sustainable work-life balance.

- **Developing Inclusive Behaviors and Cultures** – Helping leaders and teams change mindsets and behaviors by developing the Relational Intelligence to build strong relationships across difference and distance, to model inclusive leadership and to create environments where people can bring their most authentic selves to work.

- **Building Social Capital for Competitive Advantage** – Leveraging the power of quality relationships to achieve stronger bottom-line performance by raising the level of Relational Intelligence and the collective organizational capability to build strong relationships across the network of stakeholders – employees, leaders, customers, shareholders, suppliers – in order to increase social capital.

More and more, leading organizations today recognize that investing in building Relational Intelligence across the organization is both socially responsible and financially wise. As a leader, it's the right thing to do for your people, for your clients, for your stakeholders and for society at large.

For additional resources, information and help building Relational Intelligence in a work setting, visit our corporate website at: www.4habitsconsulting.com

Time for Reflection

Key Takeaways

- Strong Relational Intelligence amongst leaders is vital for employee wellbeing, mental health and productivity.

- Cultures, policies and processes might need to be created / recreated to foster an environment of strong, trusting relationships across differences and distances.

- Whatever the existing culture, leaders can create their own micro-environment of K-A-R-E: *Know the team; Address conflict immediately; Renegotiate priorities, availability and expectations; and Engage and encourage as individuals.*

- The business case for investing in building Relational Intelligence in the workforce is clear and compelling, both in moral and financial terms.

- Building Relational Intelligence in leaders and across the organization is best done as a natural part of professional learning and development addressing employee engagement (especially in remote teams), mental health and wellbeing, and inclusive leadership.

Chapter Sixteen

Taking responsibility as a society

*'To succeed as individuals – and as a society –
we must become intentional about learning
to do relationships well.'*

In the year 2020, for a brief moment in history, we all embraced our humanity and stood together on the same side, supporting and comforting each other as we shared the raw emotions of fear, grief and loss in the battle to get the COVID-19 virus under control. In the months that followed, we drew collective strength in the hope that together, we could conquer the global pandemic. We encouraged and cheered-on our front-line workers, eternally grateful for their service and sacrifice.

We allowed ourselves to be human, to connect as humans, to show care for each other as humans, to step up to the plate and do whatever we could to help those around us without regard for skin color or political persuasion. We were together in the fight against a common enemy that was destroying our health and taking our loved ones – and for a while, that was all that mattered.

Those were moments of innovation and inspiration as people offered the strengths and skills in their hands and found creative ways to serve others, without fear of judgement or attack. That was a glimpse of the possible – moments of human-to-human interactions as equals, all in this together and giving the best of ourselves in the fight against the virus.

Unfortunately, though, a few months on, with the battle against the virus still raging, for many the magic disappeared. All of a sudden, we were back to battling each other – across our individual differences, across our ideologies and politics, and across the issue of our skin color.

Sadly 'healthy relationships' is not the global default setting – not at home, not at work and not in society. Most of us turn up to jobs, to relationships and to life with the skills we picked up as children. Instead of proactively building skills for successful relationships as adults, we either carry the emotional strength and resilience of relationships done well or the baggage of relationships done badly, based on the luck of the draw of the role models we had. And it seems our luck has been running out.

Across the world we are now paying a high price for broken relationships – physically, financially, emotionally and mentally. The effects and repercussions are being felt by everyone, everywhere. From friends to work colleagues, from couples to families, from classrooms to boardrooms, relationship breakdown is hurting individuals, families, companies and nations.

Relationship breakdown is killing us, literally

As we already shared in the introduction to this book, the breakdown rate for couple relationships is, on average, 50 percent in much of the developed world. Everybody knows somebody who has been through separation or divorce. Everybody has seen the devastation and costs of relationship and family breakdown and too many are experiencing this first-hand.

And as if that isn't bad enough, perhaps even more heart-wrenching is the impact of relationship breakdown on the innocent bystanders – children on the receiving end are more likely to end up with mental health issues in their teens. According to research by think tank Marriage Foundation,[101] this tends to show up in girls as emotional problems and in boys as behavioral problems – which probably helps explain the increasing national concern over teen mental health and why there are so many angry young men in prisons. It would appear that family breakdown is the number-one driver of teenage mental health problems.

The reality for the UK and many other nations across the globe is that poor-quality relationships lie at the heart of many of their biggest social challenges – family breakdown, homelessness, mental health issues and suicide.

Relationship breakdown, it seems, is literally killing us.

As the 2016 Mental Health Foundation report concluded *'with urgency we **must** invest in building quality relationships and remove any obstacles to achieving this'* (our emphasis added).

If we don't, our future as a society is at risk. If current trends continue, the prediction is that half of all children being born in the UK today will be living with only one birth parent by the time they are preparing for their end of compulsory secondary school exams (GCSEs) at the age of 16. Statistically, this means that as a society we are heading into a future with a population at higher risk of mental health issues, lower educational achievements, lower wage incomes, higher poverty, higher addictions and higher crime.

Struggles with racism, inequalities and injustice

The killing of George Floyd in the USA on May 25, 2020 by a policeman kneeling on his neck for 8 minutes and 46 seconds was recorded on a smartphone and witnessed the world over. During the final two minutes, Floyd lay motionless on the ground and had no pulse. Though the officers called for medical assistance, they took no action to treat him. The official autopsy confirmed Floyd's death as a homicide. This harsh reminder of the very dark history that is still all too prevalent in the lived experience of many African Americans and other black people across the world today sparked a global movement of protest, with blacks, whites and every color in between marching for justice, equality and

346 | The 4 Habits of all Successful Relationships

genuine inclusion for the black community. It seems our urgent call for people to develop Habit #2: BE CAREFUL, not crushing in conflict situations was more prophetic than we realized.

Often, people talk about the issues of inequality, racism and systemic injustice as if they are only problems 'out there' to be solved. Over the years, the UK and other parts of the western world have made valiant inroads through attempts to address inequality, promote equity, embrace diversity, become more aware of unconscious bias and develop cultures that foster inclusion and belonging. However, as long as the solution to the problem lies outside the individual – with governments, with legal systems, with the Diversity and Inclusion department, with affinity groups for 'them' – we cannot get much further. While there is much work to be done by governments and institutions at a systemic level, in a very real sense, inclusion needs to start with each of us. As Shakespeare once famously said, *'the fault, dear Brutus, is not in our stars, but in ourselves . . .'*

Instead of acting out stereotypes or lazily absorbing beliefs that have been fed to us, we can choose to 'show up' well and treat people well, with the same level of value and respect that we would desire. Yes, we need new norms and systems that do not favor white people while disadvantaging people of color. Yes, it is a shocking disgrace that in some countries black people are nearly 10 times more likely than white people to be stopped and searched, and twice as likely as Asians. Yes, the issues often feel so big that they make us feel impotent. But we can't wait for laws and systems to change to play our part. We can start right where we are. We each have the power in us to make people, no matter how different to us, feel valued and respected and included.

In a very real way, we each need to recognize that inclusion starts with me.

It's true, everyone smiles in the same language. The challenge is we each turn up to our interactions with 'other people' with assumptions about 'them'. We each have our own emotional baggage, our unconscious biases. What this means, is that to address inequalities, racism and injustice, we each need to step up to the plate, examine our own assumptions and behaviors and choose ones that build relationships across difference, rather than continue to damage them.

Rather than focusing on the things that divide, we can focus on developing the skills that help us improve our one-on-one interactions with people who are different to us. As one TED speaker highlighted, building relationships with people who are different to us provides the vaccine that inoculates us against our own racism.[102]

Inclusion is everyone's 'response-ability'

Equipping people with the Relational Intelligence to push past prejudices and build strong relationships will help remove the underlying tensions that keep all too many of us stuck tip-toeing around each other and walking on eggshells in an effort to be politically correct. In fact, many of us are so afraid of saying the 'wrong thing' that it has crippled our ability to have any meaningful conversations at all. We have spent so long talking about our differences and inequalities and biases that we are more focused on not getting things wrong than trying to establish a relationship at all. So, we end up with a room full of 'diversity' – with people who are noticeably different and made to feel awkward because nobody is really attempting to form a genuine human-to-human friendship.

Yet, as the early days of the pandemic showed, we each have it in us to push past our differences and find ways to connect and build meaningful relationships. We can choose to educate ourselves about history and learn the words that come loaded with negative emotions for traditionally marginalized groups. We can have caring conversations with people very different to us, one-on-one over coffee (or tea or wine!) to understand the issues and concerns of under-represented groups and hear their distinct voices. Technically, there is no such thing as a BAME ethnic group. BAME is simply a way of grouping Black, Asian and Minority Ethnics, but the reality is that the histories and lived experiences of each of those individual ethnicities differ in very significant ways. The biggest thing these groups have in common is that they are not white . . .

Instead of fearing getting it wrong we can focus on developing the heart to want to do better . . . to love better . . . to build genuine relationships across difference. We can focus on treating people with respect, getting to know them as individuals and not stereotyping and having assumptions about 'people like them'.

Beyond *not* discriminating against or *not* excluding certain people, it's important that we all learn to actively include them.

Inclusion is everyone's response-ability.

There are six simple steps you can take to help people B-E-L-O-N-G:

- **B** - Be aware of your own biases

- **E** - Educate yourself on the issues and concerns

- **L** - Listen with empathy to the distinct voices

- **O** - Offer help and ideas for better inclusion

- **N** - Never tolerate inequity and injustice. Call people out. 'I don't understand – what do you mean by . . .'

- **G** - Get personal (build one-on-one relationships)

The 4 Habits® for building relationships across difference

Apart from their general application to Relationships, The 4 Habits® that we share in this book also provide practical suggestions for getting better at building one-on-one relationships across difference:

Habit #1: BE CURIOUS, not critical

Instead of judging and criticizing difference, give people the 'space and grace' to be who they are and treasure hunt for the strength they bring to complement yours. There is always strength in difference. Our job is to be open enough to find it.

Habit #2: BE CAREFUL, not crushing

The more different we are, the easier it is to misunderstand each other's intentions, especially where there is a lot of history and baggage. Choose your battles – not everything needs to escalate into a conflict. But if it does become a conflict, treat people carefully, don't crush them.

Habit #3: ASK, don't assume

We all have assumptions and biases that, sometimes, we don't even know exist, yet still they drive the way we think and behave. Sometimes we say things that offend someone hugely and we don't know why. The only way to find out is to ask them, rather than assume. Sometimes what is said or done offends us and we react disproportionately – in a deep-seated, 'nerve-touching' kind of way. Whenever you find yourself with an intense gut reaction to something that someone said or did, investigate the feeling. Try to look internally to find out what actually provoked such a strong response and think about what you would like to be different, then ASK them for it. It takes courage, but the better we get at talking about these deep-seated issues one-on-one, the more we can build relationships of mutual respect and trust. And the more we create strong relationships across difference, even if we get things wrong from time to time, we can keep the conversation going and keep learning until we get it right. If relationships remain weak, we will just keep digging deeper trenches.

Habit #4: CONNECT, before you correct

It is so easy to point fingers, cast blame and offer 'constructive criticism' of what other people do. But we are not so good at balancing criticism with making people feel valued, appreciated and loved – assuming we are interested in doing that at all. But to quote Theodore Roosevelt again, *'People don't care how much you know, until they know how much you care.'* Just listening and genuinely wanting to hear someone's story – their thoughts, feelings, pain – without judging and criticizing, is a great place to start to show care and build connection with someone different to you. When you help people feel validated, heard and cared for, they are likely to be far more open to your story and your input on what needs to change. We only earn the right to correct, when we have genuinely connected.

In its simplest form, all we need to do is allow ourselves to be human again, to care again and to reach out and build relationships again. It doesn't cost anything to offer a smile and talk with someone in a way that makes them smile and feel included. No matter how different you might feel the other person is, we all share the same humanity. If nothing else, strike up a conversation with someone different to you with the simple goal of making them smile. You will both feel better off for it.

Building Relational Intelligence for a better future

As the early days of the pandemic reminded us, when we stand strong together without fear of each other, we become our most creative, innovative, inspiring selves. What could we really achieve if we were able to recreate those moments of genuine human-to-human connections – without another pandemic? What could we achieve as individuals, families, societies and nations if we were able to build strong, meaningful relationships?

Leaving our level of relationship skills to chance will continue to hurt our wellbeing, our families, our children, our future, until we decide to become proactive and strategic in our approach.

In order to stem the tide and crippling impact of relationship breakdown in all its guises, we need to shift mindsets to the point where building Relational Intelligence is a natural part of personal learning and development.

What if everyone was equipped early – in schools, universities, communities, places of worship, places of work – ideally before starting relationships and definitely before they got into trouble? What if everyone learned the fundamentals of relationships and how to successfully get over the common hurdles?

What if, instead of just pouring money into fixing the mess of relationship breakdown, we equipped people at those transition points in life that tend to put more pressure on relationships? In a home context, this could include times like getting married, moving in together, having a baby or even working from home. At work, this would include times like starting a new job, taking on more management responsibility, going off on a long-term overseas assignment, retirement, or transitions to a remote environment.

Organizations are already spending huge budgets on helping their people improve mental health and wellbeing, but many are missing the relationship piece of the puzzle. As a society we could have a more joined-up approach across the public sector, the private sector and the third sector to shift mindsets so that learning to do relationships well becomes the aspirational and achievable goal for everyone.

The quality of our relationships determines the quality of our life — not just as individuals and families but as societies and nations. Strong Relational Intelligence for ALL must become our strategic priority.

To succeed as individuals — and as a society — we must become intentional about learning to do relationships well.

When we make the conscious and deliberate choice to do relationships better:

- we learn the skills to build great relationships;
- we turn up better in how we treat each other;
- we become better versions of ourselves;
- our marriages, partnerships and friendships are strengthened;
- our children flourish; our communities and workplaces thrive;
- and our nations are all the healthier for it.

We might question how our tiny contribution can make a difference to global problems. Well, it's not the whole answer, but one thing is for certain: if we want a more human world, it has to start with the relationships in our own backyard.

If we learn to become more CURIOUS about how we may differ from each other . . . (Habit #1)

. . . then we can become more CAREFUL about how we treat each other. (Habit #2)

If we learn to ASK, in order to understand each other more deeply . . . (Habit #3)

. . . then we can work out how to CONNECT with each other more genuinely.[103] (Habit #4)

And together, we will make the world a better place.

Are you ready?

Time for Reflection

Key Takeaways

- Relationship breakdown is literally killing us as a society and is the common thread through major societal concerns around family breakdown, mental health, homelessness and suicide, and global concerns around inequality and injustice.

- Inclusion is our response-ability and we can each make a difference right where we are.

- We need to shift mindsets and become more proactive in equipping people with Relational Intelligence as a natural part of personal and professional development and at key life transition stages.

- We must learn to do relationships well – our future depends on it.

Appendices

Start/Stop/Continue/Change - Exercise
(Download this template for free at: www.the4habits.com/downloads)

Instructions:

1. Write down at least one thing you plan to Start Doing / Stop Doing / Continue Doing or Change to reflect your new learning on: _____ (topic)
2. Today's date is: _____/_____/_____. Two weeks from today will be _____/_____/_____. Make a note in your diary to check in then to see how well you're doing.
3. Also, review this sheet every month for the next 6 months to ensure the new habits remain fresh in your mind. Next review check due *one month from now*, on _____/_____/_____.

Start Doing ▶	Continue Doing ▶▶
Stop Doing ■	**Change** ✕

Scheduling based on Values – Exercise

(Andrea talks you through how she does it, *personally*)

What you'll need

- A blank Weekly Schedule Template, with one-hour slots of time from an early start (say 5am) to a late finish (say 11pm). You will find a blank template immediately following these guidance notes, together with a real example of one of my actual planning templates!

- You will need six or seven different colored pens, depending on the number of roles / priorities you need to highlight.

Thinking time

- Spend time giving real thought to the things that are important to you that you want to reflect in your schedule on a regular basis. It's too easy to go through life fire-fighting and spinning plates. If you could schedule your *ideal* week, what would you do, when and with whom? Once you start allocating time you will be forced to decide which things you need to drop, even if they are all 'good things' to do.

- **Quick tip** – If, like me, the idea of planning and scheduling makes you feel like you've been put in a straight-jacket, here is the trick that works for me. In the days pre-COVID-19 when we could move around freely (and hoping they will return again soon) I quite often escape to the lounge or coffee bar in a beautiful nearby hotel for a morning or afternoon where my sole mission is to get the planning done before I leave, while the beautiful surroundings feed my soul and the waiters / waitresses are on hand to feed my body! :)

Put pen (highlighter!) to paper

- Use different colored highlighter pens to physically highlight where in the week you want to invest the time to live the values important to you. So, in the example, I have colored in 5:00-6:30am as quiet time for building my faith, feeding my soul and planning ahead. On a Tuesday afternoon and a Thursday evening I colored in a red heart to show time to spend one-on-one with Jon (our date night), giving my relationship priority in my diary and so on, as reflected in the color code at the bottom of the schedule.

- Think about your peak periods and when you are most creative. For me, 'thinking and writing' or more creative work is scheduled in before lunch.

- Once you have created the schedule of your ideal week, the trick is to plan each week's appointments and activities following the template as closely as possible. Have a sense for what general commitments for the month look like so you can balance time across the priorities if any particular week is out of kilter, as happens when I have 'full day' consulting assignments.

- For each key role, jot down the things you need to get done that week and work out when those things will be scheduled, so every one gets considered.

- Instead of having an unending to-do list that keeps rolling, I suggest having 'one big thing' that must be done each day and a handful of other things that can be fit into nooks and crannies. So, for me, a big thing might be a client workshop, presentation or article that must be written, and I focus on that to the exclusion of everything else until it's done. Then I fit the smaller things like making a handful of calls, sending a specific email or popping to the cleaners or the local shop, into nooks and crannies.

- Depending on your lifestyle, expect that your ideal week might only be relevant for a couple of months. Mine changes often around school holidays.

Remember why you're doing this

- Commit to putting First Things First by scheduling them into your diary so that day by day you get closer and closer to living the life of your dreams.

Weekly Schedule Template – Example

See color version at https://the4habits.com/downloads

(Download this template for free at: www.the4habits.com/downloads)

Phase 2 Lockdown Schedule

Weekly Schedule Template

For the period: 06/20 to 07/20

Time	Monday	Tuesday	Wednesday	Thursday	Friday	Saturday	Sunday
05:00							
06:00							
07:00	PLANNING & PREP	WORKSHOP DELIVERY	COURSE DEVELOPMENT	WORKSHOP DELIVERY	BOOK	BOOK	
08:00							
09:00							CHURCH
10:00							
11:00						FAMILY	FAMILY
12:00							
13:00	FAMILY LUNCH TIME						
14:00	BUSINESS DEVELOPMENT	FOLLOW-UPS	COURSE DEVELOPMENT	MEETINGS	FOLLOW-UPS	CHORES	SABBATH
15:00							
16:00							
17:00							
18:00	FAMILY DINNER TIME					FAMILY MOVIE NIGHT	REST
19:00		ISAAC TIME	ISAAC TIME		SAM TIME		
20:00							
21:00					FRIENDS		
22:00							
23:00							

COLOUR CODE: Quiet Time/Planning | Partner | Children/Family | Work | Exercise | Children/Family | Gardening Passion/Hobby/Chores | Chores | Charity | Other

©Andrea Taylor-Cummings 2020. Used with permission.

Weekly Schedule Template

(Download this template for free at: www.the4habits.com/downloads)

THE 4 HABITS

Weekly Schedule Template

For the period: mm / yy to mm / yy

Time	Monday	Tuesday	Wednesday	Thursday	Friday	Saturday	Sunday
05:00							
06:00							
07:00							
08:00							
09:00							
10:00							
11:00							
12:00							
13:00							
14:00							
15:00							
16:00							
17:00							
18:00							
19:00							
20:00							
21:00							
22:00							
23:00							

COLOUR CODE: Quiet Time/Planning   Partner   Children/Family   Work   Exercise   Passion/Hobby/Charity   _____ Other

©Andrea Taylor-Cummings 2020, Used with permission.

Value *Your* Values - Exercise

(Download this template for free at: www.the4habits.com/downloads)

1. What is 'the thing' that you promise you will do 'one day'?

2. What 'grates' on the inside? Where do you feel the balance might be off for you?

3. If you could create your ideal day, what would you do, where would you be and who would you be with?

4. If you were given six months to live, how would you spend it?

5. What words would you hope people would use to describe you in your eulogy?

6. Reflecting on what you have written above, what do you value most?

Useful Links

- UK Freephone National Domestic Abuse Helpline
  - 0808 2000 247

- USA National Domestic Abuse Hotline
  - 737-225-3150
  - https://www.thehotline.org

- Stop the Traffik. People Shouldn't Be Bought & Sold
  - https://www.stopthetraffik.org/help-and-support/

- UK help for family life matters/counselling support or signposting
  - https://www.careforthefamily.org.uk/family-life/ careline

Footnotes and References

CHAPTER 2

[1] CPP Global Human Capital Report, (July 2008), 'Workplace Conflict and How Businesses Can Harness it to Thrive', retrieved on March 20, 2021 from https://www.themyersbriggs.com/download/item/f39a8b7fb4fe4daface552d9f485c825

[2] Marriage Foundation, (January 2018), 'Cost of Family Breakdown', retrieved on March 20, 2021 from https://marriagefoundation.org.uk/research/cost-of-family-breakdown/

[3] The American Institute of Stress, (March 2020), 'Stress Management Industry: Global Trends', retrieved on March 20, 2021 from https://www.stress.org/stress-management-industry-global-trends

[4] Malins, J., (ca. 1895), 'A Fence or an Ambulance', retrieved on March 20, 2021, from https://allpoetry.com/poem/13223676-A-Fence-or-an-Ambulance-by-Joseph-Malins

[5] Goleman, D., (September 1996), *Emotional Intelligence: Why it Can Matter More Than IQ*, (Bloomsbury Publishing), page 34. Used with permission.

[6] Big Think, (April 2012) *Daniel Goleman Introduces Emotional Intelligence* [Video], retrieved on March 20, 2021 from https://youtu.be/Y7m9eNoB3NU

CHAPTER 3

[7] Although no one seems to be able to say for certain, it seems these words are a paraphrase of something Albert Einstein once said.

[8] Mental Health Foundation (2016), 'Relationships in the 21st Century', retrieved on March 20, 2021 from https://www.mentalhealth.org.uk/publications/relationships-21st-century-forgotten-foundation-mental-health-and-wellbeing

CHAPTER 4

[9] Chartered Institute of Personnel & Development (CIPD), (January 2020), 'Managing conflict in the modern workplace', retrieved on March 20, 2021 from https://www.cipd.co.uk/Images/managing-conflict-in-the-workplace-1_tcm18-70655.pdf

[10] Science Daily, (January 22, 2005), 'Intelligence In Men And Women Is A Gray And White Matter', University Of California, Irvine, retrieved March 20, 2021 from: https://www.sciencedaily.com/releases/2005/01/050121100142.htm

[11] Witelson, S., (November 20, 1999), 'The Exceptional Brain of Albert Einstein', *The Lancet* (Volume 354, Issue 9192, Page 1821), retrieved March 20, 2021 from: https://www.thelancet.com/journals/lancet/article/PIIS0140673698103276/fulltext

[12] Fisher, H., (February 2006), 'Why we love, why we cheat' [Video], TED Conferences. https://www.ted.com/talks/helen_fisher_why_we_love_why_we_cheat/transcript

[13] Tanner, D., (1 January 2016), *You Just Don't Understand: Women and Men in Conversation* (HarperCollins).

[14] World Economic Forum, (January 2016), 'The Future of Jobs', retrieved on March 20, 2021 from http://www3.weforum.org/docs/WEF_Future_of_Jobs.pdf

[15] Catalyst Research, (August 11, 2020), 'Women in Management: Quick Take', retrieved on March 20, 2021 from https://www.catalyst.org/research/women-in-management/

[16] Prison Reform Trust, (Bromley Briefings Summer 2013), 'Prison: the facts', retrieved on March 20, 2021 from http://www.prisonreformtrust.org.uk/portals/0/documents/prisonthefacts.pdf

CHAPTER 5

[17] Trent, J. and Smalley, G., (2019), *The Two Sides of Love* [Enlarged edition], (Focus on the Family). Used with permission.

[18] For more information on The Animal Personality Model (and Lions, Otters, Golden Retrievers and Beavers – LOGB®, visit www.strongfamilies.com and *The Two Sides of Love*. For more information on the full version of the Connect Assessment® visit jt.connectassessment.com.

[19] Obsessive Compulsive Disorder

[20] CNBC, (September 2018), 'This is the real reason why employees quit, according to LinkedIn CEO' [Video], retrieved on March 20, 2021 from https://www.cnbc.com/video/2018/09/14/linkedin-ceo-jeff-weiner-advice-managers-employees-quitting-jobs-workers.html

CHAPTER 6

[21] Tuckman, B., (1965), 'Developmental Sequence in Small Groups', *Psychological Bulletin*, retrieved on March 20, 2021 from http://web.mit.edu/curhan/www/docs/Articles/15341_Readings/Group_Dynamics/Tuckman_1965_Developmental_sequence_in_small_groups.pdf

[22] Tuckman, B., and Jensen, M., (1977), 'Stages of small group development revisited', *Group and Organizational Management*, retrieved March 20, 2021 from https://journals.sagepub.com/doi/10.1177/105960117700200404

[23] Peters, S., (January 5, 2012), *The Chimp Paradox: The Mind Management Programme to Help You Achieve Success, Confidence and Happiness* [First Edition], (Vermillion). Used with permission.

[24] *McKinsey Quarterly*, (July 23, 2020), 'Making a daily "to be" list: How a hospital system CEO is navigating the coronavirus crisis, retrieved on March 20, 2021 from https://www.mckinsey.com/business-functions/strategy-and-corporate-finance/our-insights/making-a-daily-to-be-list-how-a-hospital-system-ceo-is-navigating-the-coronavirus-crisis

CHAPTER 7

[25] Golden, B., (June 15, 2016), *Overcoming Destructive Anger: Strategies That Work* [Illustrated edition], (John Hopkins University Press).

[26] Proverbs 18:21, *Holy Bible,* The Authorised (King Kames) Version. Rights in the Authorised Version in the United Kingdom are vested in the Crown. Reproduced by permission of the Crown's patentee, Cambridge University Press.

[27] Mehrabian, A. and Ferris, S., (1967), 'Inference of attitudes from nonverbal communication in two Channels' (31, 248-252), *Journal of Consulting Psychology*, retrieved on March 20, 2021 from https://psycnet.apa.org/record/1967-10403-001

AND Mehrabian, A. and Weiner, M., (1967) 'Decoding of inconsistent communications' (6, 109-114), *Journal of Personality and Social Psychology*, retrieved on March 20, 2021 from https://psycnet.apa.org/record/1967-08861-001

[28] Sherman, M., (June 20 2014), 'Why We Don't Give Each Other a Break', *Psychology Today*, retrieved on March 20, 2021 from https://www.psychologytoday.com/us/blog/real-men-dont-write-blogs/201406/why-we-dont-give-each-other-break

[29] *Mere Christianity* by CS Lewis © copyright CS Lewis Pte Ltd 1942, 1943, 1944, 1952. Used with permission.

[30] Gass, Bob and Debby, (August 8, 2020), 'How to Deal With Difficult people (4)', *The UCB Word For Today*, retrieved on March 20, 2021 from https://www.ucb.co.uk/word-for-today/56165

[31] Chapman, G. and Thomas, J., (April 12, 2013), *When Sorry Isn't Enough: Making Things Right with Those You Love*, (Moody Press). Used by permission of Moody Publishers.

[32] As cited on Quote Investigator, retrieved on March 20, 2021 from https://quoteinvestigator.com/2014/04/06/they-feel/

CHAPTER 8

[33] IBM, Wikipedia, retrieved on March 20, 2021 from https://en.wikipedia.org/wiki/IBM

[34] Hofstede, G., 'The 6-D model of national culture', www.geerthofstede.com, retrieved on March 20, 2021 from https://geerthofstede.com/culture-geert-hofstede-gert-jan-hofstede/6d-model-of-national-culture/

[35] Volini, E., et al., (May 15, 2020), 'The postgenerational workforce: From millennials to perennials', *Deloitte Insights*, retrieved on March 20, 2021 from https://www2.deloitte.com/us/en/insights/focus/human-capital-trends/2020/leading-a-multi-generational-workforce.html

[36] Shavelson, M. (Director), (2005), *Yours, Mine and Ours* [Film] (Desilu-Walden Productions).

[37] Sandberg, S., (March 12, 2013), *Lean In: Women, Work, and the Will to Lead*, (WH Allen).

[38] Sanford, S., (November 2018), 'How to design gender bias out of your workplace' [Video], TED Conferences https://www.ted.com/talks/sara_sanford_how_to_design_gender_bias_out_of_your_workplace

CHAPTER 9

[39] Kelly, R., (March 10, 2017), 'BBC dad: Interview with Robert Kelly interrupted by children live on air' [Video], *BBC News*, https://www.bbc.co.uk/news/av/world-39232538

[40] Mental Health Foundation, (May 2016), *Relationships in the 21st Century*, (London: Mental Health Foundation) https://www.mentalhealth.org.uk/publications/relationships-21st-century-forgotten-foundation-mental-health-and-wellbeing

[41] Howard Kennedy et al., (January 2020), 'Relationship Breakdown and the Workplace: How personal relationship difficulties affect work amongst high earners', retrieved on March 20, 2021 from https://the4habits.com/relationship-breakdown-and-the-workplace/

[42] Jenkins, R., (January 8, 2018), 'This is Why Millennials Care so Much About Work-Life Balance', Inc., retrieved on March 20, 2021 from https://www.inc.com/ryan-jenkins/this-is-what-millennials-value-most-in-a-job-why.html

[43] Bick, R. et al., (March 2020), 'A Blueprint for remote working: Lessons from China', McKinsey Digital, retrieved on March 20, 2021 from https://www.mckinsey.com/~/media/McKinsey/Business Functions/McKinsey Digital/Our Insights/A blueprint for remote working Lessons from China/A-blueprint-for-remote-working-Lessons-from-China-vF.pdf

[44] Asmundson, G., (October 29, 2020), 'COVID Stress syndrome: 5 ways the pandemic is affecting mental health', Medical Xpress, retrieved on March 20, 2021 from https://medicalxpress.com/news/2020-10-covid-stress-syndrome-ways-pandemic.html

[45] Marsh, S., (June 15, 2020), 'Married Britons report higher anxiety levels during lockdown', *The Guardian*, retrieved on March 20, 2021 https://www.theguardian.com/world/2020/jun/15/married-people-report-higher-anxiety-levels-during-lockdown

[46] Lavietes, M., (July 6, 2020), 'Covid-19 could wipe out gains in equality for women at work' – U.N. [World Economic Forum], Thomson Reuters Foundation, retrieved on March 20, 2021 from https://www.weforum.org/agenda/2020/07/u-n-warns-covid-19-could-wipe-out-gains-in-equality-for-women-at-work

[47] Bingham, R., (June 9, 2006), 'Find out why we're addicted to love with anthropologist Helen Fisher', The Science Network, retrieved on March 20, 2021 from http://thesciencenetwork. org/media/videos/35/Transcript.pdf

[48] ONS, (November 10, 2016), 'Women shoulder the responsibility of "unpaid work"', Office for National Statistics [UK], retrieved on March 20, 2021 from https://www.ons.gov.uk/ employmentandlabourmarket/peopleinwork/earnings andworkinghours/articles/womenshouldertheresponsibility ofunpaidwork/2016-11-10

[49] Addati, L. et al., (June 28, 2018), 'Care work and care jobs for the future of decent work', International Labour Organization, retrieved on March 20, 2021 from https: https://www.ilo.org/ global/publications/books/WCMS_633135/lang--en/index.htm

[50] Andrew, A. et al., (May 27, 2020), 'Parents, especially mothers, paying heavy price for lockdown', Institute for Fiscal Studies, retrieved on March 20, 2021 from https://www.ifs.org.uk/ publications/14861

[51] Collins, C. et al., (July 02, 2020), 'COVID-19 and the gender gap in work hours', Wiley Online Library, retrieved on March 20, 2021 from https://onlinelibrary.wiley.com/doi/full/10.1111/ gwao.12506

[52] Coury, S. et al., (September 30, 2020), 'Women in the Workplace 2020', LeanIn.Org in partnership with McKinsey, retrieved on March 20, 2021 from https://www.mckinsey. com/featured-insights/diversity-and-inclusion/women-in-the-workplace

[53] Ruppanner, L. et al., (January 4, 2017), 'Does Unequal Housework Lead to Divorce? Evidence from Sweden', SAGE Journals, retrieved on March 20, 2021 from https://journals. sagepub.com/doi/full/10.1177/0038038516674664

[54] Carlson, D. et al., (May 25, 2016), 'The Gendered Division of Housework and Couples' Sexual Relationships: A Reexamination', *Journal of Marriage and Family*, retrieved on March 20, 2021 from https://onlinelibrary.wiley.com/doi/abs/10.1111/jomf.12313

[55] Relate, (July 20, 2020), 'A nation divided: new statistics show UK's lockdown "relationship realisations"', Relate, retrieved on March 20, 2021 from https://www.relate.org.uk/about-us/media-centre/press-releases/2020/7/20/nation-divided-new-statistics-show-uks-lockdown-relationship-realisations

[56] Relate, (June 24, 2020), 'Lockdown creates a wave of "Turbo Relationships", with new couples quicker to commit', Relate, Retrieved on March 20, 2021 from https://www.relate.org.uk/about-us/media-centre/press-releases/2020/6/24/lockdown-creates-wave-turbo-relationships-new-couples-quicker-commit-0

[57] CIPD, *CIPD Good Work Index*, www.CIPD.co.uk, retrieved on March 20, 2021 from https://www.cipd.co.uk/knowledge/work/trends/goodwork

[58] Boland, B. et al., (June 8, 2020), 'Reimagining the office and work life after COVID-19', McKinsey & Company, retrieved on March 20, 2021 from https://www.mckinsey.com/business-functions/organization/our-insights/reimagining-the-office-and-work-life-after-covid-19

CHAPTER 10

[59] As cited by Zeeb, B., (October 17, 2019), 'There is No Growth in the Comfort Zone and No Comfort in the Growth Zone', Infinitas, retrieved on March 20, 2021 from https://www.linkedin.com/pulse/growth-comfort-zone-bill-zeeb-玄奘/

[60] Ziglar, T., *The Wheel of Life*, www.ziglar.com, retrieved on March 20, 2021 from https://www.ziglar.com/articles/the-wheel-of-life/

61 Batz, P. and Schmidt, T., (January 19, 2011), *What Really Works: Blending the 7 Fs for the Life You Imagine*, (Beaver's Pond Press).

62 Harnish, V. and the team at Gazelles, (October 21, 2014), *Scaling Up: How a Few Companies Make It . . . and Why the Rest Don't*, (Gazelles Inc.), page 44.

63 Ziglar, Z., As cited on goodreads.com, retrieved on March 20, 2021 from https://www.goodreads.com/quotes/309132-money-isn-t-the-most-important-thing-in-life-but-it-s.

64 Siedle, E., (May 20 2013), *The Greatest Retirement Crisis in American History*, (Forbes), retrieved on March 20, 2021 from http://www.forbes.com/sites/edwardsiedle/2013/03/20/the-greatest-retirement-crisis-in-american-history/#1dc9614d1b88

65 Gladwell, M., (November 18, 2008), *Outliers: The Story of Success*, (Little Brown and Company), page 40.

66 Leaf, C., (September 2013), *Switch on Your Brain: The Key to Peak Happiness, Thinking, and Health*, (Baker Books), page 84. Used with permission.

67 Rohn, J., 'Half-Dozen Things' [Video], YouTube, retrieved on March 20, 2021 from https://www.youtube.com/watch?v=5rlURWrkhnw

68 Benson, H. and McKay, S., (August 2018), *Mummy's Boys, Daddy's Girls and Teenage Mental Health*, (Marriage Foundation), retrieved on March 20, 2021 from https://marriagefoundation.org.uk/research/mummys-boys-daddys-girls-and-teenage-mental-health/

69 Stanley, A. and Stanley, S., 'Parent Unscripted' – NPCC Week 1 [Video], NPCC, retrieved on March 20, 2021 from https://vimeo.com/207165655

70 Covey, S. R., (May 19, 2020), *The 7 Habits of Highly Effective People* [Revised and Updated: 30th Anniversary Edition], (Simon & Schuster UK).

[71] Comer, J. M., (October 31, 2019), *The Ruthless Elimination of Hurry: How to stay emotionally healthy and spiritually alive in the chaos of the modern world*, (Hodder & Stoughton).

[72] Collins, J. C., (October 16, 2001), *Good to Great: Why Some Companies Make the Leap . . . and Others Don't*, (Harper Business).

CHAPTER 11

[73] Ziglar, T., *If you do what you need to do when you need to do it* [Zig Ziglar Quote], Ziglar.com, retrieved on March 20, 2021 from https://www.ziglar.com/articles/if-you-do-what-you-need-to-do-when-you-need-to-do-it/

[74] Covey, S., (Reissue edition January 4, 1999), *First Things First*, (Simon & Schuster UK).

[75] Rohn, J., as cited on goodreads.com, retrieved on March 20, 2021 from https://www.goodreads.com/quotes/209560-we-must-all-suffer-from-one-of-two-pains-the

[76] Stone, D., Patton, B. and Heen, S., (November 02, 2010), *Difficult Conversations: How to Discuss What Matters Most*, (Penguin Books).

CHAPTER 12

[77] McLeod, S., 'Maslow's Hierarchy of Needs' [updated December 29, 2020], *Simply Psychology*, retrieved on March 20, 2021 from https://www.simplypsychology.org/maslow.html#gsc.tab=0

[78] Ryff, C. D., (1989), 'Happiness is everything, or is it? Explorations on the meaning of psychological well-being' [(57(6), 1069–1081)], *Journal of Personality and Social Psychology*, retrieved on March 20, 2021 from https://psycnet.apa.org/record/1990-12288-001

[79] ONS, (April 25, 2018), 'Measuring National Well-being: Quality of Life in the UK, 2018', Office for National Statistics [UK], retrieved on March 20, 2021 from https://www.ons.gov.uk/peoplepopulationandcommunity/wellbeing/articles/measuringnationalwellbeing/qualityoflifeintheuk2018

[80] Mental Health, (August 2019), 'Ensuring mental health and well-being in an adolescent's formative years can foster a better transition from childhood to adulthood', Unicef Data, retrieved on March 20, 2021 from https://data.unicef.org/topic/child-health/mental-health/

[81] Carlyle, R., (October 24, 2010), 'What's going on in your teenager's brain?', *Express*, retrieved on March 20, 2021 from https://www.express.co.uk/expressyourself/208129/What-s-going-on-in-your-teenager-s-brain

[82] White, P., (April 1, 2019) 'The value of appreciation: convincing skeptics', Appreciation at Work, retrieved on March 20, 2021 from https://www.appreciationatwork.com/blog/the-value-of-appreciation-convincing-skeptics/

CHAPTER 13

[83] Rosenberg, M., (November 17, 2011), 'Author Brené Brown Discusses Embracing Our Ordinariness', Huffpost, retrieved on March 20, 2021 from https://www.huffpost.com/entry/embracing-our-ordinariness_b_802808

[84] Nelson, A., (April 27, 2014), 'Why You Stand Side-by-Side or Face-to-Face', *Psychology Today*, retrieved on March 20, 2021 from https://www.psychologytoday.com/gb/blog/he-speaks-she-speaks/201404/why-you-stand-side-side-or-face-face

[85] Bungay Stanier, M., (2016), *The Coaching Habit: Say Less, Ask More & Change the Way You Lead Forever*, (Box of Crayons Press).

[86] Chapman, G. (1992), *The 5 Love Languages: The Secret to Love That Lasts*, (Northfield Publishing).

[87] Chapman, G. and White, P., (2011), *The 5 Languages of Appreciation in the Workplace*, (Northfield Publishing).

[88] All references to *The 5 Love Languages* and *The 5 Languages of Appreciation in the Workplace* are made here with permission from Moody Publishers.

PART C

[89] Probably one of Winston Churchill's most remembered quotes, this was the title of a speech he delivered in 1943 during the height of the blitzkrieg attacks of the Nazis and Fascists in Europe. The speech serves as an illuminating light that gave hope to the Allied Forces.

CHAPTER 14

[90] While this quote is generally attributed to English poet John Dryden who died in 1700, Quote Investigator reveals that it's possible this is a misreading. Their research, though not conclusive, suggests religious writer Frederick Langbridge's work in 1888 as the more likely original source, retrieved on March 20, 2021 from https://quoteinvestigator.com/2016/12/19/habits-make/

[91] Soulmates Academy Foundation is a charity registered in England and Wales with the Charity Commission, Registration Number: 1189169, https://soulmatesacademyfoundation.org

[92] Ramis, H. (Director), (1993), *Groundhog Day* [Film], (Columbia Pictures).

[93] Fuller, T., (1650), *A Pisgah Of Palestine And The Confines Thereof (It is always darkest just before the Day dawneth)*.

[94] Ecclesiastes 4:9-10, *Holy Bible,* Revised Standard Version, copyright © 1946, 1952, and 1971 the Division of Christian Education of the National Council of the Churches of Christ in the United States of America. Used by permission. All rights reserved.

CHAPTER 15

[95] Maxwell, J., www.johnmaxwell.com, retrieved on March 20, 2021 from https://www.johnmaxwell.com/blog/category/vision/

[96] *BBC News*, (February 12, 2021), 'KPMG boss Bill Michael quits after "stop moaning" row', retrieved on March 20, 2021 from https://www.bbc.co.uk/news/business-56038215

[97] Case Western Reserve University, (October 2012), 'Empathy represses analytic thought, and vice versa: Brain physiology limits simultaneous use of both networks', Science Daily, retrieved on March 20, 2021 from https://www.sciencedaily.com/releases/2012/10/121030161416.htm

[98] Authors' note: We do know how to spell 'care', really!

[99] The Fear of Missing Out.

[100] O'Carroll, L. et al., (August 13, 2019), 'Revealed: mental health crisis at Hinkley Point C construction site', *The Guardian*, retrieved on March 20, 2021 from https://www.theguardian.com/uk-news/2019/aug/13/revealed-suicide-alarm-hinkley-point-c-construction-site

CHAPTER 16

[101] Benson, H. and McKay, S., (November 2017), 'Family breakdown and teenage mental health', Marriage Foundation, retrieved on March 20, 2021 from https://marriagefoundation.org.uk/research/family-breakdown-has-a-major-influence-on-teen-mental-health/

102 Cekic, Ö., (September 2018), 'Why I have coffee with people who send me hate mail' [Video], TED Conferences. https://www.ted.com/talks/ozlem_cekic_why_i_have_coffee_with_people_who_send_me_hate_mail

103 Thanks to our friend and expert Communications Consultant, Charlie Simpson for helping summarise our key message into two sentences.

Acknowledgements

Our heartfelt thanks to Dr John Trent and Dr Gary Chapman for their significant contributions to the field of relationship education. Your work had a powerful impact in our lives when we struggled in our own relationship over 25 years ago and since then continues to shape who we become as individuals and as a couple. You are the giants on whose shoulders we stand, influencing everything we've been doing in relationship education over the years. Grateful thanks to you both and your publishers for allowing us to include highlights from your work in our book.

Thank you to our dear friends (too many to mention but you know we love you!), who have supported us on this journey over the years, attending workshops and seminars, being our willing guinea pigs with new material and championing the work we do. Special thanks to Jeremy and Debbie Lindley and Dawid and Rachel Konotey-Ahulu for being our solid supporters and sounding boards, helping to keep us sane through all the ups and downs.

Thank you to our church families at Riverside Community Church and St Albans Vineyard Church for your belief in us and for giving us a platform over the years to share our message and hone our craft. Our ongoing gratitude to Pastor Bediako Bosque-Hamilton who from day one has been our strong voice of encouragement and continues to champion all we do in equipping people to build strong relationships.

Our love and appreciation to our parents for their example, wisdom and positive influence in our lives and particularly to our now widowed mothers – Dearma and Grandy – for their continued support, encouragement and belief in us, even when we decided to give up the safety of City careers to pursue this passion and call.

To our wonderful siblings and their spouses who have also become our additional siblings over the years – Carrie and Tim, Karen and James, Bev and Sean, Denise and Glenn, Andy, Diane – we have walked this path of doing relationships as siblings, as couples, as parents, as employed professionals, as friends, as confidantes. May we all continue to learn and grow together, hold each other accountable for modelling great relationships to our beautiful children and together ignite a relationship revolution in the next generation.

To our nieces and nephews – Joshua, Caleb, Jaydon, Alexandra, Emma, Joanna, Matthew, Laura and Elly – you bring the richness of personalities, love and laughter to our family relationships and our prayer is that you create even stronger relationships, marriages and family bonds in your generation.

To the wonderful souls we've been blessed to parent, Sam and Isaac, thank you for your patience, your sacrifice, your belief, your loving support, your courage and your confidence to challenge us to live the principles we teach about relationships. May all the seeds we have sown become your great inheritance in strong, quality relationships first with God, with each other, in all the relationships around you and in mutually satisfying marriages in your lives and the lives of all the generations to come through you.

And thanks be to the Lord God Almighty who had the amazing plan to bring Andrea from Jamaica and Jon from Sierra Leone, to meet at Oxford all those decades ago and embark on this unbelievable journey to improve the quality of relationships across the globe, starting with our own. The journey continues and we rest in the knowledge that our future is in His hands.

Made in the USA
Las Vegas, NV
24 March 2024

87708081R00213